The Future of Difference

The Future of Difference

Beyond the Toxic Entanglement
of Racism, Sexism and Feminism

Sabine Hark and Paula-Irene Villa

Translated by Sophie Lewis

VERSO
London • New York

The translation of this work was partially funded by Technische Universität Berlin.

This English-language edition published by Verso 2020
Originally published in German as *Unterscheiden und herrschen:*
Ein Essay zu den ambivalenten Verflechtungen von Rassismus,
Sexismus und Feminismus in der Gegenwart
© transcript Verlag 2017
Translation © Sophie Lewis 2020

1 3 5 7 9 10 8 6 4 2

Verso
UK: 6 Meard Street, London W1F 0EG
US: 20 Jay Street, Suite 1010, Brooklyn, NY 11201
versobooks.com

Verso is the imprint of New Left Books

ISBN-13: 978-1-78873-802-6
ISBN-13: 978-1-78873-801-9 (HBK)
ISBN-13: 978-1-78873-803-3 (UK EBK)
ISBN-13: 978-1-78873-804-0 (US EBK)

British Library Cataloguing in Publication Data
A catalogue record for this book is available from the British Library

Library of Congress Control Number
2020932047

Typeset in Minion Pro by Hewer Text UK Ltd, Edinburgh
Printed and bound by CPI Group (UK) Ltd, Croydon CR0 4YY

Contents

Preface to the English Edition

'Germany shocked by Cologne New Year gang assaults on women', reported *BBC News* on 5 January 2016 after the assaults had taken place against women in Cologne.[1] The *New York Times*, for its part, declared 'Germany on the Brink'.[2] These were just two of many international headlines covering the incidents in Germany's fourth most populous city on New Year's Eve 2015, during the festivities of which hundreds of women are thought to have been mugged and/or sexually attacked, including raped. Over the course of the following days, the 'Night That Changed Everything',[3] as the German daily *Welt am Sonntag* decided to dub it, went global. All too quickly, 'Cologne' became an internationally recognized shorthand for the already heated debate seething at the nexus of gender, migration, religion, race, and sexuality. So, what, if anything, *did* change on that infamous 'night that changed everything'? That is the question we pursue in this book.

But is it really still necessary, especially for those of us beyond Germany's borders, four years after the event, to concern ourselves with 'Cologne'? Is 'Cologne' really something people uninvested in domestic German politics should concern themselves with, readers in the Anglosphere might well ask. We think the answer is 'yes'. As we see it, 'Cologne' has become a universal referent in the global spectacle that is the 'migration crisis', the flashpoint around which, in Kobena Mercer's words, 'ethnic chauvinisms, neonationalisms and numerous fundamentalisms strive to close down the symbolic boundaries of group belonging.'[4] 'Cologne' is not just a cipher, then, but a caesura: it stands for the alleged failure of refugees to integrate, for the supposed collapse of multiculturalist daydreaming into a living nightmare of violence and insecurity, and for the putative erosion of 'our' public order by the excessive presence of those of African, Muslim or otherwise somehow 'not German' origin.

The stage for this 'clash of civilizations' (in Samuel Huntington's model) was Cologne's Domplatte – the space around Cologne Cathedral. And, as we hope to show, it was no coincidence that the clash occurred along the fault lines of sexuality and gender. As Michel Foucault contends in his *History of Sexuality* (1980), gender and sexuality should not be understood as antitheses of politics and power, but precisely as 'dense transfer points for relations of power'.[5] It is in no small part in relation to these two terms that humanity's collective coexistence is presently being negotiated. Sexuality, Foucault shows, 'is not the most intractable element in power relations, but rather one of those endowed with the greatest instrumentality: useful for the greatest number of manoeuvres and capable of serving as a point of support, as a linchpin, for the most varied strategies'.[6]

As with sexuality, so with gender. Certainly, there are several other fields of experience relevant to everyday life that could lay claim to such instrumentality, such as 'crime', 'violence' and 'terrorism' (categories whose very diffuseness seems to make them more effective). Yet sexuality and gender seem to be especially amenable for use as a container for other, affectively charged, intensely controversial questions. They are social order issues: determining how we live alongside one another, in general, and particularly in public; which is to say, they are questions of ethical coexistence. How will – how can – we live together? How shall we accomplish this, when it comes down to it? How shall people in a pluralistic democracy speak to one another about this, including when it is necessary to really thrash things out? How do we *want* to speak? Who can, and who will, participate in this conversation in a globalized world shot through, whether we like it or not, with inequality, danger, precarity, religion and borders? Ultimately, these are the disquieting, difficult and fundamental questions that Cologne highlighted anew.

And these are the debates to which we – as sociologists, feminists and politically committed citizens – wished to contribute in writing this book. It seemed to us that public political discourse around the big questions of our time, post-Cologne, had become incredibly toxic: frequently (albeit not always) enacting the mere appearance of a debate. This was equally true of mainstream news features and talk shows; formal reportage and the blogosphere, vlogs, Twitter and other social media; parliamentary debates, seminar discussions, conference panels; political rallies, and posters brandished at demonstrations – all across the political spectrum. What was missing across the board, from our point of view, was and remains a certain quality of collective critical reflection that might enable a – controversial, yes, but deeply needful – series of debates about the practicalities of living alongside one another. Topics up for debate would necessarily include: the meaning of sexual freedom; relations between the sexes; bodily autonomy; the freedom to move around without constraint; freedom to love, pray, dress a certain way, and be sexually active – or not; and the right to be more than the object of public discussion, that is to say, to participate critically in public debates.

We could not agree more that what happened on the Cologne Domplatte on New Year's Eve is not something we can dismiss with just a few pithy platitudes. None of the available cynical reactions, be it 'nothing happened', 'we all know what happened – nothing special', or 'boys will be boys' (i.e., men having fun will necessarily be men harassing women), are remotely appropriate responses. Of course, the popular blanket statements profiling 'the' Arab or Muslim man as a harasser of 'our' women – while pretending that such things do not happen in Germany, in the West, or within Christianity – are every bit as inappropriate. Without a doubt, sexual violence was perpetrated that night, and this represents a grave problem. At the time, it made both of us feel helpless and angry. We were angry that women, in 2016, could not move around in public space without risking molestation. We were angry that the police (as a committee of parliamentary inquiry for the North Rhine–Westphalia region later determined[7]) completely failed to predict the situation and, as a result, acted negligently. We were angry that the women who reported what was done to them to the police were not believed. But all this anger and dismay, fostered by that particular occasion, has the potential to make us forget that nothing about it was either new or rare in Germany – quite the reverse. Misogynist and often sexualized violence is part of

German normality – not only against women, but also against queers, gays and lesbians, trans and intersex individuals, children and adolescents of all sexes, and structurally vulnerable people generally. Unfortunately, as international and transnational studies have shown time and again, sexual violence, misogyny and sexism are global phenomena: just think of #MeToo and #NiUnaMenos.[8] But violence is nevertheless not an ahistorical, transcultural human disposition, nor even an anthropological constant, simply to be accepted as a fact of nature. It must always be apprehended in a context-specific manner, for its expression from place to place is far from uniform. By establishing this, we are by no means relativizing bad deeds and values: we mean it as an empirical statement, denoting a general epistemic starting point.

It would be difficult to overstate the hypocrisy of those countless German commentators who, in delivering their Cologne-related verdicts, suddenly now discovered themselves to be feminists – but only insofar as the criminals were thought to be non-German and (specifically) 'Arab-born'. As vital and important as it is to fight sexism, and especially to struggle against sexual and gender-based violence, if that commitment becomes racist, xenophobic, or narrowly culturalist, it becomes destructive. And it is precisely *that* coupling, between feminism and cultural racism, that quickly became the dominant form of discourse concerning Cologne, both within Germany and internationally. Racism and culturalist stereotyping, in fact, *became the condition* for mainstream articulations of the problem of sexual violence. Or, to put it the other way around: sexual politics became, once more, a terrain for racist knowledge production. Openly racist and xenophobic rhetoric was now not just possible, nor even simply legitimate: it was now, seemingly, required in order to protect 'our' women, as part of the defence of 'Western values' and sexual equality.

Resistance to migration, in Germany, has always been racist insofar as it cannot be disentangled from the long history of normalizing divisions between those who belong to the national community – the *Volk* – and those who not only *do not belong* but actively threaten the community by their very presence. One particular form of racism experienced a substantial boost after the Cologne 'sex mob' events: *feminist* racism (or racist feminism). We saw the widespread co-optation of feminist arguments in the service of Europe's border regime. We saw notions of gender- and sexuality-related emancipation, not to mention LGBTQ rights, mobilized to justify the primacy of European culture. Indeed, xenophobic, ultranationalist, and nativist movements, parties, and governments all over Europe have increasingly adopted concepts of sexual equality for their fundamentalist purposes ever since. They claim, for example, that male Muslim citizens (and non-Western male migrants generally) are incapable of respecting the rights of women and queers. It was our intense irritation about this that first initiated our thinking about Cologne.

We are not in the least interested in denying that violence was practiced that night. It remains an appalling reality in our society that victims of sexual violence are systematically disbelieved: accused of having somehow provoked or consented to what they endured, or else implied to be outright making it up. The fact that, more than four years after the events on New Year's Eve 2015, only two people have been convicted for 'sexual assault', according to Cologne's District Court, and only one for 'groping', does not indicate to us that there was an absence of violence. That particular tally merely indicates that charges could not be brought, because the majority of the offences reported could not be confidently assigned by name to known persons. A further aggravating factor came from the fact that, at the time, the majority of the sexual offences reported were not even punishable under German sexual criminal law. Nevertheless, we find it concerning that more than three-quarters of the original 1,200 criminal complaints were lodged against 'Unknown', and that, in the almost 300 proceedings initiated against named parties, only a few cases resulted in an indictment and conviction.

Superficially, at least, these figures contradict the attitude of total certitude that still characterizes the vast majority of commentaries on the 'night that changed everything'. The sheer certainty with which civil society discussed, for instance, who was loitering outside Cologne

Hauptbahnhof that night, who was the perpetrator, who the victim, what criminally prosecutable acts and violent actions took place, for what motive and why, was and remains truly remarkable. For many people – including many feminists – it remains a foregone conclusion that among the thousands of revellers who met up outside Cologne Cathedral that evening, there numbered 'around 2,000 young men, predominantly Algerians, Moroccans, North Africans', as Alice Schwarzer, editor of Germany's oldest feminist magazine, *EMMA*, claimed once again in April 2019.[9] Schwarzer contends, in her unbearably generalizing style, that 'what we are dealing with' is 'uprooted, socially unaffiliated young men, most of them undocumented' – a group of people who, according to Schwarzer, will 'always cause problems' for 'us' by seeking to import their violent and brutal misogynist methods (inculcated in them from childhood!) 'into the heart of Europe'. Is this really the case? Is this a meaningful interpretation of the 'Night in Cologne'? Our inquiry, in a sense, starts here.

At the outset, two things were painfully clear to us. First: yes, we, too, do not know what actually happened around the cathedral that night, and we, too, are deeply upset about the extent of the sexual violence. At the same time, we contend, thinking about how these acts form part of our present does not amount to a failure to take their implications seriously: quite the reverse. If we want to make sense of the relationship sexual violence holds to our present, in a context of migration, globalization and political volatility, and particularly in view of the mounting (parliamentary as well as extra-parliamentary) political successes of new authoritarian, xenophobic, racist and antisemitic tendencies, we will have to assume the relationship is much less simple than it was typically presented to be in the hegemonic discourse on Cologne.

Then what exactly is the problem of 'Cologne', according to us, if it is not (primarily) a global culture of everyday sexism and misogyny that makes violent excesses like this possible, indeed, inevitable? What is it, if not 'toxic masculinity', letting off steam in public by harassing women who are simply trying to enjoy themselves at New Year's Eve celebrations, at carnival, football matches, military parades and beer festivals? What, if not something about the devout religiosity imputed – or, rather, naturalized as inherent – to the men involved (i.e., the perpetrators), something ingrained that means they scarcely know how to behave otherwise? How could their place of origin (supposed or actual) not be part of the problem? Our essay considers how the problem of 'Cologne' was defined, what exactly is being negotiated in it, and by whom.

Second, we, too, did not talk to any of the victims. It would have been irresponsible for us to try, since neither of us has journalistic training, and this is not a book based on first-hand empirical sociological research. Our methods can plausibly be criticized on that basis: indeed, they have been (in the course of the book's German-speaking reception). In Chapter 5, via a dialogue, we reflect on these and related issues self-critically. However, we hope that our approach is one that also contributes to the task of making sexism and sexualized violence visible and legible without falling into racist reifications or objectifications.

Instead of leaving the links between things sinisterly implicit, we seek to determine: What are the concrete effects of one explanation of (or *use* of) sexuality compared to another? Whose discourses of naturalized – ostensibly traditional – logics of sexual violence are successfully put to work, with reference to *whose* violence, and how? How are notions of sexual freedom, equality between the sexes, secularism, enlightenment, emancipation, liberty and individualism themselves freighted with particular conceptions of sexuality? And how, in historic context, are these meanings sutured and shifted? Lastly, how do certain recourses to – and versions of – sexuality organize our very perception: our sensitivities, our receptivities? What politics, what judgments, are prone to emerge on that basis? The purpose of our treatise is to confront such questions. We believe they are just as relevant to a non-German readership as they are to ours, and we hope our rumination helps to clarify them. It is, indeed, urgent to grasp how the loci of gender and sexuality are functioning, in specific contexts, to draw and redraw the boundaries constitutive of social order: inside/outside, moral/amoral, vulnerable/dangerous, own/alien, us/them.

xiv   THE FUTURE OF DIFFERENCE

To reflect properly on Cologne is to be willing to regard social effects that might appear (from a feminist perspective) to be positive developments as profoundly ambivalent. For example: the explosive rise to prominence of the theme of sexual violence resulted in reforms of German sexual criminal law that feminist legal activists had long been calling for – albeit the topic was racially charged. To be sure, the legislative sea change was not due solely to the Cologne events and the ensuing controversy. It was brought about, in part, by decades' worth of feminist struggles eking out partial victories. In the years immediately prior to Cologne, from 2013 on, mobilizations such as #Aufschrei[10] had contributed to this trend, both online and offline. Nevertheless, it seems an 'event' was needed to implement the social redefinition of sexual violence already effected in German sexual criminal law. In the absence of those struggles, on the part of people in Germany and all around the world, the reform would not have been possible. For this reason, we want our book to be understood in the context of mobilizations against sexual violence all over the world: #MeToo, #NiUnaMenos, #SenDeAnlat, #BalanceTonPorc, #GamAni and more. These struggles – which go far beyond hashtags and 'clicktivism' – have been instrumental in making visible the scope and the local character of sexual violence globally. Behind each hashtag lies a multitude of stories, experiences, battles and flavors of sexual violence. And even in these mass mobilizations, what people are naming and negotiating is, more often than not, the difficult questions of the relation of the general to the particular, the specific to the common.[11]

There is no way to grasp 'Cologne' without reference to what the media were calling, at the time, 'the long summer of migration': the summer of 2015. The Syrian Civil War had raged, at that point, for five years. Eleven million Syrians had been displaced; almost 4 million of them became refugees. Syria's neighbours had already exhausted their capacity to accommodate them. So, asylum seekers started to make their way to Europe – via the 'Balkan Route'. Following Angela Merkel's decision not to close the nation's borders, Germany gave refuge to approximately 1 million people.[12]

But it wasn't only the numbers of those seeking to enter Europe that increased dramatically that summer. Simple awareness of the realities of war spread rapidly during that time across Western European populations that had hitherto largely enjoyed obliviousness in this regard – at least ever since the so-called Yugoslav Wars of the 1990s, during which Germany took in just under 400,000 refugees. Now thousands of people – mothers carrying small children, elderly people, entire families – sought to escape the conflict on foot, leaving everything they had behind, waiting for days on end in makeshift camps in Greece, at train stations in Hungary, at motorway rest stops in Serbia, on riverbanks and roadsides and next to walls and fences, hastily erected at the EU's external perimeter, that they were prevented from passing through by Serbian, Croatian, Hungarian, Czech, Polish and Austrian border security forces. They drowned, wretchedly, trying to make the crossing to Greece or Italy. The Mediterranean Sea, that romantic destination, that paradise beloved of northwestern Europe's middle classes, turned into a mass grave.

All this took place under conditions of 'real time' visibility, made possible by the new mass digital media – causing what Navid Kermani termed an 'irruption of reality into our consciousness'.[13] The German public, just like the global public, consumed the spectacle of desperate human beings on the verge of drowning in the Mediterranean, hoping for rescue. We were mesmerized. We saw the mountains of life jackets on Greek island beaches. We watched the people trek through the landscapes of southeastern Europe, in lines often miles long. Life vests and emergency warming foil ('space blankets') became readily recognizable symbols of a humanitarian catastrophe that was no longer unfolding far away, back then, over there, a long way away from us – but rather here, now, among us, where we are. The image of the three-year-old Alan Kurdi, whose body washed ashore on 2 September 2015, showed him lying on his belly on the sand, as though sleeping soundly. He was lying on the very same surf – the coast of Greece, Italy and Turkey – where middle-class German, French, Swedish and English holidaymakers love to work on their tans. We Europeans, with our money and our passports that provide unrestricted access to almost every country in the world, we for whom 'mobility' has exclusively positive resonances: we were confronted that summer with the deadly dimension of *compulsory* mobility. Was it also perhaps, in part, the historic traumas of the Shoah that were returning to German living rooms and intruding upon our smartphones? Did the images recall the ungrieved abominations of the Holocaust – or, perhaps, the 'refugee treks' of the late 1940s, whereby Germans were expelled from the so-called Eastern Territories after World War II? No doubt, many in Europe cannot stand to recognize themselves and their own families in the images of people and *their* families fleeing Syria and Libya.

Alan Kurdi, so the famous photograph informed us unequivocally, drowned during an attempt on the part of his family (who come from Aleppo) to cross from Turkey to the Greek island of Kos, which is part of the EU. When the photo in question was published, it was hailed everywhere in the mainstream media – paradoxically – as 'a photograph fit to silence the world'.[14] As though the world had not already kept silent long enough on the subject of the ordeal endured, for years, by the Syrian people! Still, *Die Zeit* recommended that one should 'be silent' in response to the image – and perhaps also, 'insofar as one is human, weep'.[15] The intention here, clearly, was to invoke an empathic silence: a silence of grief, bewilderment and, in all probability, respect for others' suffering. But, instead of making space for grieving – instead of acknowledging that this suffering has something to do with us, does something to us, touches us, alters us – when Cologne happened, Germany took the opportunity to turn the page. Society did not tarry to consider the extent to which grieving *is* politics – in that some lives have the right to be grieved, to be recognized as valuable, while others aren't even granted access to the sphere of the grievable and the human. Instead of looking and learning from the inseparability of 'us' (in Germany) and 'them' (the refugees at Europe's borders), the affective and political atmosphere took a turn for the worse.

Even as Germany's racist and ultranationalist voices grew louder and louder, in the public imagination, the 'long summer of migration' was marked, perhaps above all, by *Willkommenskultur* (a culture of welcome).[16] As we discuss in Chapter 2 of this book, this 'culture' included elements of genuine civil politicization, intense and sustained mutual aid and, yes, kitsch charitable naivety. But Cologne provoked the ascendance of already existing tendencies to cynically question universal human rights via xenophobic and nationalist common-places, fuelling the already intensifying appetite for *völkisch*, populist and belligerent public discourses. And what the 'night that changed everything' actually changed, according to these discourses, is the viability of this dangerously naive *Willkommenskultur* – an ideology that supposedly asks too much, both of individuals and of country – promulgated by people that could now be derided shamelessly as 'do-gooders'. It is telling that '*Gutmensch*' (i.e., Good Samaritan) could become a pejorative term in this context. It was even voted '*Unwort des Jahres*' (ghastly neologism of the year) in 2015. As reported in *Der Spiegel*, the jury in the competition deemed '*Gutmensch*' and '*Gutmenschentum*' (alternatively: *Gutbürger*) to be words that 'vilify helpfulness, kindness and tolerance in generalizing terms as naive, unworldly and stupid; as symptoms of moral imperialism; or as stemming from some kind of 'white knight' (rescuer) complex'.[17] The good, in short, became a target for mockery. This was a key element of the transformation in German society effected by and through Cologne.

Further, Germany's entire policy orientation on refugees, asylum and migration was rewritten in the shadow of Cologne. The idea that Cologne had revealed that those 'we' longed to call 'welcome' were abusing 'our values' – because they hail from patriarchal and misogy-nistic cultures, societies riven with violence that had made, of these young male refugees, woman-hating brutes – was now acceptable currency among state officials. We personally will never be able to forget the spectacle of Horst Seehofer, the then–Bavarian prime minister (and, at the time of writing, Germany's minister for the inte-rior and home affairs) – a man who was still, as it happens, calling migration 'the mother of all political problems'[18] in the summer of 2018 – flirting with making 'abuse of the asylum system' a criminal offence, and generally agitating against refugees in the late summer of 2015.[19] Subsequently, Germany moved to make asylum and migration policy (even) more restrictive: tightening asylum law generally and, in particular, tightening regulations concerning accommodation for refugees; facilitating deportations; and militarizing the German side of intra-European borders (e.g., between Germany and Austria).

This course of action reflected, and worked in tandem with, a new direction in citizenship law embodied by the Nationality Act (*Staatsangehörigkeitsgesetz*), which targeted Muslim 'criminals' and perpetrators specifically, requiring that claimants to German citizenship now be not only non-criminal but 'integrated into the German way of life'.[20] What on earth the 'German way of life' might be – who gets to define it, and how? – is a question that seems to us to have been left open on purpose, just like the question of what might happen to Germans who do not live that way. The presence of the *völkisch*, ethnonationalist dog whistle is unmistakable. For many years, at this point, Germany has been conducting a debate on the subjects of '*Heimat*' (homeland) and '*Herkunft*' (ancestry): a debate that could, in theory, prove quite useful and interesting, were it not so strongly determined by fundamentalizing conceptual foreclosures and ethnicized, identitarian preconceptions. Nonetheless, post-Cologne, there is an increased presence of new and alternative voices in this debate: polyphone, often post-migrant voices, interested in justice and equality rather than integration and assimilation. They/we are demanding to be listened to and insisting that their/our perspectives matter.[21]

It has long been clear to us that racism is a part of German culture as a whole: not only behind closed doors and not only among homespun '*Stammtisch*' regulars in traditional taverns. Nevertheless, we experience the aforementioned poisonous and restrictive political direction, its simplistic ideological generalities and the attendant erosion of the human right to asylum as almost unbearable, especially in light of Germany's particular responsibilities vis-à-vis history. Racist and xenophobic – also antisemitic – attitudes were never absent from Germany, in West or East; they were never even fully marginalized. Besides the remarkable continuity of Nazi elites in politics, economy, jurisdiction and cultural realms in

West Germany, the white-supremacist assassinations carried out by the National Socialist Underground[22] between 2000 and 2007 bear witness to such ideology – as does the well-documented participation of German law-enforcement officers and constitutional authorities in far-right networks. The pogroms targeting refugee shelters and hostels housing asylum seekers in Hoyerswerda[23] in September 1991 – and in Rostock-Lichtenhagen[24] in August 1992 – bear witness to the prevalence of racism in Germany. The racist murders in Mölln[25] in November 1992 and in Solingen[26] in May 1993 bear witness to it. The racist murder of Marwa El-Sherbini on July 1, 2009, in a German courtroom in Dresden bears witness to it.[27] And the innumerable, sometimes subtle, sometimes clearly and openly articulated aggressions and microaggressions that characterize German everyday life – in all areas of society and all institutions, be they schools or universities, public bureaucracies or sporting arenas – bear witness to it. Such is the day-to-day reality, the normal state of existence, for everyone who does not present the ethnicized image of the 'real German'. In Germany, too, Jewish institutions, such as schools and synagogues, have required police protections and armed security for decades. While we were finishing the English edition of this book, the synagogue in Halle was violently attacked on Yom Kippur (9 October) 2019 by a young German man, who on the self-recorded video he uploaded on social media during his terror spray identifies as a misogynist, anti-feminist, anti-Semitic and racist Holocaust denier. Luckily, the door of the synagogue resisted. But others weren't as fortunate; the shooter gunned down a woman passing by outside the synagogue and killed a man in an Arab fast-food shop nearby. We mourn for all lost lives and are once again infuriated by the comments of many leading German politicians for their rhetoric of surprise and shock. As if this attack came out of the blue, fully unexpected. As if more or less violent anti-Semitism weren't part of German normality.

In the German-speaking world, our book has experienced a gratifyingly broad and serious reception. At the time of publication, we gave a great number of readings and participated in many discussions. These always proved lively and often even explosive. In essence, this itself tended to clarify what was at stake and confirm to us the value of what we are advocating, namely the art of thinking-in-difference: a practice of differentiation, of differentiating thought. On the one hand, speaking and arguing, controversy and debate, are needed now more than ever before. At the same time, they're rendered more difficult through the prevalence of discursive authoritarianisms and fundamentalisms: discourses that foreclose things even as they posit them. For example, we have found it unreasonably arduous in practice to go about criticizing certain contemporary feminist positions. Certainly, feminist speech has always been structurally subject to devaluations and attacks, and it is reasonable to demand that criticisms be carefully formulated with the utmost sensitivity to context and effect. But we have noticed that people too often experience ambivalences and nuances as unendurable, literally: as too much to 'endure'. We lay out the specifics of this in Chapter 4, with our critique of 'toxic feminisms' – a genre epitomized for us, inter alia, by Alice Schwarzer. An active and influential figure in the German-speaking world, Schwarzer founded *EMMA* in 1977 (a magazine she still retains control over today, as editor in chief); and she is probably, as it happens, the only really well-known German second-wave feminist.

Over the last few years, our criticisms of Schwarzer's feminism have been repeatedly interpreted as inadmissible speech – as denigration of the person of Alice Schwarzer herself and as a lack of respect for her lifelong efforts on behalf of the ostensibly unitary category 'feminism'. This assumption shows that in contemporary political space, persons and positions are all too often elided. If nothing else, we hope we have identified *that* tendency – across the political spectrum, from right to left – and treated it with the seriousness it deserves. In short, individuals themselves, and their political attitudes (whether avowed and/or ascribed), are often equated with their ascribed social positions, which is to say: their group, class, religion, gender, sexual orientation or cultural milieu. We call this epistemic operation 'positional fundamentalism'. Its prevalence betokens how difficult it has become to describe realities (for example, political and social realities) in all their complexity and nuance. Discursive traps are sprung and snapped shut. Debates are too tightly hemmed in between binary formulas, antagonisms and oversimplifications. Acts of recognition, in and despite difference and critique, become impossible.

What we hoped to achieve with our book, in the final analysis, is to have contributed to our collective understanding of the contemporary entanglements between sexism, (cultural) racism and feminism: between, on the one hand, the battle against what a transnational and heterogeneous alliance now calls 'gender ideology' and the fight, on the other hand, against the so-called Islamization of the West.

The 'anti-gender alliance' – the subject of our previous book, *Anti-Genderism* (*Anti-Genderismus*, 2015) – encompasses the Vatican as well as a number of related conservative Catholic groups devoted to the defence of tradition, family and the sanctity of private property. But its actors also include the Catholic women's movement in Poland; a number of evangelical churches around the world; La Manif Pour Tous ('The Demo for Everyone') in France; Pegida in Germany ('Patriotic Europeans Against the Islamization of the Occident'); entire political parties, such as Alternative für Deutschland (the AfD) in Germany, Rassemblement National ('National Rally', formerly Le Front National) in France, and Geert Wilders's Partij Voor de Vrijheid ('Party for Freedom') in the Netherlands; organized groupings of 'concerned parents' who campaign against the alleged 'sexualization of children'; neoconservative men's rights campaigners and other identitarian movements; self-appointed defenders of the 'right to life'; conservative environmentalists; assorted masculinist and high-profile journalists and bloggers calling themselves scholars or scientists; and outright fascist entities such as the extreme-right National Democratic Party of Germany (NPD).

For these rather heterogenous constellations and actors, the pushback against modernization, sexual diversity, gender theory, migration, and Islam (all together) form a potential platform for coalitions. They offer points of entry even within the educated, liberal spectrum. What is actually conjured is a version of 'the people', an entity that is being contaminated by things alien to its essence and whose existence is threatened by a superfluity of foreigners. This is the threat the aforementioned mobilize when they claim to be safeguarding the values and achievements of the West, of Christianity, of the Enlightenment against 'Islamization' and against the purported 'genderization' of the Western world; against fundamentalist terror and ethnic 'swamping'; against migrants and refugees; against intellectual elites; against freedom of academic speech; against 'liars' in the press; or against the state and its representatives *tout court*. The favored method is shutdown (first cultural and subsequently legal and political) as a way of defending the achievements of whichever 'we' is at stake – the nation, the people, the nuclear family, Christianity – against outsiders. The world is interpreted in Manichaean dichotomies, in antagonisms between inside and outside, and these are aligned with distinctions between the valuable and the valueless, between those who may live and those who may not.

It is a revolt that builds upon – or breathes life into – the notion that the state's task should be to protect the interests, the morality, the lifestyles of its 'own' group, regarded as the only one with legitimacy or an entitlement to stake any claim. The state, such is the constantly repeated complaint, is failing to fulfil that obligation. Instead, 'the establishment' extends its hand not to our own people but to the outsiders, allocating cheap housing and social welfare to refugees and adding insult to injury by urging us to practice compassion. 'The system' is guilty of betrayal. In this sense, the sometimes preposterous agitation against migrants, 'Islam', 'dirty Green and lefty do-gooders', and equally against what the German activists call the 'genderistas', must also be counted as part of a well-orchestrated vendetta against the establishment and a release from the affective and linguistic norms of politically correct behaviour that, in the last instance, has as its target the abolition of liberal democracy itself.

In pursuit of that goal, these groups mobilize patterns that have sedimented into society's unconscious over centuries: forms of segmentation and distinction between human beings for the purposes of stigmatization, exclusion or segregation, along with the xenophobic hostility located deep in the foundations of modern societies.

The 'enlightened fundamentalism' (Liz Fekete) of the European populist right is not only to be found in the instrumentalization of

women, lesbians, gay men and other 'minorities' on behalf of xenophobic policies; it also informs the antagonistic and embattled attitude that typifies toxic racist speech. Regarding feminism, the front
line is dual and contradictory. A particular form of feminism is
co-opted for populism's own ends – on the one hand, to agitate against
migration, Islam and the foreigners; on the other, to wage war on
particular other feminisms, namely those that interrogate hegemonic
gender and sexual norms. Western achievements such as the legal
near-equality of the sexes or the criminalization of sexual violence,
but even more importantly the concepts of gender duality, heterosexuality and family, are defended against both outward and inward
enemies: outwardly against those whom the culturally essentialist
imagination sees as uncivilized and retrograde, or as an uncontrollable sex mob, and inwardly against the 'genderistas' and queers who, so
the story goes, wish to force their ideas of how to live gender and
sexuality down ordinary Germans' throats. The othering of those
considered alien, with the intention of keeping them at a distance, is
therefore directly connected with the vilification of sexual and gender
minorities and dissident feminists. The AfD and Pegida go into battle
not only against the 'Islamization' of the West, but also against what
they call its 'genderization'.

We see here the revival of unequivocal friend-enemy dichotomies, the demonization of the other, and an insistence on the supposed
self that must be defended against all that is alien to it – the return of
concepts that in Germany are strongly associated with Nazi discourse,
such as *Volk*, 'nation', or 'race', along with a recourse to 'homeland',
'culture', and 'identity'. There is talk of foreigners 'crushing' or 'flood-
ing' our country, destabilizing our social systems, flouting our values,
and unfairly receiving things that rightly belong to 'us' alone. All this
indicates just how drastically the boundaries of what can be said have
shifted towards the authoritarian and neoreactionary, away from an
orientation towards democracy, universal human rights and political
pluralism. Disrespect, hate speech and verbal derision, threats of
violence, and violent acts including racist murders have become firm
components of social coexistence – a brutalization of civic life. This

crude discourse manifests a grammar of harshness, of imputation and suspicion, of ostracism and obloquy, all of which increasingly define commentary in the public sphere. It is a way of thinking interested neither in analytical precision nor in critiquing the parochial partiality of one's own perspective. It is also a way of thinking that disregards the individual person and the circumstances in which they find themselves, that ascribes characteristics, totalizing them and making them synonymous with the person as a whole; one that distills social verdicts out of abstractions and locates itself on the moral high ground above those it has identified as responsible for the hated state of affairs.

This is a language that is both unambiguous and global and that is not the language of dialogue and nonviolence, the language of democracy and freedom, the language of conversation between different people who are nevertheless one another's equals. *The Future of Difference* is our attempt to counteract this violence, which is as epistemic as it is lethal, for it is the language of disaster, which, as Maurice Blanchot put it many years ago in *The Writing of the Disaster*, 'ruins everything, all the while leaving everything intact'.[28]

Preface: Other and Rule

'When time stops, truth can be declared.'

– Joan Wallach Scott[1]

The night of New Year's Eve 2015 in Cologne, it is supposed, simply 'speaks for itself'. 'Cologne' – the incident – has become an epochal signifier. All of us claim to know exactly what transpired that night. Now, when we speak of 'Cologne', we are invoking an event generally understood to have a clear, well-defined shape. We all know, don't we, that women were sexually harassed en masse on the streets of a German metropolis. Furthermore, the harassment was carried out by non-German men, that much seems certain: by migrants or foreigners. Some would even confirm it was carried out specifically by 'Nafris', the North Rhine-Westphalia Police Department's internal designation and radio shorthand for 'criminals of North African descent'.[2]

Yet, at the same time, 'Cologne' is the name for an infamously ill-understood occurrence: a cipher freighted with resonances, circulating persistently through time and space, generating fresh meanings. It is a node in which, to borrow a formula from Ernesto Laclau and Chantal Mouffe, the event itself merges and coalesces together with our speech about the event, becoming a *discourse*: a 'differential system of positions' made up of a mix of linguistic and non-linguistic elements.[3] Ultimately, what happened on the night in question remains uncertain. But this uncertainty is precisely why 'Cologne', as a blank surface, has lent itself so well to projections – projections such as those encouraged by *Zeitmagazin*'s editorship when, in June 2016, it simply printed the loaded question: 'What REALLY happened?'.[4] 'Cologne', then, is simultaneously an empty signifier and one brimming with meaning.[5] It can act as a disciplining power, and it even transforms prevalent discourses retroactively.

Predictably, in this moment, we are hearing proclamations on all sides of the inevitable collapse of the (supposedly naive and misguided) *Willkommenskultur* in Germany. Didn't Cologne prove plainly that these individuals 'we' had hitherto welcomed in were neither willing nor able to respect 'our' values? (Our values, by the way, means equality between men and women.) Cologne is supposed to have definitively laid bare the fact that Germany's excessive tolerance vis-à-vis men from 'the Arab world' (whatever that is) poses a danger and a threat to 'our' liberal, egalitarian, Western consensus. And particularly to 'our' women.

In other words, 'Cologne' has come to stand for the assertion that certain migrants cannot be integrated – *they do not want to integrate themselves* – simply because, in the end, there are insuperable differences between the cultures in question. Furthermore, Cologne establishes (or so it would appear) the need for comprehensive CCTV surveillance. It can be deemed responsible for the resurgence of populist political parties and for the erosion of civil society across Germany. Finally, Cologne seems to have secured a far greater degree of cultural receptivity to feminist concerns, although this new regard for feminism is intimately entangled with the culturalization of social inequalities, that is to say, with new forms of racism.

Paradoxically, we are seeing the mobilization of feminism and women's rights by nationalist, nativist, xenophobic and populist parties and platforms – as well as by right-wing governments such as Hungary's, Denmark's or Poland's – in justification of Islamophobic and anti-migrant policies. 'Cologne', in this sense, epitomizes the ambiguous inter-imbrications that exist in our present moment between racism, sexism and feminism. It symbolizes the urgent necessity of grappling uncompromisingly with these three terms, teasing out their differences and, perhaps, inherent entanglements.

In this book, we seek to do just that. We ask: How did this notion of an 'incompatibility' – between Islam and feminism, feminists and migrants, Germanness and sexism – come into being? What role has Cologne played here? What is the nature of the cultural fight this cipher mediates – sometimes tacitly, sometimes explicitly? And how is it that Cologne became what Jacques Lacan calls a *'point de capiton'*, a quilting point of signification in which the normal ambiguity of linguistic reference is stopped? Because that is exactly what Cologne now is: a privileged signifier; a static fixture within a xenophobic security discourse; a matter on which everyone supposedly agrees, even if elsewhere – about other matters – there can still be discussion and uncertainty.

The initial impetus to dwell with these questions came from our perception that Cologne had much to do with the rapid and radical polarization of public speech in Germany. We wanted to find out if our hunch was right and get a handle on the phenomenon, if so. At the time of writing, even those preconceptions about the event 'Cologne' now seem somewhat problematic – that is, they have become problematic in our eyes. But the book that follows tries to treat this difficulty as a challenge and an opportunity. It seeks to advance the (feminist) enlightenment of the present, in a time of increasing discursive nebulousness. Committed to a politics of inter-sectionality, informed by sociological insights, we argue against the narrowing of the window of political debate in the hope of contribut-ing to the revival of 'debate culture' worthy of the name. Our goal is, in the first instance, to determine what our attitude should be vis-à-vis the aforementioned phenomenon and all the questions it raises. We do not ask after the 'objective truth' of the night in Cologne. Our text is neither a piece of reportage nor a properly academic study. Rather, it is an explicitly speculative reflection on what 'Cologne' stands for in the political domain of the Federal Republic of Germany. We certainly do not pretend to have exhausted the topic, nor to have avoided any glaring gaps.

One such gap, a troubling one, is the fact that we, too, have largely ignored the experience of those who were subjected to sexualized violence on the New Year's Eve in question. This omission comes down to our being primarily concerned with the tenor of public conversation about 'Cologne' and the question of the social and epochal shifts reflected therein. Once again, 'the women' had to be deemed irrelevant. This, of course, reproduces the social treatment of

xxviii   THE FUTURE OF DIFFERENCE

sexualized violence generally – and that it does so is not something we wish to downplay.

How are the voices of those who have survived sexual abuse – domestic, public or military sexual violence – to be made audible? This is a hugely important question. And although we do not explicitly pursue it here, we believe our text has something to contribute to the articulation of conditions of possibility for this audibleness. We firmly believe these voices deserve more of a platform, more care, and more attention generally – far more than the structure of this book allows. What follows simply pursues a different question, namely that of the violent, fundamentalizing logic of differentiation: the logic we call 'other and rule'.

By 'fundamentalizing', we mean those discourses that routinely close down meaning itself through generalization and authoritarian reductionism: speech which tries to immunize itself against ambiguity and self-reflection. We are designating – to take up Lacan's terminology again – those 'quilting points' in language where something has been firmly anchored as though through multi-layered tissue. In the context of Cologne, this involved setting up (implicitly, at least), a priori, the essential valences of groups of people, and the alleged 'reality' of their relating. By pre-establishing such commonsense knowledge, the mechanism generates useful shortcuts for reading causality into events: the actions of any given player can easily be extrapolated from the type. Basically, discursive fundamentalization is all about shoring up fixed cultural identities and their intrinsic connection to specific values – for example, the assertion that freedom, democracy, equality and enlightenment are exclusively Western values, and that the Islamic or Arab worlds, conversely, constitutively lack the ability to emerge, politically speaking, beyond their self-incurred minority.

The essentializing force characteristic of 'fundamentalizing' discourse becomes all intensified when it is oriented towards the active construction of difference. It is obviously at its most intense when the framework for distinguishing between things is restricted to, for example, them and us, foreigner and native, black and white. That is to say, selective specification in the description of a situation goes hand in hand with an equally selective de-specification of the complexity that is always – at least potentially – at the heart of any matter.

In the construction of these Manichaean differences, what is perhaps most striking is the heightening of polarized and polarizing attributions – what Gudrun-Axeli Knapp theorizes in terms of 'reduction to a characteristic'. When the media reported on issues regarding the politics of sexuality, freedom of movement, gender, migration and culture, in connection with Cologne, they often did so in the terms – noted by Hedwig Dohm (on whom more later) – of a mass typologization of populations. As such, we were always hearing about 'the' refugees, 'the' women, 'the' Arab men, and 'our' culture.

The use of such terms obstructs our ability to perceive internal differences. Relationships, modes of existence and experiences that don't fit into their typescript – because they are of a more inherently complex (which is to say, intersectional) nature – are rendered invisible, even though they are, empirically speaking, in the vast majority. But there is much else that these static, simplistic concepts of difference render invisible, namely the dynamics of differentiation as a *process*. Our vocabularies of difference tend to depict, as though already accomplished, the fact of one thing being different from another. They do not represent that thing coming into being. Depending on context, then, a decision to speak about gender*ing* rather than gender, or about cultur*ation* rather than culture, can make a big difference.

This is not to say that concepts denoting difference are wrong, per se. Differentiation is neither meaningless nor dangerous in and of itself. It is, in fact, vital that we differentiate! We constantly rely on differences in order to operate on the most basic level, for without them, thinking and acting would be impossible. Differences are the product of social practices, and, as such, they form the basic structure for whole societies, which in turn makes them the enabling framework for social practices. However, there are fundamentally different kinds of differential assertion, and contrasting modes of differentiation, that need to be distinguished from one another – that is to say, differentiated.

Furthermore, the *contexts* in which differences are (differentially) put to use differ as well. Whether it is trivial or meaningful, merely informative or existentially freighted to articulate a single marker of difference – for example, male and female, young and old, hetero- and homosexual, native and foreign, self and other – will very much depend on the context and on the agency and powers of interpretation of the people or groups involved (whose own 'differences' are, as such, rendered relevant). What it means to designate somebody as gay or lesbian, for example – and make them publicly legible in this way – is entirely context-dependent. It could be vital information, an instance of discrimination, an irrelevant detail, or even a death sentence.

In order to understand how reality itself is constituted by means of markers of difference, we must grasp the mechanism by which subjects (in all their social complexity) merge into only one difference. This is to say, we should ask ourselves: What single difference is it that all the actors typically mentioned in connection with Cologne are supposed to embody? In answering this, we propose to apprehend 'Cologne', following Mouffe and Laclau, as a nodal point – that is, a nexus linking linguistic and non-linguistic elements, discourses, and practices in such a way as to call us into being as subjects according to a set of sexual, gendered and racializing hierarchies.[6] What options for subjectivization, then, does Cologne call up? Which people does this 'node' render perceptible, visible, socially recognizable, audible – and *as* who, or as what? And how does that, in turn, end up shaping the potential for solidarity? What moral obligations does it establish, and towards whom?

We regard this book as a contribution to the understanding of culture and society initiated by Birgit Rommelspacher in her theorization of the matrix of domination. Her term *Dominanzkultur* refers to the structuring of the social as a vast network of – multitudinous, intertwined – dimensions of power, organizing our entire way of life into the binary categories of superiority and subordination and thereby determining our very actions, attitudes and feelings. One of our main emphases, in this book, is on the fact that there is no such thing as 'Arab', 'patriarchal', 'Christian', 'Western', 'German' or 'liberal-democratic' culture: that is to say, a cultural 'status quo' never actually exists in any homogeneous or secure sense. Culture is better regarded, instead, as the social space in which meaning arises and the process through which meaning gets generated. And, as a process of meaning production, it even includes all negotiations and contestations *about* signification and meaning. Culture is our making sense of the world and, thus, of ourselves. Culture, in other words, is contexts. And, once again, the contexts in question are culturally produced. They are, as we all know, ambiguous and ill-defined. They are without beginning or end, without clear boundaries, and without authenticity. Yet they cannot be silenced.

As glib as this riff on 'culture' may seem, we believe its substance is all-important. It is our duty to really grasp that culture is *not* the essential property, spirit or nature of a region, religion, 'race' or gender. For whenever we claim that something, say, a piece of our past, some quality or essence, is 'our property', we have already, in that moment – as the historian Joan Wallach Scott says – forsaken the future. Any attempt to 'revise or reinterpret' the identity thus suspended can then only be perceived as a threat to the very existence of 'a national or racial or ethnic or sexual or individual self' and not as an opening, that is to say, a possibility containing the promise that things could be different.[7]

We set forth our polyphonic thoughts against all those who think that the diversity of the world is, in and of itself, already marked by clear distinctions, clear divisions between good and evil, right and wrong, black and white, male and female, hetero- and homosexual. We seek to blast our 'basso continuo' of sheer scepticism – scepticism about the validity of any and all differential assertion – in targeted opposition to the unanimous refrain of all the different currents of fundamentalism that imagine themselves today as victims of some kind of censorship, aggressively corralled into a 'political correctness' by a fantasy feminist or hegemonic gay 'lobby'. (Such fundamentalisms are typically religious, nationalist, white-supremacist, conservative and right-wing, but they can also be left-wing or progressive-identitarian.)

Our commitment to polyglossia – and to an attitude of consistent scepticism – thrives on the fact that we, as authors, espouse different perspectives. We have, in fact, consciously allowed these different points of view to remain visible in the text, instead of downplaying and restraining them in our composition and editing processes. They are interesting differences, differences shaped by our different institutional affiliations, personal affinities and social positions: our disparate ways of being in the world. They are in themselves very much a part of our political and personal relationship, our professional and collegial friendship, which has matured over the course of many years, and whose most important distillation is, we believe, this very experiment in 'common thinking' in different voices.

It is the experimental character of our collaboration that comes across most clearly in our essayistic writing. It is explorative, tentative, incomplete. It was an exercise in 'thinking without a banister', as Hannah Arendt put it[8] – the results of which, we hope, are pleasurable to read. Created on paper and on screens, but also through chatting both online and across the kitchen table; in concentrated solitude; and through talking simultaneously, in parallel, with others, as well as to one another. Ours was a thought process actualized in the 'in-between': in the space between us two authors by the light of those differences that distinguish us (but do not separate us). It represents a merging of our thinking, our speaking, our writing, while we tried out ideas. What a risk for us academically trained as social scientists. What a departure, too, from our academic training as social scientists that would have us bolster every argument from all sides with 'hard' (empirical) evidence.[9] What's more, while writing, we found we could barely keep up with the accelerative dynamic of contemporary politics, and we felt dismayed by the shrinking duration of any given event or debate's 'half-life'.

What else have we learned through trying to not mutually silence one another; trying to actualize a commitment to tarrying with complexity instead of striving (even with the best critical intentions) to reduce it and square it away? Once again, that differences, distinctions and categories per se are *not the problem*. On the contrary. It is precisely because we value differences that we must pinpoint how they are deployed for the purposes of domination, how they get pressed into service in the reproduction of social inequalities, of the uneven distribution of precariousness.

What function does the state-authored production and politics of cultural difference serve? It seems to have become, once more, central to how societies make and remake themselves. This is the question to which we hope to contribute a partial answer, and its range cannot be overestimated. We are acutely aware that if this book were to set out to, somehow, *comprehensively* reconstruct the phenomenology and internal mechanisms of two constitutive configurations of power – racism and sexism – as well as their ambiguous link with feminism – it would constitutively fail.[10]

What we do hope to contribute, however, is a reminder that racism and sexism cannot in any way be extrapolated from the various groups or individuals their prejudice designates. Neither race nor gender are realities inherent to bodies, even though they are coupled with specific physical traits, written (and read) into bodies, and ontologized as corporeal.[11] The challenge is to understand sexism and racism as highly agile, heterogeneous, dynamic, constantly mutating figurations; expansive representations; power practices that can be linked together in diverse and even contradictory ways.[12] With this challenge in mind, we direct our inquiry into the power-freighted business of the production of differences in contemporary German society. What are the circumstances in which they are made 'relevant'?

Above all, it is important for us to remember that cultures are 'humanly made structures of both authority and participation, benevolent in what they include, incorporate, and validate, less benevolent in what they exclude and demote,' as Edward Said contends in *Culture and Imperialism*.[13] Dissident imaginations grow – like politics – in the field of power. Culture is not, after all, an 'iron cage'[14] that condemns us to behave in accordance with the rule. Culture can be, among other things, reflective, sceptical and critical; it comprises not just conformity but dissident action. Instead of thinking about identity in terms of difference, then, we want above all to *differentiate* between differences and think about differences *within* difference. In this sense, it would be a gross (and, it has to be said, symptomatic) misunderstanding if our criticism of 'fundamentalist' language were to be read as a plea for silence or an endorsement of censorship. On the contrary: take this as a call to talk . . . about the way we talk.

Acknowledgments

A book never owes its existence to its authors alone, and this is definitely the case with our book. We have registered, as references, the traces of myriad others, but we cannot and do not claim to have provided a definitive map of all the knowledge on which we built. Our editor, Mascha Jacobs, accepted the challenge of crafting a coherent text out of a manuscript in two voices, ensuring that both voices remained distinctly audible. Ina Kerner, Ilona Pache, Jasmin Siri, Imke Schmincke and Michaela Volkmann read our first drafts and provided comments: we would like to thank them for their ever-critical, ever-comradely support. Sabine Hark thanks Ilona Pache in particular for her incessant encouragement and unwavering confidence in the relevance of our project, and for the sheer serenity of her shared life with this author. Paula-Irene Villa thanks Michael Cysouw for much in general, and for his kind enabling of her intensive writing periods in particular. Karin Werner and Anke Poppen from transcript publishing house, who came up with the idea for this book. Without them it would not have been written. Last but not least, we would like to thank Sophie Lewis for her thoughtful and considerate translation.

1

'The Rotten Present': A Plea for Friendship with the World

'I wish to defend this entire rotten age, the rotten present. It's all we've got. It's the only life that is available to us. It, and no other, harbours the substances that may unleash our powers.'[1]

– Christina Thürmer-Rohr, 1987

'SEEING WHAT'S BEFORE US'

'Can't you *see* what's before you?'[2] What it means to be asked this question, typically in tones of irritation, is a matter the philosopher Nelson Goodman discusses in his book *Ways of Worldmaking*. He personally liked to answer the question: 'That depends.' That is to say, the statement 'the earth moves' is just as true as the statement 'the earth stands still', since both statements simply depend on their own distinct frame of reference.[3] Is Goodman here legitimating the 'post-truth' era in which, according to a great number of journalists and commentators, we now live, defining truth in terms of whatever generates the most clicks? On the contrary: what may appear at first glance to be a radically relativistic position that does not *want* to know the difference between opinions and facts is, in reality, a conscious exercise in 'irritating those fundamentalists who know very well that facts are found, not made, that facts constitute the one and only real world, and that knowledge consists of believing the facts.'[4]

Above all, Goodman's reflections constitute a plea for examining the conditions that make statements of fact possible, for clarifying 'what is before us' in the first place and guarding against the 'view from nowhere'. Second, despite or perhaps because of the growing importance of a certain epochal 'post-facticity', Goodman makes it possible to think about what it means that facts are not simply given: that is, that they are not outside the social unfolding of history. We create 'world-versions' – and thus facts – he writes, 'with words, numerals, pictures, sounds, or other symbols of any kind in any medium'.[5] And, Friedrich Nietzsche reminds us, 'it is enough to create new names and estimations and probabilities in order to create new things in the long run'.[6] Although we do contend, therefore, that worlds are *produced* and not simply found, we do not espouse the view, critically described by Pierre Bourdieu and Judith Butler, that the existence of things depends entirely on their names, that is, on 'performativity's social magic'.[7] We simply deem that our perception of the world, and the way we designate it, shapes what we perceive and how, at a fundamental level; and that it determines what, as far as we are concerned, it *really is*. Indeed, according to philosopher John Searle, our 'entire institutional reality' is created by 'linguistic representation'.[8]

The consequences of this are no more, and no less, than this: reality and language, perception and truth, facts and interpretations are not only interlinked, but *constitutive* of one another. That is no trivial insight, and it demands awareness of the complexity and, sometimes, inscrutability of the relationship – inscrutability being, as it is, one of the essential characteristics of the modern era. The philosopher Bernhard Waldenfels contends that, in modernity, there is no longer any form of order that exists a priori while still encompassing the observer.[9] Waldenfels, here, is essentially describing the condition of contingency. That is: it is equally possible for all things to be one way as it is for them to be another, because there is no necessary reason for anything existing. Not our actions alone, but even the sphere in which these actions take place, contain a multiplicity of possible versions of themselves. And, ultimately, this quality of impenetrability, which marks the very practice of modern science, demands that we understand the production of knowledge as always open-ended and provisional – the latter being a paradigmatic expression of the norm of 'organized skepticism' advanced by Robert Merton.[10] The opacity in question may even have intensified in recent years as a result of the increasing – or, at least, increasingly noticeable – complexity of the social.[11]

THE COLOGNE INCIDENT

Seeing what's before us and determining what matters – that is the concern of this book. The occasion for it? Whatever transpired on New Year's Eve 2015 in Cologne: a night that stands for a tectonic shift in Germany's social fabric, albeit one whose reach remains as yet unknown. As we have noted, whatever actually transpired soon crystallized into an 'event', far in excess of the real incident(s). 'Cologne' is now the name of that event: the name for an ensemble made up of 'words, numerals, pictures, sounds, or other symbols' that has acquired the capacity to 'create new things in the long run'.

Following Stuart Hall, we apprehend 'Cologne' as one element in a 'regime of representation' that encompasses 'the entire repertoire of imagery and visual effects' by which 'difference' is represented at any historical moment.[12] Within any such regime, everyday differences – ethnic and cultural labels, for instance, or gender markers – are (re)arranged in complex ways so as to bring them under a unified provisional structure. It is by referring to this unified structure that people are able to make meaning and organize the world for themselves. 'Cologne' is the name of one such structure. But what is it, specifically, then, that 'Cologne' renders legible? 'Cologne' organizes the difference between 'us and them', which is to say, in Hall's famous formulation, the relationship between 'the West and the rest'.[13]

Regimes of representation, as Hall understands them, do not simply *describe* differences. On the contrary: the defining feature of any regime of representation is the way it *produces* difference. Regimes of representation govern by virtue of the fact that differences are given to us *in any case*. We grapple extensively with this question of the distribution of the sensible in this book: that is to say, with the texts through which 'Cologne' was made visible. In this task, we understand texts and images, with Alex Demirović, as active 'intervening' entities which 'seek to create constellations and contexts'.[14]

However, to assert that differences are performative – that is to say, made visible by texts and images – is not the whole story. For

Demirović, a text or an image is always 'fundamentally dialogic – practice-based – because its emergence inevitably *changes* the constellation of already-existing texts, the relationship between the said and the unsayable, and thus, the context itself'. Texts and images do not, therefore, acquire meaning by themselves, in themselves or for themselves; they do so only 'as discursive processes, as specific events in a constellation'. By 'being part of a force-field, they are themselves co-producing and shaping', they 'respond to one problem or another, arising in order to take something up, displace it, override it or change it'. Lastly, we will state a truism, but an essential one: images and texts determine neither perception nor reality. They *co-constitute* both, and this constituting depends in turn on people's actual practices of appropriation in specific contexts.

It took less than a year from the emergence of that node called 'Cologne' for it to become part of Germany's 'objective' history. 'After Cologne' is now a dividing line in our calendars that frames the time that has passed since – and possibly the time before it, too. In any case, that New Year's Eve was the moment when the parameters of all kinds of debates shifted irrevocably: debates around culture, 'race', gender, religion, and morality; on the management of migration and asylum; on matters of sexuality and gender; on criminal prosecution policy around sexual violence; on the rights of immigrants; on relations between native Germans and foreigners; on the interconnectedness of racism, sexism and feminism; and on immigration, integration, and internal security.

The effects precipitated were complex and difficult to summarize under the heading of one common denominator. Upon closer inspection, though, it seems safe to say that the dynamics unleashed by Cologne have been characterized by a certain core *ambivalence* that is, in practice at least, always controlled and regulated by fundamentalist rhetorics. We are fascinated by these rhetorics. As we hope to show in the following chapters, sexual politics has once again become active in the service of the production of racist truths.[15] Feminism is once more being used to bear witness to the 'incompatibility' of Islam with Western values (such as gender equality or tolerance for

LGBTQI* existence and lifestyles) and to legitimize the violence of European border regimes.[16]

There is nothing remotely new about the construction of a zero-sum game involving feminism and the foreigner; nothing original about mobilizing resentment off the back of an imagined dichotomy between women's rights (and those of other sexual and gender minorities), on the one hand, and everything non-Western or foreign, on the other. The unforgettable populist rallying cry of the German minister of the interior, Thomas de Maizière, in April 2015, 'Wir sind nicht Burka' – 'We are not burka' – was but one among a slew of fresh examples.[17] To de Maizière and many others, 'Cologne' was the definitive proof and manifestation of Samuel Huntington's otherwise widely repudiated view that the source of all twenty-first-century conflicts lies in 'culture' (the 'clash of civilizations' hypothesis).[18] As that camp has, ever since, made a habit of asserting, any prospect of harmonious European or American coexistence with immigrants (especially Muslims) from the Global South is unfortunately fatally compromised – by 'cultural differences'.

AMBIGUOUS ENTANGLEMENTS: RACISM, SEXISM, FEMINISM

This book represents our attempt to gain some purchase on these contemporary entanglements, these ambiguous imbrications of racism, sexism and feminism in the present moment. We regard it as an exercise in critical thinking in which we bring together our sociological knowledge with feminist theory, postcolonial analysis, queer and critical race studies, and border or migration studies. These fields are all part of the West's internal critical tradition, a tradition which, as Foucault argues in *Discourse and Truth*, calls into question the very mechanisms by which the 'truth' is culturally produced.[19] The paradigmatic starting point these academic domains hold in common (at least in theory) is essentially Marx's insight that critique is always *immanent*, that is, it must appreciate that it is itself part of what it criticizes, such that the critique itself becomes subject to critique. In Gayatri Chakravorty Spivak's words:

'This impossible "no" to a structure which one critiques, yet inhabits intimately, is the deconstructive philosophical position.'[20] In our view, it is the heterogeneous field of feminist thought, more than any other theoretical project, that has set itself the challenge of grappling with the aporias that arise when we acknowledge the immanence of critique, paying attention, in particular, to the risk of reinscribing an axis of difference – sexual and gender difference – in the very act of questioning it.

Feminist theory, therefore, has always considered 'the critique of *all* discourses concerning gender' vital to feminism, '*including* those produced or promoted as feminist' – to quote Teresa de Lauretis.[21] It has therefore not only rejected the concept of 'the woman in general'[22] but sought to ask who is actually represented by specific usages of the category 'woman', making the production of that sign of difference and discrimination *itself* the object of inquiry. The history of feminism is rich in examples of what we mean, dating back to the mid-nineteenth century. Famously, in 1851, at a gathering of white bourgeois American women fighting for women's suffrage, the black abolitionist and former slave Sojourner Truth approached the congregation demanding to know whether or not she qualified as a woman. The question put to the gathering of women's rights activists – 'Ain't I a woman?' – drew logically from Truth's experiences of toiling as hard and eating as much as any man, being flogged, and never once experiencing any of the paternalistic gallantry the white majority took for granted on the basis of *their* femininity.[23] Ever since then, the question 'Ain't I a woman?' has served as an effective tool for dismantling racialized, ethnocentric or heteronormative definitions of gender and femininity.[24]

Thus, 'what appear as separable categories are, rather, the conditions of articulation for each other.'[25] The resultant questions have been raised again and again in the history of feminist theory, as in Judith Butler's formulation: 'How is race lived in the modality of sexuality?' and 'How is gender lived in the modality of race?'[26] And, equally: 'How do colonial and neo-colonial nation states rehearse gender relations in the consolidation of state power?' and 'Where and how is "homosexuality" at once the imputed sexuality of the colonized, and the incipient sign of Western imperialism?'[27]

Ultimately, feminism has to be understood as a project defined by its internal contradictions, discontinuities and antagonisms; as a struggle over meanings. Feminist thought has no unitary canon, but rather represents a generative field full of disparate movements. More than the sum of its parts, feminism is not only the aggregate of disparate critical analyses of gendered social inequalities and exclusions, dominant discourses and cultural regimes; it is the materialization of a process of recognizing the situatedness of all knowledge production.

Of course, this principle of critical self-reflexivity – this fundamental methodological doubt – also informs many of the branches of the humanities and social sciences we borrow from in these pages. Indeed, all the 'critical traditions' (by which we mean disciplines that cleave to Marx's orientation towards immanence in the broadest sense) – as well as the newer fields of systems theory, actor-network theory, science and technology studies, and cultural studies – direct their practitioners not to reify their own categories and to be wary of their (at least implicit) normative power. And yet, unfortunately, 'problematic' categories (and what would an unproblematic category look like, anyway?) do not simply give up and go away. Quite the contrary. We are stuck with negotiating the manifold problems of categorization and classification precisely because we know their power to generate worlds, and because, in the end, we think that concepts can actually mount a resistance to power.

Our reflections, in summary, are guided by the hypothesis that 'Cologne' is bound up in a series of highly effective ideological operations – mainly objectifications of difference – which now serve to shore up social hierarchies in Germany. We will test this hypothesis in the following chapters. Once again, we do not argue for denying differences, ignoring them, or even abolishing them. Quite the reverse: we urge remembrance of the fact that sociality itself would be impossible without differences – even as it is governed by them. The point, for us, then, is to develop an ethics of difference that is aware of its own sociality: an ethics that does not pretend differences exist in and of themselves, outside of social practice. This mode of relating would defend against the dehumanizing operations of contemporary fundamentalist differentiation which give us, for instance: 'the black person', 'the asylum seeker', 'woman', and 'man'. It would simultaneously value the way that differences make practice and perception – not least the practice of critical differentiation – possible.

A MATTER OF CONCERN

We seek to distance ourselves equally from those who would have us believe that the world consists of opinions as from those who deem knowledge to be a simple matter of acquainting oneself with the facts. As urgent as it is – and it is, indeed, more urgent than ever before – to combat lies with facts, in truth, reality is not (only) made up of facts. For the simple reason that facts do not make up the whole of worldly experience, as Bruno Latour contends, real-ness has to be ascribed to them. We, as authors, do not therefore rely solely on matters of fact; rather, we adopt 'a realism dealing with matters of concern'.[28]

'Cologne' is one such matter of concern, in the first place because, well, it concerns us. Second, as it clearly isn't reducible to its punctual components, the sum of certain localized happenings, it cannot be reduced to a fact. To continue with Latour's framework, however, we know that several conditions have to come together at once in order for a 'matter of concern' to take shape in a lasting way. Additional forces have to be in play; simple occurrences alone do not make reality. A 'matter of concern' comes into being as a result of media attention, political interpellation, cultural, religious, governmental and other interpretation, police action, scientific expertise, and much, much more. Since the world is not found but *made* – we make it – it behooves us to understand the mechanisms behind this making, this gathering up of the necessary components to turn mere objects into a public 'thing'. Only then will we appreciate the opportunities afforded us to remake the world *otherwise*. And, after all, we *must* do so, for, as Chimamanda Ngozi Adichie reminds us, 'It does not have to be like this.'[29]

We are constantly hearing from those who profess to know exactly what the nature of the reality we inhabit is. We, by contrast, want to start by asking nothing but questions. If it is the case that 'it is enough to create new names and estimations and probabilities in order to create new things in the long run', then we must recognize that the world is constantly evading us, reforming itself ahead of us, just outside our grasp. As researchers, we are, in fact, ourselves *part* of this very process. Our scholarship is part of the creation of new things – including new perspectives on the world. Just like public politicking and media discourse, our endeavours manufacture worlds and (in Ian Hacking's phrase) 'make people up'.[30] Words *do* things. It really cannot be stressed often enough.

Whenever words and concepts coagulate into operations of categorical classification, they risk generating what Sighard Neckel and Ferdinand Sutterlüty call 'qualitative judgments of otherness' (*qualitative Urteile der Andersartigkeit*) targeting individuals and groups – that is to say, drawing symbolic lines of membership or exclusion.[31] They produce and reproduce – in ways always intimately bound up with whatever news developments, media narratives and political agendas are circulating in the contemporary political conjuncture – entire modes of social valuation. And, ultimately, these words and concepts flow – mediated by culture – back into the social reservoir of knowledge. This collective reservoir of meanings is what all members of society then inevitably draw upon when forming their notions of 'self' and 'other': making 'judgments of otherness' and deciding who is entitled to what, what is collectively owed to whom, and who isn't even worth our attention.

INTERROGATING DIFFERENCES

Critical thinking must always, for these reasons, ensure it is not participating in the ongoing, violent process the nineteenth-century philosopher Hedwig Dohm referred to as *Versämtlichung* (otherization) of the world. *Versämtlichung* describes the epistemic mechanism by which – irrespective of the cause or political banner under which it takes place – we construct, ossify and maintain imaginary others. To avoid it, we must constantly question – indeed, call into question – all evidence, superficial or otherwise, of non-negotiable identity-based differences wherever they arise. Differences, be they markers of sexual, gendered, cultural or ethnic variation, should not be taken for granted or regarded as indisputable. Rather, we should understand them as *contingent* realities that are the product of specific historically and institutionally situated struggles. Differences, in other words, are the result of specific discursive strategies, practices and modalities of power. They are always provisional, but this does not mean they are in any way ephemeral or fleeting.

For example, in statistical and bureaucratic settings, social traits are not only *attributed to* social groups, they inevitably also act as a post-hoc *rationalization* of inequality, contributing to the consolidation of uneven geographies, especially when these (as signifiers of difference) have coagulated into full-blown categories of essentialized identity.[32] As the feminist social theorist Regina Becker-Schmidt contended some time ago, in order to really understand social inequality, we first have to understand the social force of attribution itself.[33]

To do that, it is just as vital that we learn how to liberate difference, not just from the rigid dyad of the universal versus the particular, but from *all* essentializing mystifications: the 'eternal feminine', 'Africa, the dark continent', 'men who don't listen and women who can't read maps', and so on. Hedwig Dohm was amazed at the 'incomprehensible contradictions' that characterized male judgments about women in the nineteenth century. She wrote:

> Woman is a potpourri of antagonistic qualities, a kaleidoscope that can bring forth any given nuance of character or colour if one simply shakes it up and down. According to the critical mass, the basic ground of the feminine spirit seems to be a fog of sheer chaos, a primal mist whence the voice of Man's Creator can simply call into being whatever properties Man so happens to desire.

It is thus crucial that we learn to decrypt all binaries, perceiving that they bind opposites to one another in the act of defining and separating them. This endeavour not only constitutes an end in itself (for example, this is the entirely legitimate form it takes in academia, notably in gender studies) but, further, helps disembed and make visible the mechanisms of real-life domination inherent in discursive dualism. It is not, in that sense, sufficient to grasp the process by which social actors get 'classified'; we must go beyond that and interrogate the *conditions* under which classificatory distinctions are hatched. Instead of accepting a given identity as a premise when thinking about difference – that is, presupposing that that identity exists, thereby removing it from criticism – as we've suggested, we have to think *in difference about difference*, and learn to differentiate between differences. What matters most to us is recognizing that some differences are harmless, even joyful, while others hold in place the poles of a global matrix of domination, as Donna Haraway attests.[34] So, it is not so much *whether* but, rather, the question of *how* differences are activated politically that spurred us on when writing this book.

RESPONSIBILITY, SITUATEDNESS, 'FRIENDSHIP WITH THE WORLD'

Totalizing ways of seeing – 'the Muslim', 'the woman wearing a headscarf', 'the economic migrant', not to mention 'feminists', 'identity politics', 'Germans and Islam', 'women and men', 'whites and blacks' – are, needless to say, simply not an option for us. Not only do they mask the internal heterogeneity of all things, they deny the partiality and positionality of every speaking position. And, ultimately, any view that is *not* considered 'partial' is always going to invoke 'the' unmarked category, the putatively white, male, cis, heterosexual, able-bodied subjectivity that history has enforced as a self-evident universal. The peculiar power of this unmarked position lies, paradoxically, in its structural limitations. That which is 'us', that which is 'normal' – imagined as universal – enjoys the relative lack of scrutiny afforded by its place in the shadow of the particular, the 'marked', and the divergent, which we force into the light. It is imperative to constantly ask, then, *why* what we see is what we see; where are we seeing from; and what are the limits on this seeing?

Once again: what we are describing here is a practice of critical, self-reflective positionality. By no means do we mean to vindicate, in this, a trivial relativism. At stake is our ability to see what is available for us to see, to perceive what we have been taught to perceive, and to know that something is missing. This means becoming willfully alert and curious with regard to that which is hidden (in part because we are hiding it). It means making things into matters of concern. Relativism, on the other hand, is a way of claiming to be nowhere and everywhere the same. According to Haraway, relativist accounts of the relation between identity and positionality are usually just a way of denying responsibility and of preventing us from critically responding to it.[35]

In contrast, Haraway's theorization of situatedness insists on shared responsibility for the practices that give us power – the authors of this book, for example, are called to account for our responsibility as privileged workers and intellectuals. This isn't about a 'fundamentalism of positionality' that seeks to derive an inescapable standing in the world from a given position occupied by the speaker within the space of the social.[36] 'Positionality' does not imply that a particular social position – female, Jewish, lesbian, middle class, Catholic, working class, migrant, refugee, white, Bavarian – inevitably entails any particular opinions, attitudes or beliefs stemming somehow, ineluctably, from the position in question. It certainly does not define the experiences that can be lived by individuals positioned thus. Quite the reverse: we understand positionality to be all about recognizing that social positioning does *things* to us – things we cannot really help – in dynamic and complex ways. What we *can* do, however, is adopt an attitude vis-à-vis our positionality, cognizant of the fact that it is in our power to do things with it in return. In fact, it is probably impossible not to.

The alternative to, on the one hand, epistemic totalitarianisms that lump the world into opposites and, on the other, relativisms that do not care about it at all, can only be 'partial, locatable, critical knowledges'.[37] Solidarity is the name for this web of connection in politics; in the field of epistemology, it is called dialogue, conversation, debate. Our book is committed to it. We hope this will contribute to 'a more adequate, richer, better account of a world' but also a 'critical, reflective relation to our own as well as others' practices of domination and the unequal parts of privilege and oppression that make up all positions', to quote Donna Haraway again.[38] For us, this has as much to do with ethics and politics as it does with epistemology, knowledge or truth.

Regrettably, responsibility is widely thought instead 'in terms of the obligation to answer for oneself, to be the guarantor of one's own actions', to quote Achille Mbembe's critique.[39] What we require is a different stance – seeking to think not so much *about* as *with* the world – namely, a stance of empathy qua intellectual orientation. This intellectual empathy embraces the influence of the world, neither grasping all random feeling willy-nilly nor attempting to defend itself against vulnerability, against *touch*. Nevertheless, it enacts 'resistance to that which is forced upon it', as Theodor Adorno writes in *Negative Dialectics*.[40] It raises the question, posed by Judith Butler, of whether one can 'lead a good life in a bad life' – that is, a world in which 'the good life is structurally or systematically foreclosed for so many'.[41] It demands that we do 'sciences from below', making sense of the world through epistemic processes that centre the perspective of the most marginalized.[42] One thing to centre, to give just one example, might be the phenomenon known as 'household air pollution', which, according to a World Health Organization (WHO) study, accounts for the premature death of some 4 million people annually, most of them women and children.[43] Scientifically and politically, such forms of slow violence would certainly become public 'things', 'matters of concern', under a regime of radical empathy. Christina Thürmer-Rohr had a memorable name for the epistemic commitment we are talking about. She called it 'friendship with the world'.[44]

DOUBT IN DOUBT

To espouse friendship with the world is to modulate how we *act* every bit as much as how we *think* (insofar as we would even wish to establish a difference between the two). It is to hesitate before passing judgment, but it is never indifference. It is to be sceptical of affective reactions without, however, cynically rejecting affect. Cynicism serves, in a sense, to augment its bearer, helping her gain a putative distinction vis-à-vis whatever it is othering. But it can offer nothing by way of justice to those who will suffer from the resultant loss of solidarity. The attitude to the world that we want to foster, in contrast, seeks to acknowledge what is known while, at the same time, defamiliarizing and alienating that knowledge – re-examining things from perspectives different from one's own – and thereby expanding one's perception of the world. This, in turn, demands that we challenge ourselves, as far as possible, always to spell out our reasoning, instead of relying on local and available repositories of common sense and general truths.

Hannah Arendt, following Immanuel Kant, referred to such a disposition, premised on the ability to take others' perspectives into account, as an 'expanded' practice of thought.[45] Instead of adding to the great number of *urgent diagnoses* people are producing at the moment – instead of generating value for the seemingly ever-intensifying 'attention economy'[46] – we trust ourselves, even at this troublesome juncture, to *doubt*. We are seeking to go against the grain of what Pierre Bourdieu calls 'doxa', that is, the ensemble of that which is taken for granted and unquestioned.[47] Instead of *inferring* contexts for things, we think it more apt to ask: What is it that is brought into context for us, such that an emergency, an *urgence* (urgency) or 'state of exception',[48] in Foucault's terms, is created?

And what is the precise nature of this 'emergency' situation anyway, which is supposedly caused by excessive liberality around questions of identity, too much political correctness, too little attention to the social mainstream, too much consideration for the concerns of sexual, gender and racial minorities – all of which, so its proponents claim, is what made right-wing populism possible?[49] What kind of 'emergency', when the challenges associated with immigration and integration have to be negotiated primarily as a matter of internal *security* to be tackled, among other things, by a *garment police*[50] – and when the topics of terrorism, sexual wrongdoing and Islam must be treated as an indissoluble unity?[51] Meanwhile, the right-wing violence that has long been endemic to the country, such as the murders committed by the neo-Nazi National Socialist Underground (NSU), are not regarded in this way.[52] Rather, they are routinely treated as non–ideologically motivated acts by individuals.[53] Why does the everyday, systematic dimension and massive scale of sexual violence against women, and of violence against refugees (their persons, shelters, dwellings) – including violence against people *perceived* as migrants – not constitute a 'state of emergency' in the same way as did the violent attacks in Cologne?

Should we agree that it is an 'emergency' that Germany is a divided country,[54] a society in which, as Oliver Nachtwey contends, 'collective fear of downward mobility seems to be universal'[55] – driving citizens into the arms of the far-right Pegida and AfD? Or should we not first ask: Whose precariousness is visible and perceptible to us, and whose is not? Whose vulnerability do we take seriously and understand as our own? Is the embitterment of the alienated, predominantly white, heterosexual, 'autochthonous' German middle class the only form of resentment that *counts*?

And, finally, why should we entertain for a second the idea that an individual's gender performance, deemed deviant in the eyes of the presumed majority, somehow leads to widespread insecurity, aggression and violence? If this were the case, would not lesbian, gay, bisexual, intersex, trans and genderqueer people, whose sexuality is relentlessly called into question and rendered permanently insecure, by the same logic, be especially violent and aggressive? And wouldn't everybody then have to demonstrate the utmost understanding for that aggression? In short, then, is the dominant description of a current 'state of emergency' actually an accurate or useful description? That is to say, does it provide answers to the big questions concerning the society in which we actually live: What holds it together? What links exist between inequality, domination, integration and social conflict? And how might we (re)establish social bonds?

To be frank, we do not have answers to these questions either. Nevertheless, we believe that the question of what constitutes the exception – the sense of *urgency* justifying *emergency* measures – must be made far clearer than it has been previously. That being achieved, those of us who do not want to settle for a strategy of reductivism – or who have no desire to combat facts with affects, and statistics with feelings – would be hard-pressed to avoid treating matters of concern (that is, the things that concern us) with compassion, empathy and the determination to *differentiate*.

'MORAL-SOCIAL SCIENCE'

Any good analysis of complex realities therefore requires of us an empirically oriented mode of thought – but one that is capable of appreciating the mutually contingent nature of various differences. It requires, in other words, 'a *moral-social science* in which moral considerations are not suppressed and set aside, but systematically blended with analytical reasoning', in the formula of Albert Hirschman.[56] Of course, as Christina Thürmer-Rohr already advanced thirty years ago – in her analysis of the entanglements of femininity, feminism and patriarchal rule – categories like sensitivity, care, empathy, compassion and tenderness are neither context-free nor morally innocent.[57]

Rather, they are components of a relational morality which, albeit beautiful, is ultimately an abstraction. So even values like morality, dignity and respect must be critically unpicked, *precisely because* we cannot do without them as we go about the urgent task of reviving democracy. 'In what social location', we must ask, are empathy, concern and compassion to be found? How can they be tied to analyses that take us beyond mere fleeting affect? 'Whom do they serve, whom do they benefit, who mobilizes them, whom do they fail, do they break, to whom do they turn to their opposite?'[58]

One way of summing this up is to stress, once again, the importance of understanding that our entire way of life is predicated on
relations of subordination and its opposite, superordination: the
fixing of things within endless hierarchies. These often subtle yet
violent differentiations determine almost everything – actions, attitudes and feelings – for all of us. And, as we've stated, it is not the
differences themselves that are the problem here, but the domina-
tional logic of (de)humanization that subtends them and inflects the
things they designate: man, African, victim, woman, human, queer,
foreign, citizen, and so on.

DOMINATION CULTURE

Our book seeks to contribute to an understanding of the mechanism
we call 'othering and ruling'. We are convinced that difference is not,
in and of itself, the problem: rather, the problem is the way differences
are anchored, made meaningful and roped into everyday political life.
And it is precisely for this reason that we feel it is crucial to understand the difference between at least two different kinds of differences.
On the one hand, there are differences that are themselves committed
to the knowledge that nothing on earth, especially not the human, is
thinkable in the singular; as Hannah Arendt writes, 'Not Man but
men inhabit this planet.'[59] On the other hand, differences are often
conceived and motivated by domination. The latter kind of differentiation is best understood as driven by the will to misunderstand the
many and 'reduce them to quantity – to the number one', in Christina
Thürmer-Rohr's formulation.[60]

We advance the notion of 'othering and ruling' so as to highlight
a mechanism we take to be a core part of what the German theorist
Birgit Rommelspacher calls 'domination culture'.[61] Rommelspacher's
framework designates a comprehensive social logic made up of an
intricate web of mutually interacting dimensions of power. Above all,
the term 'domination culture' focuses on the sphere of culture: the
domain in which, today perhaps more than ever, the production and
reproduction of difference, discrimination, segregation, vulnerability

and danger are negotiated. And, finally, 'domination culture' sums up Rommelspacher's contention, which we've already alluded to, that our entire way of life is couched in 'categories of subordination and super-ordination'.[62] This includes, of course, the way we create images of other people, and represents a tendency that has rapidly taken on an unprecedented virulence, what with the worldwide right-wing and populist-conservative capture of liberal democracy in recent years.

The French sociologist Michel Wieviorka, too, has long presented similar arguments, emphasizing the pre-eminence of culture. For Wieviorka, economic inequalities and social injustices aren't just things that affect people; rather, as dimensions of discrimination and segregation, they *define* the most fragile and the most vulnerable in *cultural* terms that can then all too easily be expressed as natural char-acteristics (i.e., naturalized).[63] Whenever we speak of 'cultural differ-ences', we cannot, according to Wieviorka, remain silent for long on the subject of social hierarchy, inequality and exclusion. Questions of cultural right (or rights), moreover, simply *cannot* be discussed with-out involving social injustice in the debate.

Rommelspacher understands culture in a very broad sense as the ensemble of social practices and shared mediations through which the current constitution of a society and, in particular, its political-economic structures and its history, are expressed.[64] Moreover, according to Rommelspacher, the dominant culture determines *all* behaviour – 'the attitudes and feelings of all people who live in any given society'[65] – and mediates between the individual and social structures. In Western societies, or so her book *Dominanzkultur* contends, this dominant culture is also a *domination* culture, which is to say, a culture 'primarily characterized by different traditions of domination in all their different dimensions'.[66] What we are scrutinizing, then, is these many and particular 'forms and modes of domination' which, as Beate Krais and Gunter Gebauer show, are encoded in our worldviews, constantly confirmed to us by our systems of reasoning, and transmitted to us via the social institutions that, in themselves, produce culture.[67]

Culture, then, is not a specific constellation of traditions, mores, myths and cuisines made up of various, alternately regional, religious or historical essentialisms. Culture is both the complex location and *form of production* of social knowledge and meaning. It is an unevenly available and authoritarian sphere that is productive of inequality – thus paradoxically not 'merely cultural',[68] as Judith Butler says, but linked to all kinds of concrete material issues that determine access to resources. It is also, on the other hand, a place where societies and their members make sense of these circumstances, and thus provides the (only?) possibility of changing these conditions. Culture is form that is simultaneously indestructible and always in flux. Culture is the circulation of meaning and signification, which are constantly being limned and remade anew by that circulatory movement.

Prime among the relations of inequality culture reproduces (inequality of access, of participation and of interpretation) are: sexism and heteronormativity, racism, and class. These, however, are not to be understood as social divisions operating independently, but rather analyzed as a complex intersectional constellation. It does not make sense to categorize them, as many have unsuccessfully sought to do, in terms of 'primary' and 'secondary' contradictions; nor to classify them, for example, as 'vertical' versus 'horizontal' axes of inequality; 'ascriptive' traits as opposed to socio-structural inequalities; or neatly partitioned struggles for 'recognition' on the one hand and 'redistribution' on the other. This is a decidedly erroneous approach that fails to recognize the extent to which visibility, recognition and representation are systematically connected to the flow of resources, power and opportunity.

For the aforementioned French sociologist Michel Wieviorka, the cultural and the social are always already 'mixed' to begin with when it comes to the contemporary formulation of the social.[69] Power relations simply cannot be mapped according to a hierarchy in which the precise configuration of 'primary' and 'secondary' contradictions can be precisely established. People are never simply one thing or the other, never 'first' a privileged researcher and only then female, lesbian or heterosexual, for example, with or without living children, with or without proletarian roots or 'some kind of migration background'. Identities – understood as relations to the self, as the question 'who am I?' – are not constative things: they are neither given nor fixed. Rather, they are expressions of social relations. It's up to us what we do with them.

NO BLUEPRINTS

For all these reasons, we strongly oppose any attempt to interpret a given social position as a blueprint for an identity, or even for attitudes. If you are white, for example, you may not necessarily think or act in racist ways, but you have to acknowledge that you benefit from the accrual of a racist dividend. This dividend will differ again, depending on your positioning along other axes such as age, physical appearance, religion, gender, sexual orientation, education level and citizenship. Again, those who belong to an educated elite do not necessarily have to 'be' elitist; the point is that they should acknowledge and strive to be accountable to the fact that they systematically benefit from these privileges, even where they are not consciously deployed. Institutional privileges do not function in the same way for everybody.

In a spirit of friendship with the world, we must recognize one thing – a necessary and often unmanageably complex-seeming characteristic of this 'rotten present' – namely, that one is always *multiply* situated within these constellations. That one exists within an educational elite does not, for example, simply negate one's 'migration background' or a childhood spent among a majority-Catholic German rural proletariat; likewise, being a lesbian does not negate one's whiteness. In keeping with this complexity, the conversation about difference must free itself once and for all from the 'positional fundamentalism' that is currently spreading its reach on both the Right and the Left. The question of the inter-imbrication of divergent, often equally intimate, sometimes contradictory divisions in contemporary society must finally be brought to the centre of the discussion.

Modes of scholarship dedicated to the use and development of the Marxian concept of 'articulation' strike us as particularly useful here. Given the enormous wealth of theoretical literature and empirical research premised on 'articulation', we will only gloss the concept very summarily. The important thing to note is that what we (in the German context) would call 'articulation theory' deals in conditions, relations and dynamics rather than categories and group identities. It inquires above all into the contingent social production of difference, for example, via race, nation, geography or gender.

Instead of beginning with a preconstituted category of female oppression, for example, articulation theory focuses on precise historical instantiations of that relation, pinpointing specific institutions, forms of knowledge, practices and norms that produce 'woman' as a racialized (and heterosexualized) category. The same goes for the category 'race'. Racism, argues race theorist Avtar Brah, 'is neither reducible to social class or gender, nor wholly autonomous. Racisms have variable historical origins but they articulate with patriarchal class structures in specific ways under given historical conditions.'[70]

Articulation refers to a *practice*: a practice of linking two or more 'relational figurations', for instance, gender, class or ethnicity. It is, to be precise, a form of connection-making that does not necessarily give rise to any unity; and if it does do so, that unity needs to be understood as neither essential nor determinate nor necessary nor permanent, as Stuart Hall shows.[71] Articulation denotes, then, not so much a straightforward relation between given entities as a nexus transforming the identity of the linked elements.

Articulation itself is a transformative process. For example, when they become articulated, gender and race do not remain unchanged; they are never simply *added together*. Our social identities are not merely the sum of the social positions to which we belong, such that one might boil oneself down to an additive equation [white + female = me]. Rather, the 'I' of any subject is (re)produced as white within shifting parameters of femininity and masculinity, and rendered female within shifting parameters of race, sexuality and class.

Laclau and Mouffe emphasize another dimension of articulation we've already touched upon, that is, the construction of 'nodal points'. The function of nodal points is, to fix meaning, to get the incessant movement of the social to stand still, to foster new differences and call up new subjectivities. Nodal points provide us with a reality, or rather a way of seeing. It is through nodal points that realities *become* reality. For Fredric Jameson, the articulation 'is thus a punctual and sometimes even ephemeral totalization, in which the planes of race, gender, class, ethnicity, and sexuality intersect to form an operative structure'.[72]

Nodal points (to use Mouffe and Laclau's term), or operative structures (to use Jameson's), are all about drawing social boundaries vested with the power to determine who does and does not come into contact with whom and how. They are what sets up any given society in a given way. They organize all our doings, our thoughts, and our very feelings. 'Cologne' is poised to become the newest name for one such operative structure, the name of a specific articulation of racism, sexism and feminism, through which society will be remade. Hence why Cologne is a 'matter of concern', that is, a thing that very much concerns us.

2

'The Night That Changed Everything': Othering and Ruling

> I have never lived, nor has any of us, in a world in which race did not matter . . . How to be both free and situated; how to convert a racist house into a race-specific yet nonracist home. How to enunciate race while depriving it of its lethal cling?
>
> – Toni Morrison[1]

THE 'UNVARNISHED TRUTH'

'This changes everything': that was how the German newspaper *Welt am Sonntag* described Cologne's New Year's Eve night just a handful of days afterward.[2] 'Cologne', the editorial team declared in the unmistakably ominous tones of law and order,[3] was quite possibly just the 'tip of the iceberg', the visible sign of 'something' much bigger 'we aren't yet able to fathom'. They conjured a scenario in which various 'no-go zones' within German cities – 'Neukölln in Berlin, Marxloh in Duisburg, or Bremen, and just about everywhere in Cologne last New Year's Eve' – are spreading like an epidemic, while the public is being 'intentionally misled' and citizens aren't being trusted with 'the truth' about what happened in those locales. This 'truth' was, needless to say, luckily in the possession of the *Welt am Sonntag* reporters, however. They knew that, for women, that night had been a 'brutal and shocking night' filled with 'savage firings of fireworks at human beings, gang-based street robbery, and sexual violence by north African and Arab young men on a massive scale'.[4]

Admittedly, conceded the right-wing Catholic commentator Birgit Kelle on 7 January 2016 in a post for the Austrian business blog Wirtschaftswunder: 'We don't yet know very much about the identity of the young men.'[5] Nevertheless, it was already clear to her that we were dealing with 'men of Arab and African appearance' and, at any

rate, 'men with some kind of migration background'.⁶ Shortly afterwards, on 10 January the journalist Harald Martenstein informed his
readers in the Berlin *Tagesspiegel* that 'What we're dealing with has to
do with Islam, not refugees', based on his opinion that 'Islamic socialization' leads to a 'perception of women' that leads inexorably to such
crimes.⁷ His point was unmistakable: *It's the Islam, stupid!* And,
furthermore – here comes the kicker – since 'Islam is not a race, it's an
ideology', to say so is no more 'racist' than to point out the connection
'between Germans and Nazis'.⁸ Obviously, 'not all Germans, not all
men, and not all Muslims' are criminals, reasoned Martenstein; but to
relativize crimes like the Cologne attacks serves only to encourage
'tomorrow's criminals'.⁹

These are just three representative examples we've selected from
the immense quantity of articles, reports, op-eds and commentaries
published on 'Cologne' in the first weeks of 2016.¹⁰ Already, we can
spot all the key ingredients that would go on to shape political conversations and media debates in the following months, turning 'Cologne'
into a 'matter of concern' in the Latourian sense: crime, discipline,
order, public morality, domestic (specifically *national*) security,
terrorism (and the question of how to defend against it), the normalization of racist (specifically Islamophobic) generalization, the drawing of links between religion, violence and gender, and the articulation of 'feminist' concerns.¹¹ In particular, as these examples indicate,
the media coverage relentlessly focused on the origin of the alleged
perpetrators and speculated about their ethnic and cross-cultural
confusion. From that point on, they – the so-called Nafris – served as
emblems of the possibility of sexualized violence, threatening German
society from the outside.

In the first chapter, we proposed approaching 'Cologne' as a nodal
point within a new European 'articulation'. This means that, on the
one hand, it is the contingent but all too real co-production of two or
more relational figurations – in this case, racism and sexism, which
consequently became linked in a particular way; and on the other
hand, it designates a transformational movement that alters not only
the linked elements, but the ensemble of the social balance of power

in Germany (and beyond). Considered in this light, it is clear that 'Cologne' has repositioned the guard rails around mainstream political discussions about migration, asylum and sexual violence.

But, as we hope to show in this chapter, 'Cologne' signifies even more besides. It marks the revival of a morally virulent 'us and them' distinction and the (re)activation of a racially charged everyday 'common sense' (following Stuart Hall).[12] This commonsense consciousness roots itself in state-authorized forms of knowledge that are then reproduced by the practices and institutions of all socially functional systems. People refer to it to make their relationships, their political and social struggles, the very borders of their worlds, legible to themselves. Last but not least, it is our common sense that provides the moral compass for human action.

THE SOUND OF OTHERING

The phrase 'the night that changed everything' is a note repeatedly sounded about Cologne still today. It's already become an old saw. Wherever it is heard, it summons up what we call the sound of othering, and it starts up the steady beat of 'othering and ruling'.[13] It washes over society like a soothing background music legitimating any outrage, any humiliation, any act of discrimination, any gesture of marginalization, expressing the ineradicable difference between 'we' and 'they'. It wafts into our ears in a key rich with justifications for the primacy of those who claim to have been and belonged here 'first', freighted with the idea that some elements in society possess more social value than others. Its melody whispers the chauvinistic certainty that 'we' are right, 'we' are better, 'we' are ultimately more human than 'them'.

This is the sound of hatred, of active estrangement, and of dehumanization. It crops up, of course, in the speech of those who drone on about migrants' inability or unwillingness to 'integrate' and warn explicitly against Germany 'being overrun' as part of an 'Islamization of the West'. But elsewhere, too, the sound is distinctly audible. We detect it in the voices of people reacting to their own experiences of exclusion with hatred, denigration, and violence towards others; and among those who have declared a fundamentalist war against the world, a war of one kind or another in whose name they are ready to rape, maim, enslave, terrorize, plunder, torture, and even to destroy their own life.

It is a sound as old as modernity itself, freighted (as Zygmunt Bauman tells us) with 'ambivalence'.[14] In their infancy, bourgeois democracies faced a dilemma the bourgeois revolutions had brought into being themselves. In theory, these revolutions had granted equal rights to all human beings on the grounds of their 'natural' equality. On the other hand, in reality, civil rights were only extended to 'adults', which is to say, property-owning, white, heterosexual men. Women did not enjoy civil rights. They were consequently widely described as the 'other' of modernity, the infamous 'second sex'.

In her monograph on the science of sex, *Die Ordnung der Geschlechter* (The Order of the Sexes), Claudia Honegger shows that the establishment of an interpretive schema of gender difference was necessary for the formation of an era wherein male human beings acceded to the status of Modern Man, a 'universal' process in which 'woman' served as the necessary remainder and complement to man's development.[15] But the sexist dichotomy between man and woman was not the only dyad pivotal to the birth of modernity. Epochally, this was also the moment of invention of what Achille Mbembe calls 'the racial subject', of the 'the appearance of the principle of race and the latter's slow transformation into the privileged matrix for techniques of domination'.[16] (No one since, as Toni Morrison notes, has ever lived in a world where race was not deadly.) By this gesture of othering and degradation, the indigenous populations of the colonies – including the Americas – and the Africans who were enslaved and abducted across the Atlantic were thereby excluded from the framework of human and civil rights and, thus, from the very category of humanity. This is the foundational dilemma that still holds modernity in its grip – this is the European legacy. It grounds a mode of existence, a mode of being in the world, to which every one of us is accustomed – albeit in different ways. We are, in an ongoing way, very much a part of the cultural memory of imperialism, which was, as Ann Stoler contends in *Race and the Education of Desire*, elaborated 'in the heads and hearts of people in the metropole'.[17] This collective memory saturates German everyday life. One can readily track it through history by looking at our patterns of communication and physical idiom, concepts of emotion and perception, hierarchies of value, and institutions and laws – operations with real effects one can describe.

MANICHAEAN CONSTRUCTIONS

Even before Cologne, the sound of othering had grown louder within public discourse about 'immigrants' – both in politics and in the media – and not only in Germany. For the past two decades, Manichaean views of the world have been spreading all over Europe and beyond. In the United States, these ideas moved into the White House with Donald Trump; in the Kremlin, however, they have dominated politics since the early 2000s. All over the world, whether in the Netherlands or in Syria, Hungary or Turkey, Italy or India, Brazil or South Africa, Saudi Arabia or Poland, Libya or England or France, or any of the territories around the world ruled and occupied by Boko Haram, the Taliban, Al Qaeda, or Daesh – albeit, of course, in different ways and with distinctly different consequences – the plagues of xenophobia and racism torment populations. More than that, increasingly, they define the political climate.

Manichaean constructions operate on the basis of a strong 'us vs. them' antagonism and a nativist[18] conceptualization of society.[19] Above all, they set up an emotionally – and, increasingly, racially – charged opposition between 'the people' and 'the establishment', or 'the people' and some other, demonized outsider.[20] This is because, according to Chantal Mouffe, the collective dimension could not be eliminated from politics. Thus:

> If they were not available through traditional parties, collective identities were likely to be provided in other forms. This is clearly what is

happening with right-wing populist discourse, which is replacing the weakened left/right opposition by a new type of we/they constructed around an opposition between 'the people' and 'the establishment'.[21]

While the rhetorical *forms* exclusion, stigma and villainization take remain surprisingly constant, the demons themselves, the logic whereby they are ostracized, and even what is done to them vary in accordance with the requirements of the day. Sometimes it's Jews, sometimes communists, sometimes queers, or Blacks, or witches, or Catholics, or Muslims, or lesbians.

The contours of the 'we' group remain, on the other hand, every bit as vague as the figure of the 'other' is detailed, stereotypical and vivid. For instance, what Germany, France, Europe, Denmark or Poland must *not* be, under any circumstances, is a much clearer matter than what they actually *are*. As Zygmunt Bauman pointed out in the last essay he ever wrote – 'The new anti-establishment hatred and the yearning for an enemy' – it is often more expedient to 'seek, find, or invent an enemy closer to home and above all inside the gate'.[22] In the Middle Ages, for instance, 'the function of the enemy in the case of Christian states was perfectly performed by heretics, Saracens, and Jews – all residing inside the realms of dynasties and churches by which they had been appointed.'[23] Today, according to Bauman, 'in the era that favours exclusion over inclusion while the first (but not the second) is fast becoming a routine measure to which well-nigh mechanically to resort, internal choices [of enemy] assume yet more attraction and facility.'[24]

GOVERNMENT OF DIFFERENCE

At the national and EU level, ever since the end of the Cold War, the effort to create a German and European identity along racialized, as well as gendered and heterosexualized, lines – and to expand 'Fortress Europe' – has sharply intensified. Central to this effort is the construction of a mass of 'foreigners' who threaten national security, overburden the economy and swamp labour markets. Indeed, discourse analyses of parliamentary debates on immigration in six European countries – Austria, England, the Netherlands, Spain, France and Italy – have demonstrated that, since the early 2000s, 'foreigners' are only deemed welcome if they are bringing in 'economically useful' competencies along with them.[25]

Over time, these discursive norms and speech patterns legitimize and lend credence to the need for exclusionary measures and discriminatory differentiations between citizens, aliens, and 'denizens'.[26] Combined with what Wendy Brown has called 'neoliberalism's stealth revolution'[27] – her term for the far-reaching political and economic transformations of recent decades – they have fundamentally changed the conditions for political and social participation and, thus, warped the very structure of democracy: a development Peter Wagner characterizes as 'the postliberal compromise'.[28] Laws, regulations, state directives and policies now, more than ever, manufacture intricate hierarchies of different categories of people, thereby establishing a complex system of differential participation.[29] Each group has rights granted to it (and obligations imposed upon it) according to its place on a hierarchized civic spectrum, which ranges from the status of 'full citizen', endowed with all possible rights, all the way down to that of refugee, rightfully stripped of rights, here at best on sufferance, or else held in detention.

THE AMBIVALENT RETURN OF SEXISM

Already in the 1990s, the sound of othering was typically presaged by some special gesture towards sexism. The linguist Margarete Jäger, who identified this nexus at the time, called it the 'racist ethnicization of sexism' – with reference to Germans' systematic production of the notion that sexism is somehow an inherent part of Muslim or predominantly Arab communities.[30] For Jäger, it was clear that almost everyone was familiar with 'the notion that Turkish or Muslim men are especially sexist – that they oppress women in a particularly bad way'. And this argument, according to her, served readily as a reason for

Germans believing that 'living together with Turks and Muslims is difficult, for us – or even impossible'.[31]

What a comeback for sexism as a hot-button issue! After all, sexism had been declared a thing of the past, a problem considered politically resolved ever since women's liberation politics were 'nationalized' institutionally in the 1980s. Had not a plethora of laws and regulations officially aimed, ever since, to eradicate gender inequality? Don't an ever-growing international body of both governmental and non-governmental organizations dedicate their energies to enforcing 'women's rights'? Aren't supranational (European Union) as well as national 'gender mainstreaming' policies in effect? More Western nations than not today extend equal rights to men and women. Therefore, even though feminists have continued to denounce sexism and violence against women all the while, they have been widely ridiculed as killjoys and frustrated nags. Sexism? Surely that was all *so* last year!? In fact, no – in the discourses Jäger investigated, she found that a whole new articulation of feminism had emerged. This time around, the scandal of sexism would loom very prominently in society, yet its function would be ambivalent in that it could serve, above all, as a justification for anti-Muslim racism.

We can now name a toxic link that exists between racism and anti-sexism, dreadful proof of just how flexible and dynamic both formations can be. Tragically, this link can be weaponized, under favorable political circumstances, towards nefarious political ends. Relevantly, critical race scholars have of late put forward the concept of 'reflexive Eurocentrism'.[32] As an ideological project, reflexive racism involves mobilizing oppositional and critical discourses – in this case, the critique of gender oppression – in order to repudiate unenlightened 'others' all the more effectively thanks to that 'progressive' arsenal: using feminism, in other words, to denounce foreigners' 'backwards' views and 'wrong' behaviours.

Within the 'racist ethnicization of sexism', a particularly harsh spotlight has been shone on so-called hyphenated Germans[33] and their putative failure to integrate (especially German-Turkish and German-Kurdish people, some of whom have been living in Germany for generations). But, since Cologne, a new group has been targeted for sexism's ethnicization: a group deemed even less capable of integration – indeed, whose very existence threatens public order, national security, social cohesion and morality itself – namely male persons 'of refugee or migrant experience'.

A NEW CONFIGURATION OF THE FAMILY

Next, an imagined family constellation, an imagined household, which had been placed in the crosshairs of a hostile (yet somehow also 'feminist') discourse about gender and migration, was expanded to include a wider cast of racist characters. Hitherto, it had only really consisted of the image of the Muslim woman wearing a headscarf (hijab), veil (niqab) or, later, also, full burka. Initially, it was extended only to include the figures of the tradition-bound, misogynist Muslim patriarch, and of the elder son who watches relentlessly over his sisters' honor.[34] Now, however, it was further supplemented to include one final, completing figure. This last figure was the figure of untrammeled or at least insufficiently restrained raw sexual instinct: embodied in the lowly young Muslim man without family attachments or parental control.[35] We've now added to the family picture the figure of the 'lost son'.

The role of sexuality and sexualization within racial discourses has always been prominent, as historically oriented theorists like Ann Stoler, María do Mar Castro Varela and Paul Mecheril contend.[36] What we are confronting today, in that sense, is nothing new: rather, it's an all-too-familiar and efficacious type of discourse on 'civilization' that has simply been given a makeover. What makes others 'uncivilized' has long been, and remains today, the idea that they are unable to control their sexual desire. Indeed, this particular ideological operation is one that, in Castro Varela and Mecheril's terms, 'lacks both temporal boundaries and a specific goal'.

On account of their innate savagery – according to the colonial-racist worldview – these 'others' are essentially incapable of progressing beyond the polymorphous perversity of infancy. In contrast, the

European subject is constitutively characterized by the fact that 'he masters his desire', keeping it strictly within the bounds of heteronormativity while also respecting class-based and racial segregation. The European subject exerts control over his own desire with respect to both quantity (sex is to be enjoyed in moderation) and quality (sex should be oriented towards reproduction more than pleasure). By the same token, non-European *others* are unfit to govern themselves politically, as a collective,[37] *because* they are incapable of managing themselves sexually, as individuals.[38]

The discursive articulation of the Cologne attacks was designed, in the first place, to shore up the construction of the dangerous, sexually incontinent male Arab or Muslim refugee. But equally, as Gabriele Dietze has pointed out, it mobilized that figure's antithesis: 'the fantasy of western liberal-democratic freedom, tolerance and secularism, paired with western citizens' willingness and ability to make rational use of the freedoms granted to them'.[39] They alone, according to this fantasy, are capable of self-government. They alone have found their way out of the darkness of immaturity.

The Manichaeism in play is clearly visible here. The West occupies the spotlight as a place where women have been emancipated and masculinity 'detoxified'. It becomes, in Gabriele Dietze's words, 'the blueprint of perfection for all possible civilizations'.[40] This intensely ideological construct of Western liberal democracy depends, furthermore, on being permanently threatened by a brutish barbarian: a wild, retrograde specter of masculinity who, in assaulting the nation's own white heterosexual women (who *must* be defended), attacks the very essence of liberal democracy itself.[41]

One might think that the times had collectively moved on from 'Me Tarzan, you Jane'. But it is precisely this old formula that Stefanie Mayer, Iztok Šori and Birgit Sauer locate at the heart of European right-wing populism. In their view, 'the most important discursive construction is the (young) foreign criminal and violent perpetrator' who attacks the 'native girl'.[42] True enough, all over Europe, xenophobic nationalist parties are using principles of gender equality to formulate the claim that male Muslims – and non-Western male immigrants generally – do not and will never respect women's rights nor (increasingly) queer rights.

On her personal website, the AfD politician Beatrix von Storch has published an 'Annual Review of 2016', in which she describes Cologne as 'emblematic of a failed immigration policy, of the erosion of public security and of a policy of silence and trivialization on the part of the media and the political powers who are responsible for this.'[43] In her view, these powers are responsible for hiding and minimizing the fact that German immigration policy is 'bringing in men who do not respect women and for whom gender equality is a foreign concept'. It was for similar reasons that Birgit Kelle asked (with unmistakable malice) why feminists had barely cried out over the events in Cologne. Writing on 5 January, just four days after the attacks, Kelle first posed and then answered this rhetorical question with complete confidence: 'The reason is simple: the culprits in question were the wrong ones.' Wrong for the feminist narrative, she alleged, because they were migrants.[44]

In the face of these volleys, it took a surprisingly long time for the voices of feminists dedicated to apprehending racism and sexism as co-constitutive social divisions – feminists interrogating how racism is articulated in the language of anti-sexism – to make themselves heard. The German Women Lawyers Association issued a press release on 8 January. A feminist alliance eventually formed under the banner '#ausnahmslos' (the word for 'unexceptional', translated by the activists as 'not surprised', as in: 'we are not surprised'). Under the credo 'against sexualized violence and racism: always and everywhere', #ausnahmslos brought together Muslim, secular, Black and white feminists including Kübra Gümüşay, Anne Wizorek, Keshia Fredua-Mensah and Stefanie Lohaus, with signatories include Manuela Schwesig, Milo Rau, Angela Davis, Claudia Roth, Judith Holofernes, Emine Aslan, Azize Tank and Chandra Talpade Mohanty.[45] Their platform attracted quite a bit of media attention but, on the whole, intersectional-feminist perspectives have been marginalized on the matter of Cologne.

The centre of gravity in this debate has never been with those of us who insist that sexism is a far-reaching and transversal phenomenon

– a historically and culturally specific yet globally generalized dynamic of 'masculine domination'[46] (over women *and* men). Rather, the hegemonic framework is one in which sexism represents a naturally occurring property of Muslims or Arabs. The fact that male supremacist culture is not imported into Europe along with human migration – it is produced just as much in Germany and Norway as it is in Morocco or India – has once again become a minoritarian viewpoint.[47]

At the same time, it has become very rare to address the actual specifics of sexist practices and patriarchal values in Islamic contexts. This trend is fatal in that this silence repeats, like a negative mirror image, the dynamic of reductive generalization and othering (Hedwig Dohm's *Versämtlichung*) it intends to oppose. Moreover, it is fatal because it 'only plays into the hands of those who have always been a thorn in the side of gender equality', as the Frankfurt-based scholar of gender and Islam Susanne Schröter argues.[48] The alternative to racial or culturalist accounts of sexism can therefore *only* be a thoroughgoing analysis of the continuity of male supremacy and how it is maintained, namely via the interweaving of cultural, religious, and sociostructural dynamics with superstructural 'constants' and mechanisms that reproduce male domination on a world scale.

A FEMINIST NATION?

But it was the racist and racializing fundamentalist worldview that defined large swaths of the press and TV coverage of Cologne – certainly in the first few weeks of 2016.[49] Even the executive wing of the state purported to know for sure what had happened, who the perpetrators were, and where they had come from – significantly before concrete results of the police investigation had become available, let alone anybody convicted. The government seemed to take the position that there was only one possible reaction to the event(s). The justice minister, Heiko Maas, declared that the perpetrators would have to be deported.[50] It had been Maas, too – with astonishing swiftness – who called the events in Cologne a 'civilizational rupture' in his first statements to *Der Spiegel* on 7 January.[51] The 'Asylum Package I' of October 2015 was accordingly replaced, in February 2016, by the 'Asylum Package II', which declared Morocco, Algeria and Tunisia 'safe countries of origin' and promptly suspended – for two years – the right to immigrate to Germany that had previously been extended to family members and dependents entitled to subsidy protections (including those in war and disaster zones).[52]

But there were other legislative changes, too. For years, feminists had called for reforms to Germany's criminal law on sexual violence ($177 StGB) and been denied. After Cologne, however, on 7 July 2016, the German Bundestag voted to adopt a far-reaching reform of sex-offence legislation, which took up an old slogan from the women's movement: 'no means no'. Absence of consent was hereby established as the central factor in criminal liability for sexual violence. Other factors, such as the presence of threat, surprise, other forms of violence, more than one perpetrator, or opportunism vis-à-vis someone's vulnerability, were now legally rendered as elements that could potentially augment a sentence.

But let's not be fooled. Cologne undoubtedly brought some life into the long march to reform sex crime legislation. However, feminist lawyers' attempts to stop the gaps in German criminal laws' power to protect diverse groups against sexual violence has met with formidable opposition from every part of the political spectrum.[53] The very existence of these gaps is, to this day, not widely acknowledged. Nevertheless, at the time of the events in Cologne, reforms geared towards fixing them had actually long since begun, not least because the Federal Republic of Germany had, a few years earlier, adopted a series of international conventions on sexual violence, sexual exploitation and sexual abuse of women and children that required these changes.[54] In 2007, for example, Germany became a signatory to the Lanzarote Convention: the Council of Europe's Convention for the Protection of Children against Sexual Exploitation and Sexual Abuse.[55] And, in 2014, the federal government signed the Istanbul Convention on preventing and combating violence against women and domestic violence[56] – though this was only ratified in March 2017, on International Women's Day.[57]

This ultimately meant that, on New Year's Day of 2016, the mandates imposed by these Council of Europe conventions had yet to be carried over into national law.[58] Human rights and women's organizations had mobilized protests and issued statements on the matter throughout the preceding years, pushing for immediate implementation of the changes in German sex-crime law necessary to render the country compliant with the Istanbul Convention.[59] For example, Frauen gegen Gewalt (bff), the federation of women's counseling centres and rape crisis centres, launched a campaign in 2014 calling for the reform of §177 StGB.[60] All manner of lawyers and anti-violence NGOs spoke publicly in this period about the fact that existing laws rendered all kinds of sexual assault essentially unpunishable in Germany.[61]

Thus, as a matter of fact, the majority of the Cologne attacks did not constitute a criminal offence according to the existing laws. Under Germany's criminal code at the time, non-consensual sexual acts were only regarded as criminal offences if they were perpetrated either by force, under threat of immediate violence posing danger to life and limb, or through exploitation of a person's incapacitation (or otherwise vulnerable condition). In February 2015 – that is to say, almost a whole year before 'Cologne' – the Federal Ministry of Justice and Consumer Protection (BMJV) had set up a commission for the reform of the law on sex offences.[62] It had a draft worked out, by means of which these loopholes were to be closed.[63]

Regarded in the light of this sorry saga, Cologne looks less and less like a bolt out of the blue, less and less like the emblematic occasion, unconnected to everyday realities, whereby Germany became a feminist nation 'overnight'. The contention that feminism gained countless allies that night is, ultimately, a myth; the notion that conservative politicians somehow experienced an intersectional-feminist coming-to-consciousness en masse, committing themselves to the cause of antipatriarchy, is a fantasy.[64] In reality, the slew of sexual assaults perpetrated on women in Cologne was brandished as incontrovertible proof that the so-called Summer of Welcome – the opening of Germany's borders in the late summer of 2015 – was a mistake from the outset, one which had to be abruptly and irrevocably terminated.

In other words, the project, in that moment, involved rolling back 'hospitality culture'.[65] Although activated (not to say actualized) via its expressive association with the summer of 2015 in Germany, this ideal of 'hospitality culture' – Willkommenskultur in German – resonated far beyond the borders of Germany, its moral and collective inspiration proving contagious. The phrase, inaugurated long before 2015, conjures a civil society centred around gestures of openness towards others and upon a willingness to 'build a world that we share', as Achille Mbembe writes: 'reassembling broken parts, repairing broken links, relaunching the forms of reciprocity without which there can be no progress for humanity'.[66]

We do not wish to be misunderstood here. By no means are we insinuating that the potential for a 'hospitality culture', glimpsed in its barest outlines in the 'Summer of Welcome', turned Germany into a decolonized, anti-racist, feminist nation. Not even close! In no small part, anyway, the show of welcome was 'characterized by the cultivation and enjoyment of a national attitude of bountiful graciousness', as Paul Mecheril notes.[67] Furthermore, the civic mobilization of hospitality did not prevent the federal government from passing 'Asylum Package I'. The German government lent its support to widespread efforts to close Europe's borders, which intensified.[68] Right-wing violence against refugees and their dwellings increased, and more people drowned in the Mediterranean in 2015 than ever before.[69]

Unwittingly, 'hospitality culture' contributed in its own way to Germany's ability to hold a fig leaf over its anti-migrant policies of violent exclusion and deportation. By enabling the Federal Republic to present itself as a Willkommenskultur, it made it increasingly difficult for activists to make visible 'the everyday racist mechanisms and attitudes that remain at work in policies, law and administrative practices'.[70] At the same time, it is undeniable that many people experienced that long summer, the summer of 2015, as a sea change: a conjuncture capable of – in Gramscian terms – shifting the existing 'alignment of social forces'.[71] That is precisely why a reaction was necessary.

SEX POLITICS AND THE PRODUCTION OF RACIST 'TRUTH'

Xenophobic hostility – including antipathy towards immigration and fears concerning open borders – is embedded in the foundations of modern societies. The European tendency to subdivide and distinguish between people in order to stigmatize, exclude and segregate, has become sedimented over the course of centuries in what Erich Fromm termed 'the social unconscious'.[72] And, with Cologne, the ancient topos of the 'sexually threatening Muslim'[73] was able to revive with impressive force and efficacy. The revival meant that sexual politics had once again become the terrain for *the production of racist truth* (or truths). In German civil society, speaking openly in racial terms was now not only possible, but necessary and legitimate in the name of defending Western values, gender equality, and the well-being of 'our' women.

Judging by the logic that seemed to govern the overwhelming majority of articles and radio and television shows across the German media – especially in 2016 – the sine qua non for participation in public debate about sexism in Germany at the time was an attitude of concern for the sexual safety of German women combined with a willingness to speculate about 'foreign men from foreign lands' as culprits in the erosion of German standards of gender equality.[74] This formation – of moral panic – had actually been stimulated before, as we shall detail. It certainly did not click into place for the first time in response to New Year's Eve in Cologne. However, it is probably true to say that a moral panic had never before saturated discourse to the extent that Cologne did – to the point that 'Cologne' *became* a discourse.

Part of why Cologne was able to become a kind of synonym for sexual violence –perpetrated by a 'sex mob' of 'young men of North African and Arab descent' against 'native' women and girls – was the fact that the upsurge of moral panic fell into the lap of an interpretive community that was, as Dietze puts it, already possessed by 'a fixation with sexual and political bogeymen'.[75] Just a few months earlier, in *Der Spiegel* online, the journalist Jakob Augstein had listed the key points of this discursive community's perspective on their scapegoat: 'Young. Aggressive. Macho. Medieval ideas about women. Treats them like fair game.'[76]

In whipping up the spectre of the bogeyman on the streets, 'Cologne' reinscribed what feminist lawyers have identified as the foundational paradox about the fear of crime and the desire for 'law and order' as it pertains to women. Public space gets set up conceptually as naturally and intuitively dangerous for women – which is why they are, supposedly, better off being looked after in the home, where they are protected. The empirical reality, however, is that women's physical health, their sexual integrity and their bodily autonomy are all more at risk of violence within the household than they are in public.[77]

Fatima El-Tayeb shows in *Undeutsch: Die Konstruktion des Anderen in der postmigrantischen Gesellschaft* (*UnGerman: The Construct of the Other in Post-Migration Society*)[78] that the contemporary repudiation of migration is closely linked to a long history in Germany of drawing hierarchical distinctions between those who belong to the national community and those who do *not* belong and thereby outright endanger it through their very presence. This construct – of an insider/outsider dyad (be it German/unGerman or Italian/unItalian, etc.) – plays a key role in the discourses of right-wing and far-right populist movements across Europe. Mayer, Šori and Sauer conclude that 'arguments in the intersection of ethnicity and gender are vital to construct a contradiction between 'their' and 'our' values, which fosters the construction of migrants, especially Muslims, as uncivilized and a threat to European societies.'[79]

Our argument is that 'Cologne' has functioned as an apparatus of racist truth production. But one objection that could be raised here is the fact that sexual violence is *always* a controversial topic whose mediation by mainstream news organs is, again and again, characterized by trivialization and reductionism or else sensationalism.[80] And this is, actually, partly due to a core characteristic of violence itself. 'Violence is a leveller; it flattens things out', contends Carol Hagemann-White, who has been researching sexual violence since the 1970s.[81]

Furthermore, the presence of violence seems to demand unequivocal representations, which is to say, clear and forthright judgments. In this respect, reporting on Cologne conformed to well-established patterns in media coverage of 'scandals'. So far, so familiar.

But 'Cologne' went further. It immediately inserted itself into a long-established tradition of racializing practices devoted to 'attributing collective quasi-biological and/or cultural characteristics to people to foster a perception of these particular groups not *belonging*', in El-Tayeb's analysis. The culturalization and ethnicization of sexism plays an essential part in this. Be it allusions to what is putatively an Arab culture of patriarchal 'honour',[82] be it in the quiz questions posed in citizenship tests in Baden-Württemberg between 2006 and 2011 (on gender equality and acceptance of homosexuality), or in the headscarf debates raging since the turn of the millennium (most recently around the February 2017 judgment of a Berlin labour court affirming Berlin's 'neutrality' laws[83] in the case of a schoolteacher) – it is always a question of amassing evidence for the failure of these strangers, these others, to integrate.

A RESERVOIR OF IMPERIAL AFFECT

The racist appropriations of the discourse 'Cologne' draws on the largely unacknowledged *reservoir of imperial affect*, and the imperial modes of knowing, whence our typical 'justifications for the arithmetic of racial domination'[84] are drawn. As Gloria Wekker writes in *White Innocence: Paradoxes of Colonialism and Race*, this 'imperial racist economy, with its gendered, sexualized and classed intersections'[85] has shaped the relationship between the West and the rest, between Europe and the colony, for four centuries now – and it is far from over. As an affective economy, it is fundamentally a matter of elevating the perspective of an enlightened, advanced – in other words, *superior* – civilization in order to assess the alleged deficits of other, 'backward' cultures.

Today, our world is still a 'world of races',[86] Achille Mbembe notes, even though we rarely acknowledge it. 'The twenty-first century is, of course, not the nineteenth century', and yet, 'encouraged by processes of globalization and the contradictory effects they provoke, the problematic of race has once again burst into contemporary consciousness.'[87] What Mbembe calls 'procedures of differentiation, classification, and hierarchization aimed at exclusion, expulsion, and even eradication', he writes, 'have been reinvigorated everywhere'. At the same time, he continues, 'new voices have emerged proclaiming, on the one hand, that there is no such thing as a universal human being or, on the other, that the universal is common to some human beings but not to all.'[88]

AGAINST 'VERSÄMTLICHUNG'

'Cologne', as a mechanism we perceive at work in the present, is not entirely reducible, however, to this process of racist we/they differentiation addressed by Mbembe – although that process is undeniably central to the regime we are calling 'other and rule'. Let us now, therefore, turn to the second aspect – the one we see as equally important in the functioning of this mechanism – namely *Versämtlichung*. As we briefly explained in the previous chapter, the term denotes the reifying, ossifying, hyperdetermining valence of othering or otherization, whereby we bury a thing (or group) under negative ascriptions. It is an epistemic operation designed to eliminate internal differences and empirical complexities, and to install homogeneity, abstraction and fungibility at the very heart of difference.

Versämtlichung is a violent – abstracting – form of thought which varies according to the individuals and the circumstances it is directed towards. At root, it simplifies attributes, ascribes properties, turns these properties into synecdoches for the whole person, and uses the results to cast social verdicts. As such, *Versämtlichung* participates in the regulation of social conditions and in the allocation of resources. Insofar as attributions of quality and of social rank contribute concretely to creating and reproducing relations of inequality, it facilitates acts of distinction and of control, and guides decisions determining who gets a chance to lead a successful life. Thus, *Versämtlichung* is not the same as the ideal of meritocracy, whereby persons are integrated (rewarded) according to the status they have earned. Nor is this a question of embodying prescribed roles and positions within a specific subsystem of the social: the role of 'employee' in an encounter with your boss, for example, or that of 'the customer' in a retail context. By *Versämtlichung*, we mean a much more essential ontologization, in the sense of a group affiliation that completely saturates a person's meaning.

Feminist thought has named and apprehended *Versämtlichung* since the beginning of the twentieth century, in which time it has very much become a central concern of feminist critique. The feminist theorist and writer Hedwig Dohm, in coining the term, analyzed the polarization of sexual attributes in the thought of her contemporaries. In her 1903 polemic *Die Mütter* (The Mothers) – subtitled 'A Comment on the Education Question' – she mapped this radicalization of the gender binary at the conceptual level directly onto concrete developments that were detrimental to the lives of women. Dohm writes:

> It seems that we conceive of Womanhood as a mold or cookie-cutter into which all feminine creatures must fit in order to become homogenized (*versämtlicht*), such that one comes out barely distinguishable from the other, according to God's will. Each of us does, feels and thinks exactly alike. Does not this brutal process of equalization amount to a mutilation? I am tempted to say it begins already in the womb (as an inheritance many generations deep). Certainly, it takes us in childhood, allowing all manner of powers and organs – perhaps earmarked by Nature for lofty things – to lapse to nothingness.[89]

The Austrian feminist and writer Rosa Mayreder turned her attention, too, to the mechanism of 'violent equalization' or othering, that is to say, *Versämtlichung*. In her 1907 essay *Zur Kritik der Weiblichkeit* (On the Critique of Femininity) – translated into English as *A Survey of the Woman Problem* in 1913 – Mayreder criticizes this mode of thought's 'generalizing methods' and scoffs at the way 'such terms as "the male" and "the female" are employed as if they expressed some actual metaphysical entity existing in and distinguishing every man from every woman.'[90]

Both Dohm and Mayreder were scrutinizing the ensemble of essentialist and mystifying norms comprising 'femininity' in their time and naming it as a medium of 'violent equalization'. And European history, as much as the present, is replete with such phantasms of femininity. They are so abundant that Virginia Woolf famously asked her readers, in her essay *A Room of One's Own*, whether they had 'any notion of how many books are written about women in the course of one year' or for that matter 'how many are written by men' – men who 'have no apparent qualification save that they are not women'.[91]

None among us who has been allocated to a community marked out as 'gendered' can avoid noticing, nor escape experiencing, the normative pressure of polarized stereotypes. These 'mutilations' of the feminine, as Hedwig Dohm called them – these culturally powerful 'alloys of femininity'[92] (*Legierungen*), to use instead the formulation of Gudrun-Axeli Knapp – remain to this day of exceeding importance for the social reproduction of gender relations, gendered society and gender order. Let us not lose sight, however, of what we argued in our first chapter: namely, that gender norms only ever appear in articulated form, inextricably entangled with race and class. Let us keep prominently in mind, in other words, the difference between privileged bodies and exposed, precarized ones. Gender-related politics – not to mention heterosexist, homo- or transphobic and racializing politics – do not affect all persons equally. Violence strikes *some* bodies, and not everybody's. Sexual norms, like other worldly norms, safeguard the lives of some while rendering others expendable.

As a mode of thought, *Versämtlichung* proceeds in three steps identified by Gudrun-Axeli Knapp, in the late 1980s, as operations of 'iconization'. In her essay 'The Forgotten Difference', which elaborates this thesis with regard to gendered norms and femininity stereotypes, Knapp enumerates three principles.[93] First, she writes, the category 'woman' is universalized by means of a *methodological imperialism*, leading to ahistorical and globalizing statements about 'women'.

Second, 'woman' is elevated and decontextualized because 'she' is idealized. This tactic of idealization, writes Knapp, obscures the historicity of women's development (and degeneration) as subjective potentials – in other words, women's made-ness and becoming, their 'ongoing entanglement' with a world riven by conflict and toxicity. And, finally, *Versämtlichung* deploys a *positivism* insofar as its conception of the 'real', says Knapp, counts only that which is self-realizing or self-realized. It discounts 'thwarted dreams and desires, secret aspirations, unrealized projects and talents that lie fallow', as though these were irrelevant characteristics of subjects. *Versämtlichung* merely registers 'facts', and encourages one to conflate the 'real' and the possible. Through these three operations – universalization, idealization, positivism – the effect of 'iconization' is achieved. The icon is 'rendered real', for Knapp, by virtue of its abstraction from history, its abstraction from concrete sociocultural contexts and, finally, its abstraction from horizons of potentiality – which is to say, 'from the possibility of resistance and change'.

One can find traces of Knapp's 'alloys of femininity', or detect the operations of 'violent equalization' she named in the 1980s all over the explosion of racist speech precipitated by Cologne on the topic of 'the' Arab, 'the' North African, 'the' Muslim, 'the' libidinally driven, mendacious young man, and so on. They define our way of speaking, for example, about the 'girl with a headscarf' who is incapable of judging or speaking for herself, not unlike (to invoke a completely different stereotype) the welfare-dependent single mom or 'welfare queen'. These tired stereotypes draw from the two-hundred-year-old well of binary gender 'scripts' that naturalize the 'gender order'. There is still, after all this time, ultimately, Man, on the one hand, who stands for the outdoors, politics and public life – the sphere of energy, strength, violence and assertiveness – and Woman, on the other – her disposition tending towards weakness, adaptiveness, devotion and dependency on account of her association with the indoors and domesticity.[94]

This, ultimately, is the dramatically impoverished caste of characters we find at work in the process of flattening and homogenizing the world. As we've seen, they consist of a threefold abstraction – from history, from geography and from the possibility of change. Being techniques of normalization and standardization, their main uses are control and domination: the undermining of social cohesion, reciprocity and responsibility in the world.

For this reason, as Knapp notes, the operations of *Versämtlichung* contain within them an ethical and epistemological challenge – the imperative to *differentiate*. They demand an attitude of friendship with the world. They call for the abandonment of the privilege of epistemological ignorance. This means we must, at the very least, make an effort to be more thoughtful and more hesitant in our embrace of definitions and our selection of terminology – searching for ways to preserve and express difference. It means not allowing statements about 'the' Muslims, 'the' blacks, 'the' women, and 'the' men, but also 'the' Germans, 'the' whites, 'the' heterosexuals, 'the' lesbians or 'the' gays, to go unchallenged. It means resisting the hypostasization of areas of possible difference and preventing them from becoming fixed as immovable properties. It means taking difference among women, or among men, just as seriously as similarity. And, finally, it means distinguishing between similarity and uniformity (for Knapp, the latter is 'the result of declassification').[95]

'COLOGNE' QUA MORAL CROSSROADS

Having laid out our understanding of othering – *Versämtlichung* – we now return to the question of what made 'Cologne' a 'matter of concern' in the sense developed in Chapter 1. We have already presented a sketch of our argument that reportage on the as-of-then still basically unknown specifics of 'Cologne' cannot simply be explained as a particularly egregious and extreme example of the media's standard sensationalization of sexual abuse. Rather, one thing after another accrued to turn the Cologne occurrences into 'Cologne'. Bruno Latour proposes that for every 'matter of concern', there is a 'whole earth and heavens that have to be gathered to hold it firmly in place'.[96] And once 'Cologne' was held in place, it gave birth to realities of its own, creating, as Nietzsche put it, 'new things in the long run'.

Specifically, Cologne contributed to the creation (or revival) of a new social thing (or 'Ding'). At the beginning of this chapter, we expressed our view that this thing was an us/them antagonism with a particular *moral* charge to it. In turning our attention to this moral dimension, we hope to shed further light on Cologne as a hub of moral experience, a moment of moral mobilization. Considering what the *performative* power here might be will prove particularly key. In our opinion, it is above all the performative power of morality that enables events to become effective 'boundary objects', be it socio-geographically, demarcating group from group, or temporally, prompting talk of a 'before' and 'after'.

What do we mean by this? In Birgit Rommelspacher's definition of 'domination culture', there were (recall) two central components. First, Rommelspacher locates domination culture in the behaviours, the attitudes and the feelings of those who live together in a given society: imperial dominance, as Ann Stoler reminds us, lives in people's minds and hearts. Second, the culture (of domination) is what weaves together the structures of the personal and the social; it mediates between the individual and the collective.[97] Thus, in order to understand how domination culture works, one must widen one's focus to include the emotional and affective undertow of society: the multifaceted and complex interrelations Birgit Sauer calls the 'political economy of affects'.[98] Relations of superiority and inferiority, for example, are not 'just' inscriptions structuring our social fabric, determining who is 'entitled' to what and who is not. They are also impressions, as Andrea Maihofer elucidates – *affects*, which mutate into feelings as a result of specific localized patterns of interpretation and categorization determining what any given sensation *means* in socio-cultural context.[99] And emotions *do* things: they 'secure collectives through the way in which they read the bodies of others', in Sara Ahmed's phrase – they 'align some subjects with some others and against other others'.[100] Ultimately, affects are the expression of being *affected* by (and with) others. Collective feelings such as 'love' for one's country, for example – or hatred, fear, disgust vis-à-vis foreigners

– are indispensable parts of the constitution of an 'us' as distinguished from some other 'them'. They contribute to the consolidation of collective identities. Emotions and affects are, in short, 'bound up with how we inhabit the world "with" others', concludes Ahmed.[101]

Feelings, then, are neither neutral nor pre-social. They are not autonomous: not confined to the individual who feels them. They are a stubborn and intrinsic part of the political. Affects mediate power relations in everyday practices and can never be entirely separated from domination. At the same time, they help people understand the social conditions and struggles in which they exist. Affects can, indeed, all too easily become a nuisance to the prevailing system of relations –think of irritation, indignation, shame and exhaustion. But, be they resistant or quiescent to power, affects are part of people's everyday consciousness: the syntax of their morality.

It is Brigitte Bargetz who points out that social relations – which is to say, relations of power and domination – always have to be 'accepted, rejected or reinterpreted at the affective level'.[102] Yet we do not tend to think of the way we feel about things, for instance, our likes and dislikes, the familiar and the strange, the feared and the trusted, that which we feel responsible for or not, that which we deem useful and harmful, supreme or subordinate, as shaped by the social. We do not tend to think of our own affects as expressions of what Andrea Maihofer calls a 'hegemonic regime of affect'.[103]

Yet, social relations of domination and subordination are closely connected with this regime. They determine, in Maihofer's words, 'what is felt (or at least what is *meant* to be felt), how, and where', providing the 'inner logic' for all kinds of different modes of feeling.[104] This question of the felt, of the 'sensible', is also fundamentally one of distribution: 'which feelings are admissible, intelligible or even viable for whom'. As Maihofer puts it, 'the hegemonic modes of feeling are in themselves hierarchical and hierarchized: both differentiated and differentiating in terms of class, race and gender.'[105]

Viewed in this light, 'Cologne' is an emotionally explosive moral 'node'. It mobilizes feelings designed to be directed towards some subjects and against others. 'Cologne' interpellates us. Through the specific way it sutures discourses and practices, it mobilizes feelings and affects, thereby hailing us as subjects within a specific, asymmetric – gendered, racially and sexually marked – moral order. For example, white, Western cisgender women are called up as morally superior subjects, but also as valuable assets. For them, Cologne represents a kind of 'VIP invitation' to the club of Western andro-centrism, a membership they have been denied, as we have seen, for over two centuries. It is an invitation to agree to a kind of 'new deal'[106] on gender, promising to keep their bodies safe. Should they accept the terms of this modern and progressive iteration of the age-old protection racket, whereby rights and privileges are conceded in exchange for white cis women's investment in a regime of racial stratification, they would, however, only be gaining a seat at the table.

With Niklas Luhmann, we understand morality to be the mode of communication[107] that organizes the distinction between good and evil, respect and disrespect, belonging and exclusion, and so on – including the drawing of demarcations not just outwardly, against others, but also internally, against oneself. Seen in this light, 'Cologne' finally becomes visible as an element in an ensemble dedicated to a wider moral mission: namely, perfecting the imperative to protect one's own self and defend against the foreign. The ensemble in question *constitutes* 'objects of concern' such as 'public order and morality', 'domestic security', 'Western values', 'Europe's borders', and 'the native girl'. It brings to life a host of moral collectives endowed with different responsibilities and burdens of care. This is the moral machine that organizes the question of who *belongs,* and who doesn't, who does and does not deserve credit or affection or empathy – being legitimately aggrieved or grievable – and who can be denied. Once again, the constitution of the affective regime, in a domination culture, will not be experienced as domination by all, at the practical level. Happily, this means that, within these ensembles, all manner of unpredictable affects – and effects – may unexpectedly arise.

HOW WE DO

If we have, so far, considered Cologne in terms of the 'sound of other-ing' that has lately grown so loud as to be impossible to block out – teasing out its morally charged mechanisms for producing us/them dichotomies – we want to round off this chapter by visiting a perspective of Hannah Arendt's that can allow us to take into account the *perpetrators* of the violence in Cologne while examining 'Cologne' as a 'moral node'. Contemplating the extermination of Europe's Jews under German National Socialism, Hannah Arendt wrote in her *Denktagebuch* entry for January 1951 that all 'morality' can really be reduced to the keeping of promises. This fundamental matter of the ability to make a promise and keep it, she proposed, ultimately has 'nothing to do with the concrete question of right and wrong, on the one hand, and the Ten Commandments on the other'.[108]

In her emphasis on 'action' – in particular, the act of promising and of keeping promises – Arendt is defining an essential, arguably *the* essential, component of morality, namely the matter of what we *do*, which is to say: ethics. For Arendt, morality is not in the first instance about norms, commandments, principles or what we believe in – be it the Ten Commandments or select surahs from the Quran. In any case, prescriptions such as these only ever enter into human lives (according to a particularly vivid passage in Arendt's diary) in moments of extreme catastrophe and circumstances of 'cataclysm, desolation and desertification of the heart' when 'life is murdered'.[109]

What matters far more to Arendt are our promises, our keeping of these promises, and the attitude that manifests in us as a result of what we do. This includes, first and foremost, the question of what attitude we choose to take in relation to a moral demand that we respect some people and relinquish others. Will we choose to follow or resist the ensemble of – often violent – mores, morals and ethical norms in whose midst we live? And how will we commit practically to the standards we decide upon? All of these are questions we are addressing to the perpetrators in Cologne, whosoever they may be, as much as anyone. They, too, had the freedom to bring violence into their encounter with women on the street – or not. They, too, were free to acquiesce – or not – to an implicit moral imperative to wound and denigrate individuals in the name of modesty and 'honour',[110] or to do violence to women's bodies. Not choosing violence is a decision we are all equipped to make – including the perpetrators in Cologne.

It was Edward Said who identified a double movement of self-affirmation and othering as inseparable from Western imperial culture.[111] But if, with Cologne, this double movement was activated again throughout (our) society, what we *do* with (and in) this situation is by no means a foregone conclusion. Here, it makes sense to recall Hannah Arendt's injunction, in her treatises on morality and ethical action, that everything depends on *how we do*. Theodor Adorno powerfully lays out what is demanded of us:

> If today we can at all say that subjectively there is something like a threshold, a distinction between a right life and a wrong one, we are likely to find it soonest in asking whether a person is just hitting out blindly at other people – while claiming that the group to which he belongs is the only positive one, and other groups should be negated – or whether by reflecting on our own limitations we can learn to do justice to those who are different, and to realize that true injustice is always to be found at the precise point where you put yourself in the right and other people in the wrong. Hence to abstain from self-assertiveness . . . seems to me to be the crucial thing to ask from individuals today.[112]

In view of this state of affairs, writes Niklas Luhmann with characteristic tartness, 'perhaps the most pressing task of ethics is to warn against morality'.[113]

3

'In the Name of Liberty, Take Off Your Clothes!' On Body Politics

> One might simplify this by saying: men act and women appear. Men look at women. Women watch themselves being looked at. This determines not only most relations between men and women but also the relation of women to themselves. The surveyor of woman in herself is male: the surveyed female. Thus, she turns herself into an object – and most particularly an object of vision: a sight.[1]
>
> – John Berger

GETTING (IN) THE PICTURE

The general public has made an image out of Cologne. On its face, this hardly seems noteworthy. Life now consists of a flood of pictures. Analogue and digital media have become omnipresent, and many people's days are rhythmed according to the Facebook statuses that accompany their early-morning coffee, the appointments they've made via Instagram and Tinder, the tweets sent of an evening. But images are no mere illustrations of factual reality; rather, they play an essential role in the constitution of meaning, perception and knowledge (in short, the world). Through pictures – including pictures of 'Cologne' – we form a 'picture' of the world by forming a world, as it were, for the pictures. Images are never simple depictions, and they do not reflect realities inherent in themselves. Rather, as John Berger teaches, images are performative. They don't only reproduce things, they *produce* them. In the modality of the image, there can be no distinction between normative interpretation and objective replication. Images are actions, as we argued in Chapter 1. Images have a life of their own.

In this sense, they are no different from texts – words, sentences, idioms, grammar – but by means of images even stronger effects can be achieved. This is because images, as the art historian W. J. T.

Mitchell argues, make *demands* of those who look at them. They demand reactions; they provoke and seduce.[2] They intervene actively in shaping things and events, particularly by furthering the transformation of doubt into certainty, subjective into objective sense, and tentative knowledge into irrefutable evidence. Pictures organize the sphere of the aesthetic and condition our perspectives, which is to say, our patterns of perception. But, perhaps most important of all, pictures mediate the *ethical* relationship between any given historical subject and his or her social and political reality.[3]

If we are to consider images, in this way, as productive of worlds – apprehending them, following Berger and Mitchell, as living entities that make demands on us – the first thing to ask would intuitively be: 'What kind of world are these images making?' Who and what do they 'give' us to see? Who and what do they make legible? Which sensitivities, if any, do they cultivate (and in relation to whom)? What kind of impulses do they call up? How and what do they make us care about or detest? And, finally, to whom do they offer the opportunity to 'gain representation, especially self-representation' – which, as Judith Butler notes, is assumed to provide 'a better chance of being humanized'?[4] Who, in this sense, tends to appear in pictures as 'like us'; and who appears alien?

When we ask after the life of images in this way – What do they want? What do they do? What networks of influence do they belong to? – we are asking about what Jacques Rancière calls the 'ethical regime of images'. This is, for Rancière, 'a matter of knowing in what way images' mode of being affects the *ethos*, the mode of being of individuals and communities'.[5] 'Ethos', here, designates not the actions of single individuals, but the structure of moral behaviour that constitutes, integrates and stabilizes the community in which we live, while at the same time separating this community from other communities.

THE CRITIQUE OF IMAGES

Images are, in this sense, particularly good for teasing out what it is that we generally consider to be our social and political reality, what is and isn't a fact, and which events count as important. Indeed, the images that circulate about Cologne provide vital information about what has been established as the 'authentic' version of this event, and how. They tell us how this event is to be regarded and what it stands for. At the same time, images and their performative power also enable us to critically question this 'authorized' version, as though inviting criticism of themselves. For images are simultaneously deter-mined and determining, and thoroughly non-innocent.

Images are inseparable from their referential contexts, which is to say, they generate meaning only through their relationship to the 'chain of significations' of which they form a part.[6] Neither are they autonomous, nor is their significance innately fixed. What they *might* mean is always an open question. This is, on the one hand, what makes pictures so essential for this book's understanding of culture (following Rommelspacher) as an 'ensemble of social practices and shared practices of meaning-making through which the current constitution of society – including its history, economy and political structures – is articulated'.[7] On the other, this tells us that culture is also precisely the mode and place in which this constitution is constantly challenged and negotiated.

Insofar as meanings are substantially generated in pictures, they can at the same time (at least potentially) be called into question by means of pictures, too. In pictures, as in texts or in speech, the limits of shared meanings can be explored, as can differences between them. And such interpretative conflict is ultimately the beating heart of culture. The ineluctable momentum of contradictory processes of meaning-making – the struggle over interpretation, in other words – *is* culture.

Every colour, every line, every pose and every image visible in photographs and illustrations today is *related* not only to earlier – simi-lar, but differently contextualized – versions of themselves, but also to possible future colours, lines, poses and images. Their meaning is inter-woven and co-constitutive through space and time. In other words, the meaning of a specific image arises from an infinite but by no means arbitrary social connection of the interpretation. 'Do things – objects, people, events in the world – carry their own, one, true meaning, fixed like number plates on their backs?' asked Stuart Hall rhetorically; no – meaning *flows* and cannot be definitively codified.[8] Just like any other kind of text, then, an image is always a quotation in that it cannot *but* refer to earlier texts. In fact, texts cannot help but refer to *future* texts, either; in the case of images, it is not material for future writing they invoke, but future *images* and representations.[9]

In short, images resonate, just like texts – just like *signs* more generally – within an indeterminate space of ceaseless meaning-making. The fundamental dynamic of this reverberating process of quotation is the deferral – sometimes to a greater, sometimes to a lesser extent – of the meaning of that which is 'quoted'. In this sense, the *production* of meaning (world-making) is every bit as inherent to pictures as is *reproduction*: images are just as capable of undermining normativity as shoring it up. To take up the perspective of a critique of representation, as advanced by the cultural queer theorist Antke Engel, is to appreciate that 'images are never isolated entities, but rather, bound up in complex processes of production, reception and circulation'.[10]

Our task in dealing with images in the spirit of an anti-essentialist ethos of difference is to remain open to their polysemy – that is, to the possibility of their plural, competing and even contradictory meanings. Where meaning is concerned, one must grasp that nobody and nothing ever has the last word. This will become clearer over the course of this chapter, as we demonstrate the unstable, polysemic character of what images have persistently referred to as 'Cologne'. As Silke Wenk enables us to appreciate, this image-based definition has once again set up 'woman' as the embodiment of culture, of nation and of Western civilization as a whole.[11] Indeed, newspaper images like those that attached themselves to the dread 'night of Cologne' force (and enable) a discussion about the ways in which – in the analysis of Nira Yuval-Davis – 'women play the roles of cultural transmitters as well as cultural signifiers of the national collectivity'.[12]

Now, it is true that repetition and change, affirmation and critique, reinforcement and destabilization are all processes that are *inherent* in pictures. But they are not equal. Caught up in history, and

in relations of power and domination, the full range of possible interpretations is never equally available or 'normal'. Not everything
constitutes 'legitimate speech',[13] as Bourdieu puts it, or for that matter
legitimate figuration. Rather, we have to contend with hegemonic
frames, into which some readings fit far more readily than do others.

The persistence of marginalized, minoritarian, less readily available readings, and of interpretations marked as particular, special or
'different' – with potentially powerful effects – cannot be underestimated. The very criticisms that we, within *this* text you have before
you, are leveling at the specific images that have composed the cipher
'Cologne' are as much a part of those very images as what we criticize
them for (namely, the weaving together of racism, sexism and feminism). Once again, however, a note of caution: the subject matter and
the critique thereof are not *equally* available to us, the general public.

There are 'normal' perspectives – or at least *normalized* ones –
versions of an event or an image that stand for the self-evident or
'majority' view. On the other hand, there are critical, sceptical, questioning voices, which arise historically from constellations of (always
only provisional) power. These are usually quieter, sometimes to the
point of inaudibility. Consequently, an act of critique or of questioning usually functions as a disruptive intervention, an imposition on
normal life, a stumbling block in the flow of the everyday. Even as the
public sphere continues to multiply and to elude singular comprehen-
sion, some images – and, thus, some 'ways of seeing' – remain
predominant and therefore normal. Others remain marginal, trickier
to find and adopt, or possibly even (aesthetically speaking) wholly
inaccessible.

COVER GIRLS: 'BROWN MAN GROPES WHITE WOMAN'

A key part of the reporting on the Cologne New Year's Eve was the
great quantity of 'documentary' images circulated in the media – at
least, images that seemed to be documentary in nature – for instance,
photographs of Cologne's iconic cathedral square (Domplatte), of
the festive New Year's Eve street scene, or of Cologne Central Station.

Special illustrations of Cologne, the event, were also made to order in great abundance. These images did not aim to depict events, nor even to depict the real places where something had supposedly taken place. Rather, they were polemical: pointed, provocative, self-consciously *interpretive* significations of what had happened. As such, they were visual interpretations of an event they were themselves constituting, or to which they were at least contributing. They were not so much 'illustrations' as expressions of prevalent social fantasies and (pre)conceptions about what had – allegedly or actually – occurred.

The pictures, then, did not simply *reflect* events, either objective or imaginary. They *defined* those events. And, apparently, the essence of the events in question was self-evident: brown men groped (and even penetrated) the bodies of white women.[14] We do not dispute that this summary probably does speak to part of what happened in Cologne that night, nor do we dispute that, as such, it should be spoken about. At the same time, it is vital that we critically reflect on the *production of evidence* for this view, as manifested in the mode of the image. To understand the effect of the pictures below is to begin to understand what had to be 'assembled' such that Cologne could become an event, a 'matter of concern'.[15]

Viele junge Muslime können nicht
entspannt dem anderen Geschlecht begegnen.
Das sind jedesmal hochsexualisierte
Situationen. Auch das ist der
Boden für den Exzess von Köln.

Already, at this juncture, the striking *ambiguity* of the above images can be turned into a question: Is reproducing them – as we are doing here, for the purposes of critical analysis – in itself a racist act? We don't know the answer to this. We would like to leave it as an open question. We are aware that the repeated display of certain images is capable of stimulating the continuance of racist image production and reception. In this case, we think it makes sense to show them, because we want to draw attention to the power of the pictures while subjecting them to critical analysis highlighting their historic entanglements. This would be very difficult to do without showing them.[16] Not showing them would, in some sense, perpetuate the invisibility of the freight racist images carry. The racism hides in plain sight precisely because such images circulate within the dazzling bandwidth of maximal visibility – the specific kind of visibility Angela McRobbie calls 'luminosity'.[17]

In the magazine cover images we have selected, we perceive one topic that is (literally) being centred, numerous subtopics and, finally, themes that contribute to the constitution of the whole event through their very absence and invisibility. Graphically speaking, the women are rendered as white, and the groping, even *penetrating* hands are made to stand for black people. Both covers ram this dichotomy home with the help of accompanying journalism that sexualizes the encounter between (young) Muslims or migrants and women (or 'the opposite sex') while promising to deliver the 'truth' ('what *really* happened').

Accordingly, there has been much talk of a 'highly sexualized situation' and of 'sex attacks'. This is an interpretation that has arisen via the medium of a multimodal representation (consisting of text and image), which in turn constitutes what has happened performatively – this thing called 'Cologne'. The event now feels concrete: a white woman has been, or *is being*, sexually assaulted by migrant hands and/or male hands of colour. In addition, one of the covers includes the reader directly in the event, suggesting that she is – that 'we' all are – co-creators of this event. The question that appears on the *Focus* cover, 'Are we still being 'tolerant', or have we already become blind?', suggests shared responsibility for what is supposed to have happened.

We are being addressed in the very act of viewing. In this way, we come to learn that we are all implicated – *in certain circumstances* – in women's struggles against sexual violence. The circumstance in question, specifically, is when white women have to defend themselves against brown men. In the same gesture, the ideas of tolerance and potential blindness are brought into a promiscuous proximity to one another: tolerance, according to the text, might really be blindness; at least, tolerance threatens to *turn* into blindness at any time. Tolerance is, therefore, *potentially, possibly, perhaps*, blind to the sexual aggression of men of colour and/or migrants towards white women.

The choice between 'still tolerant' and 'already blind' introduces, somewhat ambivalently, a certain temporality. This is a well-known chronological formula in advertising rhetoric, pioneered in 2009 by a certain mass flat-pack furniture store from Sweden for whom it proved enormously successful. In the decade since, variations on that firm's question 'Are you still doing x, or already doing y?' have been adapted to all kinds of retail contexts. The formula remains constant: the thing from the past that you might 'still' be doing is worse, and whatever it is implied some people are 'already' doing in the present is the better option. The magazine cover essentially evokes the following normative interpretation: tolerance was then, blindness is now, so why are you holding on to tolerance? This reversal of the progress-oriented logic of the publicity formula challenges the standard normative interpretation that earlier equals worse, now equals better. The cover consequently ironizes and questions this temporality defined by still/already. As we see it, in our reading of this text, it is tolerance *of* the past, too, that is positioned as a 'bad' – at least, a questionable – attitude.

Tolerance, or so *Focus* magazine's cover suggests, amounts to criminal ignorance of real dangers. And, as we mentioned in Chapter 2, this perspective perfectly aligns with the tendency towards discursive fundamentalism that got into full swing in the aftermath of Cologne. From the many, many intersecting and interrelated, mutually constitutive differences that played a role in Cologne's New Year's Eve – including education, age, class, ethnicity, gender, sexuality, migration status – only a very few were singled out, only to be partially fused with one another.

HEGEMONIC DOUBLESPEAK AND DEMONIZATIONS

As soon as it became known that sexual assaults and sexual violence generally had taken place on the Cologne Domplatte, the majority of the media coverage strongly intimated that their reporters knew very well just what had happened, namely: 'the' Arab migrants, 'the' refugees, had attacked 'our' women.[18] German women. Now, if there was some truth to this, it still remained to be seen whether it was the whole truth. Which women, exactly, were attacked – by whom? And is there any empirical basis to the claim that refugee politics and sexual violence politics can be traced together, one onto the other, in this way? Are asylum-seeking men really more responsible for sexual violence than 'native-born' German men? Police statistics do not give any indication that this is the case.[19]

In the absence of a pre-existing framework of discourse couching Islamophobia in the language of sexual politics, Cologne could not have become 'Cologne', the event, and could not have gained the purchase and the character of 'truth' that it did. The scandal – of sexual violence against women, which is indeed a scandal – would not have registered to the same extent had it not been immediately established that the story involved refugee 'others'.

The coverage and commentary on Cologne embodied a certain hegemonic doublespeak, a Janus-faced logic which had already developed in the months before the incident. On the one hand, the influx and increased visibility of migrants in Germany was greeted with a great display of discursive hospitality and *Willkommenskultur* so marked that it was in fact rapidly derided as 'do-gooder culture'.[20] On the other hand, however – often even in the same newspapers – there was a great upsurge in what Castro Varela and Mecheril call 'demonization of Others'.[21] The latter was typically expressed in gestures of performative rejection and devaluation, of which there were too many to count among the sheer volume of journalistic and essayistic speculations on the 'Arab man', 'Islamic masculinity', 'the patriarchal underpinnings of Muslim societies' and so on, not to mention social media's representations of the 'sex-starved Muslim'. This avalanche of performative rejection was habitually intensified by the use of accompanying images.

The demonology of the 'brown man' – that is to say, the narrative in which women should beware of him – figuratively fuses two axes of difference: black/white and male/female. Specifically, the figure of the brown man here forms the node in which these two axes of difference mutually essentialize one another. 'He' becomes the repository of a primitive, uncivilized cultural ontology: a specifically 'oriental' patriarchal misogyny (supposedly imbibed by 'the Arab' from childhood) which means he is only capable of seeing women as whores or saints, not as equals. Counterposed against him, in this imaginary, is the contradictory, sexually pure figure of the 'white woman' – a chaste yet at the same time (heterosexually) eroticized, simultaneously bared and covered, figure – who is being groped.

EVIDENCE AND CRITIQUE

So, what the newspaper spreads and magazine covers were generating, first and foremost, was this one crucial piece of 'evidence': the brown man–white woman dyad. However, as we've indicated, this very endeavour also generates, as a side effect, openings for its own critique. What appears in these striking images is ultimately quite simple: the sexual threat to white femininity posed by a racialized and thus implicitly migrant and aggressive masculinity. But with the publication of these images, the existing critiques of their underlying ideology also became real.[22] For our critiques are built into the images themselves, as a latent possibility, and they are now being realized in our text. Ours is a text that *situates* these images, analyzes them, and deciphers the 'evidence' they generate so as to expose the interpretations they pass off as total and show the ways in which they are, in fact, totalizing and particular. Against their visual assertion that 'things are thus', we counter by showing that myriad other accounts exist ('things are also like *this* and *this*') which they have rendered invisible.

Specifically, yes, racialized men sometimes perpetrate sexual violence upon white women. Yes, Arab men commit such acts against Arab women, be they Christian, Muslim or non-religious. White men rape and sexually assault racialized women. Men do it to men, women do it to men, and women do it to other women.[23] To say all this – to bring the fuller picture into the debate again and again, drawing attention, again and again, to the diverse specifics and the extent of sexual violence in society – is by no means to relativize concrete incidents. Individual experiences of violence should, indeed, never, ever, be relativized.

At the time of their publication, an opportunity seemed to arise from the cover images and front-page spreads of German newspapers and magazines, of which we selected two here for discussion. This was our chance! At last – the chance to name a problem. The problem in question is called sexism, sexual violence, and (as some say) 'rape culture'. As a problem, it is universal, though always context-specific. *All* extant research on violence against women strongly suggests that a sexual dimension exists all over the world, in all social contexts, strata and milieus, and across all generational constellations. At the same time, such a generalization does not really tell us much because, even though this is the case, sexual violence is always enacted in a context-specific way – and, as we've already emphasized – it also victimizes men. It is also perpetrated by women. While sexual and gendered violence is ubiquitous, then, its specific logics are concretely localized.

In that sense, one might say, the following ways of 'naming the problem' denoted by Cologne are, strictly speaking, synonymous: 'sexual violence', 'sexual assaults by migrant men against German women', 'sexual harassment in Germany', 'sexual assaults in the context of multiculturalism'. After the incident, a number of public figures, activist networks, organizations and public initiatives came forward, or formed specifically, in order to contribute to the process of naming and definition.[24] The network #ausnahmslos, for example (which we already discussed in Chapter 2), came out with its statement 'against sexual violence *and* racism, always, and everywhere' and its core demand: 'The struggle against sexual violence must become a political priority, not just now, but every day, because sexual violence is a problem that affects us all.'[25] For some time after New Year's Eve, indeed, the extent of the violence, of women's fear of and in public spaces, *was* intensively discussed in German civil society.

Equally, as discussed in Chapter 2, things also stirred in the domain of criminal law reform. But, since the impetus for change was the outrage and indignation unleashed by Cologne, this movement of integration only underlined the toxic underbelly of the (visually dominated) media representation of the matter at hand. The price of the law taking sexism seriously soon became apparent: sexism would be locked into an 'us and them' structure of ontological difference. Sexual violence would be firmly displaced onto the far side of the dividing line between our society and the 'beyond', barbarians, foreigners, strangers, *others* – those who do not belong to us and who, furthermore, do not belong.

THE BODY OF THE OTHER: MORE SEXUAL THAN HUMAN

Once again, the magazine's cover compositions are revealing. An airbrushed, post-processed, alabaster-white female anatomy[26] is being groped and dirtied (with dark handprints) by dark, masculine hands. A blonde, fair-skinned woman is being menaced by nonwhite men, whose manual invasion is located at (perhaps even penetrating) her genitals. In these images, it is Europe, the West or, indeed, simply *us* that is being embodied by this woman. Under the rules of this neo-racist iconography, she stands in for the whole of the Western world, while the racially 'other' men are 'stranger danger' personified.[27]

The construction of difference here is not one-dimensional: it is not 'only' a matter of 'woman' beset by 'man', 'male' defiling 'female'. These images stage a more complex articulation of relations defined by gender, sexuality and culturalized race. Femininity and masculinity are, indeed, portrayed as complementary (heterosexual) entities, who seemingly only exist for and in distinction to one another: she being the hunted, the aggressed, the object of his (all of their!) uncontrollable desire. Note, too, that she stands alone, while they are many. This hides from sight the wonderful diversity and plurality of women; the fact that women by no means all correspond to the particular physiology, this luminous alabaster nakedness, depicted here. At the same time, it hides from sight that 'the other side' – the racialized one – is also comprised of women, allowing the reader to forget that these 'offstage' people – these nonwhite men and women – are not primarily (certainly not solely) to be understood as sexual actors.

This particular amalgam can be described as 'ethnosexism', which, writes Gabriele Dietze, operates at the 'intersection and interaction between ethnicity and sexuality, in the way in which each defines and depends on the other for its meaning and power'.[28] Dietze defines ethnosexism as a 'culturalization of gender, discriminating against ethnically marked subjects on the grounds that they belong to an allegedly problematic or "backward" sexual order'.[29] This, in turn, carries on a long history of sexually inflected racist stereotyping.

Multiple historically marked axes (and relations) of difference coalesce in the illustrations and depictions analyzed here. It is in the mode of the image that their preliminary essentialization takes place. There is, as such, nothing arbitrary about the particular colours, genders and sexualities that come to count as evident signs of reality, as authenticity, as the plausible truth – in other words – of an event.

Sexual violence in public spaces was hardly a new or localized phenomenon, either for the city of Cologne or for the Federal Republic as a whole. Accordingly, the 'fundamentalization' of this multifaceted and deeply complex violence was achieved by equating perpetrators with darkness, maleness and migrant status, on the one hand, and victimhood with blondeness, femaleness and Germanness, on the other. Once this fundamentalized text – and image-structure – had been put in place, it became difficult to have a nuanced discussion of the generalities and specificities of sexual violence. Note, though, that discussion was not actually made *impossible*, since images are too underdetermined, open and limited in their determinative power to foreclose interpretation. It is ultimately difficult to miss the way the (demonic) image of the 'black man' in the cover composition rearticulates a very old figure – a colonial trope – connected with Europeans' enslavement of millions of people, their appropriation and exploitation of entire continents.

The 'black man' has, over time, become an efficient visualization of a phantasy, the embodiment of a particular mode of othering associated with European modernity. The 'black man' distills the foundational differences against which this white European modernity is constituted: he is 'nature', unbridled libido, primitive, ahistorical, an embodiment of authenticity in the form of pure danger and desire. Frantz Fanon writes in *Black Skin, White Masks* that 'the biological cycle begins with the black man'.[30] The black man, in his account of this psychic phantasy, is 'nothing but biological', 'fixated at the genital level'.[31] And, like other theorists of modernity, Fanon further contends that biology, here, stands for a frontier of 'nature' or an 'outside' of culture, and thus, in an era of colonialism, for the ensemble of that which must be subjugated and appropriated in order to secure civilization and history. 'Nature', in this imaginary, also stands for sexuality – at least, sexuality beyond the bounds of normative social regulation.

Moreover, this quintessentially modern form of naturalizing, racializing exoticization has always gone hand in hand with a projection of overpowering sexual potency, thus giving rise to the stereotype of the hyper-virile, excessively physical (and therefore irrational) black stud. In his critical inquiry into the racist stereotype of the figure of the black man, Kobena Mercer concludes that 'the Primal Fantasy of the big black penis projects the fear of a threat not only to white womanhood, but to civilization itself.'[32]

'The Orient had to be captured yet, at the same time, kept at a distance',[33] writes Birgit Rommelspacher in her account of early modern Orientalism's importance for contemporary Germans' ideas of 'Arab cultures' and Islam. This was achieved by conceptually reconstructing this 'Orient' wholesale, using European categories and classifying it at a lower stage of development. Examples of today's continuation of these ideas exist in abundance. Jürgen Mannke, president of the Saxony-Anhalt Philological Association, for example, worried recently that the 'young, strong, mostly Muslim men who have chosen the Federal Republic of Germany as their asylum' would seduce local girls and young German women. For the 'responsible pedagogue', he writes, it is important to be allowed to ask the question: 'How can we enlighten our young girls, ages 12 and up, in such a way that they refrain from superficial sexual adventures with Muslim men (attractive as they undeniably often are)?'[34]

In this way, both before *and* after the New Year's Eve in Cologne, myriad German voices defamed 'the young Islamic men' as irresistible – but dangerous! – testosterone bombs: creatures of instinct who put 'our' public spaces and 'our' achievements in the realm of gender equality at risk on account of their backwards and sexist (because Muslim) attitudes to the world. Equal parts voyeuristic titillation and defensiveness, this mode of sexualization of the 'foreign man' continues a centuries-long colonial pattern of racism, when, for instance, it crops up in the form of HIV tests imposed on refugees in Bavaria, seemingly without their informed consent.

By ontologizing difference, *Versämtlichung* makes complex dynamics of differentiation invisible: an effect that is particularly striking in the case of pictures, as we have shown. But *Versämtlichung* also manifests itself against bodies themselves, and it clings to the signs that attach themselves to the human body in real life. The degree of nudity of the female body, for example, was not just a *pictorial* element of the public debate around 'Cologne'. In the summer of 2016, news stories, testimonials, and all manner of sensational images circulated throughout Europe on the subject of women and their clothing choices – and this was hardly new, nor was it a coincidence. Women's bodies have historically (one is tempted to say 'always') served both as the repository for social norms and as the raw material onto which negotiations of these norms can be projected. But even the attenuated version of this statement would be too broad, too reductive, and therefore false.

But it *is* correct to say, especially in the context of migration and 'multiculturalism', asylum politics and 'diversity', women's bodies often come to function as a kind of surface for the projection of contentious discourses. In other words, it is in, through and on 'the' female body that socially constitutive differences and their normative interpretations are negotiated. 'The female body' is deliberately formulated in the singular, here, because the matter at hand is, at best, a phantasmatic projection only tangentially related to real, empirical, complex, dynamic bodies in the plural. The phantasy woman incarnates, according to the occasion, the nation, nature, virtue, purity, fertility, weakness or seductiveness. Sometimes, other symbolic freightage attaches itself to other bodies, too: witness how 'the male body', 'the black body' and 'the body of the child' serve in cultural representations as the embodiment of whole other sets of differences and values. As discussed, the black male body, for example, betokens 'the savage'.

BODY POLITICS OF THE HIJAB

The modernist mode of otherization, then, turns the bodies of 'others' into visible representations of otherness. Above all, it positions these 'others' as objects in relation to a subject: as the things that are being negotiated. As 'others' of modernity, animals, children, women and 'blacks' are, ideologically speaking, 'not quite' subjects. And the normative force of this social order is negotiated, in large part, via corporealities. Practically every wave of historical change, in modernity, has had its somatic side, its bodily dimension.

Body-politics have been an essential component of emancipatory movements under modernity, shaping struggles for equality, rights, inclusion, recognition and access to material resources. These struggles have often striven to articulate their own account of the relation between the universal and the particular, balancing the problems of recognition and visibility and asking, for example, which body is considered the universal body of culture. What kind of body embodies the citizen? Which bodies are 'normal', which 'deviant'? Which bodies are up for debate, and which go unscrutinized because they are regarded as the embodiment of a general norm? Who has power – and what sort of power – over what bodies? Whose bodies are 'appropriate' in which contexts? Bodies are, alas, never 'just' bodies, in a naive anatomical sense. They are corporealities, comprising elements like posture, hairstyle, clothing and much, much more.

One visually prominent and highly controversial element of corporeal self-presentation in the present is, of course, the headscarf or hijab. In the context of the complex differences between gender, migration, religion and sexuality, it is a particularly contested and normatively charged body sign:

> As long as it was only the woman scrubbing the school-rooms who wore a headscarf, there were no problems. Nobody thought to 'problematize' the hijab, then. No, the dispute over the headscarf only arose at the moment when students and academics were seen to be wearing it. The more successful the integration, in other words, the sharper the contestation.[35]

The subject of the 'Islamic' headscarf has provoked public disputes across Europe for decades. In fact, in Germany and neighbouring countries, a plethora of normative conversations has attended the full gamut of garments for women's concealment (regardless of their empirical prevalence among a population) – including the niqab, chador, burka – promoting fixation on the piece of cloth specifically, while simultaneously managing to draw attention to the human being who wears it. As with all forms of feminine clothing in general (and veiling in particular), the hijab is a locus for the negotiation of interweaving strands of religious belief, culture, gendered power, status, inequality, inclusion and exclusion. The veiling of women is, one might say, the visible site of a complex, always potentially conflictual and unsettled context that is always in flux.

In the lines quoted above, the sociologist Aladin El-Mafaalani gives us a crucial dimension of this dynamic in a nutshell. As long as it was merely *Gastarbeiterinnen* ('women guest workers') in western Germany who wore the headscarf – that is to say, women in the lower ranks of society who overwhelmingly perform society's 'dirty work' – the headscarf was no provocation. Possibly, he ventures, it even fit in well with widespread bourgeois preconceptions of the backwards but industrious, oppressed but diligent 'Muslim woman'. Moreover, migrant women from majority-Muslim regions of the world were no more socially invisible in the 1950s and '60s than women who didn't wear veils. There are noteworthy exceptions, however: during the Second Wave of the women's movement in West Germany in the 1970s, there were intense arguments about this very question. The Committee of Women from Turkey declared, in its founding statement:

> Here in Germany, many know us only as colourful headscarves, which often leads to prejudice. But there are people living under these headscarves! People with thoughts and feelings. We have decided to fight for our social and democratic rights ourselves.[36]

Meanwhile, in 1984, the first joint feminist congress of 'German and non-German women' took place in Frankfurt am Main.[37]

Ever since that congress, Germany's queer, (post-)immigrant and anti-racist milieus have been grappling with the complex constellations of gender, regional specificity, religion, culture, class, sexuality and nation that locate their visible sign in the headscarf. As Rommelspacher rightly notes, it ends up being a peculiarly underdetermined sign, because 'cultural codes such as the headscarf or the veil are multiply determined, that is, they have a multiplicity of meanings that are usually not explicitly visible in the discussions themselves.'[38] One thing that is often not visible in current debates, for example, is the long tradition of exoticizing 'oriental' femininity, and the role this plays in the West establishing itself as superior to it, which is to say, civilized and modern.

Another dynamic that is not always sufficiently apparent within the hegemonic discourse around the hijab is the sheer range of attitudes and positions espoused by those who actually wear it (or wear other forms of modesty-oriented, body-concealing headgear or clothing). The Islamic scholar and journalist Lamya Kaddor has spelled out what ought really to be a trivial and self-evident point: 'Just as iterations of the veil differ significantly, the decision to self-veil is made for different and individual reasons.' By force of necessity, however, Kaddor's is also one of the key voices in today's broad spectrum of feminist activism in Germany patiently and insistently pointing out that the veil (of whatever type) mainly functions today as the symbol of a negative stereotype. In other words, the hijab is totalized and totalizing: the wearer of the hijab *becomes* the hijab when she becomes, discursively, 'the veiled Muslim woman' or (among those more familiar with the terminology) 'the hijabi' or 'hijabi woman'. Emphasis on the veil implies that the object in question is the visible sign of women's oppression (and *repression*), epitomizing a culture that is completely different from ours.[39]

In our view, that the above stance represents a completely avoidable form of fundamentalist thinking about difference is indisputable. And what this fundamentalism of differences forgets is not only the diversity of ways of wearing the headscarf within Islam, but also the (uncomfortable?) overlaps between these Muslim practices of veiling and long-standing analogous practices proper to Catholicism, Judaism and Protestantism. After all, in all these religious traditions – especially, though not only, in their fundamentalist branches – the normative ordering of sexuality and gender has been reinforced by means of commandments concerning women's (and, to a lesser extent, men's) dress and attire. Even today, the Hasidic school of Judaism enforces a strict requirement that women wear wigs and men cover their heads as part of a commitment to 'chaste' attire. Similarly, the Protestant Amish in the United States observe vestimentary strictures: as with the Hasidic and Orthodox Jews, women must clothe themselves in loose-fitting skirts and shawls and may not wear trousers. Meanwhile, in the modern Catholic church, obvious norms still exist for women today, norms which include headscarves and 'modest' concealment of the body.

In short, in many parts of the world, across many religions and 'cultures' – insofar as such a thing might be said to exist – clothing norms have developed, albeit in more or less pronounced ways, with a view to emphasize sexual difference (e.g., pants for men, skirts for women) and thus to materialize and naturalize operative constructions of gender and sexuality. The trope of 'modesty', with its implicit sexualization of women and women's bodies, is truly not unique to Islam. To insist on this does not amount to denying the reality of the specifically Islamic expression of this powerful norm.

BODIES AND 'HYPER-CULTURALIZATION'

In Germany, a discourse of 'hyper-culturalization' (which makes 'culture' the single cause of all kinds of problems) increasingly obstructs any kind of reasonable debate about differences, dynamics of othering, or commonalities between traditions; in particular, sometimes successfully preventing different groups from speaking with one another.[40] The reification of a given 'culture', as we currently encounter it in the German media with regard to 'Islam' or 'the Maghreb', effectively obliterates heterogeneities and conflicts *within* regional religious contexts. For example, one would never know, to consume this media, that there has been an extensive internal Islamic feminist conversation happening for decades. These culturalizations thus hide not only the complexity of history, but the individuality and the diversity of the people who actively comprise these traditions. 'In this culturalized discourse', writes Nira Yuval-Davis, 'gendered bodies and sexuality play pivotal roles, as territories, markers and reproducers of the narratives of nations and other collectivities.'[41]

As numerous historical and cultural analyses (like Yuval-Davis's) show, the body of the 'other' is sexualized and infantilized in modernity, whose mode of otherization systematically produces embodiments of naturalness, authenticity and impulsivity. As Rommelspacher writes: 'Anti-Semitism and colonialism, Orientalism and other forms of racism all have one thing in common: a tendency to sexualize the other. All of them end up somehow with a figure of a sexually dissolute and/or perverse and threatening man, and a dangerous and sinister, yet seductive, woman.'[42]

When it comes to Orientalism and gender, women's bodies have been, and still remain, the privileged 'battlefield' for a number of culture wars (which aren't and weren't ever, as it turns out, really 'culture' wars at all). In her political collages in the late 1980s, the visual artist Barbara Kruger criticized the body politics of the new social movements in general – and the women's liberation movement in particular, especially around abortion, rape and reproductive rights. Kruger's line of analysis, condensed in the slogan 'Your Body Is a Battlefield' (the title of her series), speaks thoroughly even now to the intertwinement of Islam, gender, sexuality and regional difference.

Then as now, differences are not always asserted – and are not always made effective – in the register of a biological ontology. Sometimes the discourse operates via a subtly altered yet analogous ontologization of *culture* (e.g., 'cultural DNA'). Bodies and embodiment can then be read accordingly, not as *biologically* other but as *culturally* so (in equally visible, tangible ways).[43] Just as the pictorial deployment of the stereotypical trope of the 'black man' in the current German context rearticulates the biologically racist fantasies diagnosed by Frantz Fanon, so does the ongoing discussion around Islam, refugees, 'Nafris' and the hijab reinvigorate a hyper-culturalist, even cultural-ontological, notion of the 'Orient'. And thus, the body, especially the female body, becomes a cultural battleground once again.

BURKINIS ON THE BEACH: NAKEDNESS AS MEASURE OF LIBERTY

In Germany, politicians have periodically been bringing up the possibility of implementing a complete legal ban on full-body veiling in public (the so-called burka ban) for some time. In France, however, localized burka bans have been legal since 2011.[44] In August 2016, the city of Cannes was among a number of French municipalities that decided to prohibit the wearing of the so-called burkini on the beach, on the grounds that loose-fitting full-body wetsuits with headscarves attached do not correspond to a religiously prescribed item of clothing. Far from signaling one's faith, or so certain public officials were quoted as saying, to wear a burkini on the beach betokens one's affiliation with a terrorist network, or at least a fundamentalist creed that hates and subjugates women.

As it happens, the beachwear interdiction in Cannes was very soon lifted. In August 2016, a picture went viral around the world that seemed to show policemen on the beach in Nice in the act of forcing a woman to take off her burkini. The German newspaper *Der Spiegel* summarized the scene in astonished tones: 'The pictures are unbelievable: the seated woman seems to be stripping off under the gaze of the standing policemen, while other beach-goers, dressed in swimsuits and bikinis, simply look on in passive curiosity.'[45] It isn't surprising to most of us, given the desire for transient indignation at the heart of the 'attention economy' now structuring the media industry, with its logic of prurient clickability, that the confrontation on the beach transpired this way. And this is precisely what interests us so much about this image (or series of images): the fact that it seems so *plausible* that what happened, happened the way it did, rather than some other way.

In the summer of 2016, many people took the presented version of the 'burkini cops' incident on the beach to be the truth. Interestingly, the story was believed in equal measure by those who regarded it as an outrage and a scandal, and those moved to praise the police for their putative actions on Facebook or in comments on *Spiegel Online*, advocating 'putting "the Muslims" in their place' (which clearly means, in practice, here, making a woman *leave* a particular place – 'our' place). Regardless of its veracity, the incident – and the media attention it commanded – aptly demonstrated the extent to which biopolitical mechanisms of difference-as-*Versämtlichung* play out in, on and through the body of 'the' woman. The degree of (liberal) freedom enjoyed in the West is considered visible – and thus measurable – in the degree of women's public nudity. And the armed wing of the state *polices* this visibility among women by requiring them to become visible, which is to say, naked, for all to see. Naked in public, no less!

When these images 'work', they point to real gains that have been won by feminist movements past and present, in terms of personal freedom and emancipation. These horizons speak to the still-elusive promise of sexual self-determination for all women, our right to our own bodies and our experiences of being visible in public. In the modern era, this goal of self-determination is often pursued in the mode of self-empowerment and 'owning' one's body. This represents a shift that touches on many dimensions of struggle, including the question of sexual freedom.

There is something here worth defending: namely the right to one's own body. The struggle for this right is by no means concluded – neither for women nor for children, so-called disabled people, or, in fact, anybody departing from the norm of the adult, cis-heterosexual, white, middle-class man who still serves as modernity's 'general subject'.[46] The right to undress, to unveil one's body and show oneself, is a key part of the right to body sovereignty, the right to be the one – the only one – making decisions about one's sexuality and its visibility.

This right can by no means be taken for granted. It is a right that was won, by movements for liberation and emancipation, in a fight that is not yet complete. Moreover, it is a right that has courted controversy ever since it was first formulated. During the time of the new social movements, which included the feminist movements of the 1970s and 1980s, the merits and limits of bodily autonomy were at the heart of debates about the connections between domination, sex and violence.[47] For example, the standard understanding of 'sexual liberation' in mainstream circulation was thoroughly criticized as an extension and intensification of the sexualization of all areas of life. Feminists leveled critiques not only at compulsory heterosexuality but at compulsory sexual availability, and especially the 'orgasm imperative', which they denounced as the continuation by other means of patriarchy's reduction of women to objects of male lust.

According to one significant, immanent, historical account of the legacy of the new social movements, the victories women won in the spheres of social participation and representation were bought at the expense of an increased sexualization of increasing numbers of women and children across increasingly diverse sectors of society. This sexualization must be regarded, at minimum, as 'problematic'. Today, for women (it is perhaps more accurate to say: for feminized bodies) there exists a sexualization imperative. This imperative, of course, does not go unchallenged, nor does it affect all feminized subjects equally. But it is undeniably a part of the current conjuncture concerning women and public corporeality.

The sexualization of women is as much a part of the fundamentalist requirement that they veil their bodies as it is inherent to the other (relatively more subtle) compulsion they face – to bare their skin on the beach. In both scenarios, both in the present and in the past, women's bodies are being understood and valued as sexual, *because sexed*, and thus, the meanings of gender and sexuality are, to a certain extent, being ideologically fused.[48] In practice, this means that female bodies can only be perceived through the lens of sexualization. As the public treatment of celebrity athletes makes abundantly clear, it is only through their (hetero-)sexualization that women's bodies become 'proper' female bodies. And, at the same time, in the current debates around asylum, migration, ethnicity and gender, we are losing sight of the right to be free of sexualization, the right to not have one's body be sexualized in public space. While this narrowing of the frame is certainly contested, it remains the case that women's empowerment today – indeed, the whole question of visibility and inclusion for women – is disproportionately understood in terms of the right to self-sexualize.

PHALLIC WOMEN AND AMBIVALENT EMPOWERMENT

The hegemonic concept of freedom underlying the images that circulated under the rubric of 'Cologne' is one whose measure seems to be the degree of nakedness (or, at least, the *ideal* degree of nakedness) of a given society's women. This is unmistakable, for example, in the *repetition* of the very sexualization of the women whose sexualization is being lamented, in the *Focus* magazine cover. The naked, blonde, molested woman stands there on the cover like a visible sign of the irreducible difference between 'us', the West, and 'them', the Muslims, refugees, Arabs or North Africans (in short, the other). Further, she speaks precisely to the neoliberal Western capitalist conjuncture in which, as Angela McRobbie attests, the 'phallic woman' has become a leading trope.[49] This phallic female subject is not bound to a particular sphere or location. Rather, she represents a form of life, a way of living and (self-) 'identifying'. The phallic woman is the contemporary model, in culture, of a woman who is emancipated, modern and free; and her freedom is realized, in large part, through making herself a sex object.

The phallic woman's status as a subject, that is, her status as a self-determining actor and fully enfranchised person, flows from her sexualization of herself. Subjectivation, for the phallic woman, *is* self-sexualization. In popular culture as a whole, this effectively takes the form of 'pornographic empowerment', wherein a sense of personal autonomy is attained via the performance of specific bodily practices, such as the twerk or the duck-face selfie. The trick is to be aware of one's own sexualization – one's becoming pornography, even – and not to lament or seek to avoid or mitigate it, not to critically confront it or seek to contest it by participating in a social movement, but to lay claim to it as a gesture of self-empowerment. Self-sexualization is performatively celebrated, in these practices, as self-determined and -determining, not determined by others.[50]

CRITICAL REFLECTION

And, indeed, there *is* an element of self-empowerment in self-sexualization. After all, practices oriented towards a horizon of bodily (including sexual) self-determination have constituted a central plinth of feminist movements for decades. Such practices, of experimentation in bodily autonomy, have occupied feminism in diverse and conflictual ways. One hears, especially in queer-feminist circles, about the veritable battle – or so-called sex wars – that once raged and still continue to circle around the questions: What (if anything) is properly *political* about sex, sexualized bodies, and sexuality in general? What kind of thing (if anything) can we think of as 'autonomous' when it comes to sexual self-expression?[51]

In view of the complexity of these disputes, which naturally go into nuances of difference far beyond what we can represent here, we will simply confine our parting advice to the following: let us relearn how to *distrust* images; no more and no less. Let us distrust the visual register of corporeality that purports to mark differences such as 'us' and 'them', 'West' and 'Orient', 'black' and 'white', 'male' and 'female', 'liberated' and 'repressed', and so on, while presenting its visualizations as ontologically self-evident. This plea of ours, for scepticism, is simultaneously a plea to recognize that images and bodies, that is to say, signs and materializations of complex differences, always contain within themselves the possibility of their own critique. No image – and likewise, no body – is unambiguous. The meaning of a particular portion of exposed skin or a piece of fabric will never be a foregone conclusion. Thus, the human body, and the various means by which it is framed, concealed and clothed, is likely to continue to elicit critical reflection for a very long time to come.

4

What Might Alice Schwarzer and Birgit Kelle Have in Common? Feminism in the Maelstrom of Racial and Cultural Essentialisms

> The failure of ... feminists to recognize difference as a crucial strength is a failure to reach beyond the first patriarchal lesson. In our world, divide and conquer must become define and empower.[1]
>
> – Audre Lorde, 1979

> We are actively committed to struggling against racial, sexual, heterosexual, and class oppression, and see as our particular task the development of integrated analysis and practice based upon the fact that the major systems of oppression are interlocking. The synthesis of these oppressions creates the condition of our lives.[2]
>
> – Combahee River Collective, 1977

TOXIC FEMINISM

Among those who accepted the 'VIP invitation' from Cologne – this wordless invitation to redraw the fault lines of German society in terms of 'civilizational' clash – were the journalists Birgit Kelle and Harald Martenstein, the politicians Frauke Petry, Beatrix von Storch and Horst Seehofer, and the editor in chief of *EMMA*, Alice Schwarzer. In fact, these figures should probably be understood as part of *issuing* that invitation in the first place. And, for feminists, the last name in the above list is a hard pill to swallow. Schwarzer is a feminist! – nobody could possibly say she isn't; after all, the publication she founded in 1977 was modeled on *Ms.* magazine. But what, then, can feminism still be said to even stand for – what becomes of feminism, when Schwarzer's commentaries on the events in Cologne overflow with all the sordid elements that have made 'Cologne' *the* privileged signifier in contemporary Germany's xenophobic security discourse (as laid out in Chapter 2)? Because, in Alice Schwarzer's pronouncements, they're all there: the themes of law and order, crime, the terrorist threat, national security and public morality, as well as abundant racist generalizations, positing, for instance, religion, violence and gender as inseparable, and, finally, a slew of nativistic talking points, creatively sutured to classic feminist concerns. Can we perhaps say that these are the ingredients of a putatively *hegemonic* feminism, a *right-wing* feminism? Is this, in fact, what Alice Schwarzer advocates? Must we now, at least, get used to naming a discursive – even a *political* – kinship between Schwarzer's positions and those situated on the right, populist, racist, cultural-essentialist end of the spectrum?

To further complicate the picture, how do these positions relate to those of someone like Seyran Ateş, the feminist lawyer and journalist who made it abundantly clear in her 2008 book *The Multicultural Mistake* (*Der Multikulti-Irrtum*) that she, although a left-wing feminist, felt more kinship with conservatives than she did with the Left on the issues of 'integration, German multiculturalism, and Islam'.[3] Ateş has suffered a massive number of threats of violence from rightwing extremist Turkish and Islamist groups, both for this and for her firm stance against sexual violence. What's clear, in short, is that the situation is complex and can support neither simple solutions nor simplistic assignments like 'xenophobic' or 'multicultural'.

This said, when it comes to Alice Schwarzer, we feel comfortable affirming that her brand of feminism is 'toxic' – despite the radical-feminist register in which many of Schwarzer's texts are couched. Hers is an essentializing feminism: one that is not so much critically responding to ressentiment-filled, othering dynamics in society as it is contributing to them. Under Schwarzer, *EMMA* has advanced an anti-sexist position whose tenets are fundamentalist and fundamentalizing. For, as Ina Kerner has noted, Schwarzer is at least consistent in that she 'sees the world exclusively through sex/gender glasses'.[4] Viewed through these goggles, some things no doubt become perceptible with incredible clarity. Other things, however, blur together to the point of illegibility. The final picture is full of fuzz, more mist than light.

In the images and articles that fill the pages of *EMMA*, as part of her avowedly no-holds-barred fight against sexist violence, Schwarzer deals approvingly – enthusiastically, even – in violent abstractions concerning Muslim women, whom she presents as two-dimensional victims of Islamic patriarchy.[5] Even where comprehensible political demands *are* formulated, such as, for example, shelters for women fleeing domestic abuse, one can still hear, loud and clear, that sound that Hedwig Dohm called the 'sound of othering':

> *EMMA* has been swamped with cries for help. German women are clearly distressed. They are concerned for the women and children among the refugees, but also on their own behalf. So *EMMA* has drawn up a catalogue of demands: What will it take for the men and women who have fled their countries and come to us to respect democracy and equal rights?[6]

Schwarzer barely seems to have issued a single statement, ever, on any subject adjacent to migration, immigration or asylum that is not imbued with anti-migrant and Islamosceptic (not to say Islamophobic) sentiment; she has barely published one single text in which she does not either contend that migrants should first learn to respect 'democracy and equal rights' before they come 'here', or paint the entirety of Islam – which, for her, only exists in the singular – as irredeemably impregnated with sexism and patriarchy. Sometimes, as Ina Kerner points out, Schwarzer's disquisitions even convey the impression that Islam is the central or possibly even the *only* 'bastion of androcentrism in Germany'.[7]

POLITICS OF LOCATION

In this chapter, we explore these highly contradictory intertwinements – advanced by Alice Schwarzer – of anti-sexist positions and cultural-essentialist (i.e., racist) ones. Basically: since the knitting together of feminism and racism is evidently *possible*, we consider a careful critique of these unhappy hybrids, and the dilemmas to which they give rise, to be indispensable. And we believe this not least because it challenges us to rethink feminism from the ground up. This means not seeking to explain away Schwarzer's politics with a simple equation along the lines of 'Schwarzer + feminism = racism'. Indeed, efforts intended to 'unmask' her will ultimately, we feel, lead nowhere. The more difficult task, and the one required, is to trace the subtler ways in which Schwarzer's discourse has been contributing to racist and Islamophobic resentments for quite some time.[8] The question we're interested in is: How has its forceful advocacy for a wrongheaded type of sex-universalism succeeded at reinforcing these prejudices? The key here seems to be the complete absence of reflexivity with regard to both the content of the speech itself, and the powerful, dominant position from which Schwarzer sends forth that speech.

We will not be reinventing feminism in this chapter. How could we possibly pull off such a thing? Perhaps, for now, it is enough simply to recall that feminism has always been infinitely greater than, and different from, Alice Schwarzer, whose positions represent a portion of the German-speaking field (no more, no less). Today, more than ever, it is important to highlight the disunity of feminism, to insist that feminism does not, and never has, taken a single form. Already at the time of the first stirrings of a women's movement under the German Empire, the radical-feminist positions of Hedwig Dohm and Anita Augspurg were worlds away from the more moderate, bourgeois difference-based feminisms of Gertrud Bäumer and Helene Lange, which were, in turn, worlds away again from the socialist-feminist politics of Clara Zetkin and Pauline Staegemann. As we saw during our overview of Hedwig Dohm's and Rosa Mayreder's vivid critiques of the *Versämtlichung* effected by 'femininity' stereotypes, feminism has always contained a wealth of alternatives for pursuing critiques of essentialism instead of self-essentializing gestures. These are the alternatives from which we still draw inspiration today.

Instead of speaking from nowhere, which is to say, from a purportedly universalist standpoint, the tendencies in question have all committed to what Adrienne Rich would later term a 'politics of location'.[9] Without in the least implying (let alone demanding) a fundamentalizing fusion of position and message, the politics of location – as explored in Chapter 1 – takes the relation between positionality, knowledge and politics seriously, asking if and how the place from which we speak is likely to determine what we say, as well as what can be said. Furthermore, it's a mode of thought that seeks to establish the *responsibility* for one's own speech and actions that derives from this inquiry. For example, one might seek to exercise discursive caution, taking care never to allow the language of racism to creep into the critique of gender and never to allow sexist language to creep into the critique of race. Unfortunately, Schwarzer's publications are no more able to integrate this wisdom than she is capable of reflexiveness vis-à-vis the social relations that invest her with discursive power.

The situation, as it stands, is one in which all communication about these issues seems to be fatally poisoned, in that having recourse to pat commonplaces and denying the existence of social dynamics associated with migration and asylum both seem equally wrong. In this context, we believe interventions of the kind we are proposing here to be no small thing.[10]

How does one forge a non-racist, anti-sexist discourse that is simultaneously a non-sexist, anti-racist discourse? This is the complicated task we face. One might also rephrase it this way: How do we detoxify feminism? Or, how do we decolonize feminism? How do we free feminism from the trap of what the economist Esra Erdem calls the 'politics of ressentiment'?[11] Erdem writes that this prevalent contemporary groundswell promotes anti-Muslim racism as a proxy for tackling the social issues it itself identifies. The demands, for example, usually bear some connection to domestic violence, honour killings and forced marriages within immigrant communities, yet they have nothing to say:

Either about making victim protection services more effective, or about improving immigrant women's access to rape crisis centres, battered women's shelters and counseling. They have nothing to say when it comes to denouncing the racism within anti-violence campaign practices or promoting the development of robust cross-cultural strategies against domestic, sexual and other forms of gendered violence. Rather, they are single-mindedly focused on using the legal machinery of the border regime to punish and deter migrants who have committed violent acts.[12]

The consequences of these remarks are unmistakable. We must extricate feminism from its deep entanglement with the colonial legacy (of othering that which is 'foreign'), and from the attendant solipsism that leads it endlessly to affirm itself and its own. Today, this also means freeing it from its complicity with the politics of securitization, discipline and carcerality, and ending its promotion of xenophobic and exclusionary border regimes. How to accomplish this is a major question for our time. We must tackle it now. It is no longer the case, as it was only a few years ago, that feminism is derided as an irrelevant and toothless old fossil, set in its ways.[13] On the contrary, it is now roundly deplored by right-wing populists and reactionary centrists as a key part of how we are governed – and they're right, we are, without a doubt, governed in part by a kind of feminism![14] – while also being opportunistically enlisted (by a different faction) for the purposes of racist dog-whistling. In this context, the detoxification of feminism belongs at the very top of the agenda of feminist thought, movement and action.

A 'KIND OF TERRORISM'

Before we proceed any further, let's deal with the question of what actually constitutes the toxicity we've attributed to Schwarzer's texts by examining one of her salvos in depth. In an article entitled 'The Consequences of False Tolerance', posted online on her personal website on 5 January 2016, Schwarzer opined that 'we [sic] do these brutalized young men an injustice' by characterizing them as violent by nature. After all, they were 'not born perpetrators'.[15] Rather, she speculated, the 'experience of a violently traditionalist patriarchy within the household, paired with the civil wars raging on the streets' in their home countries had turned the young men of Cologne into 'victims *and* perpetrators'.

At first glance, Schwarzer seems to be going about providing social explanations for social problems, just as Durkheim demanded it. She appears, on the face of it, to be seeking to understand violence as a consequence of (albeit not directly caused by) violent social relations, and specifically not as an expression of some kind of putative male human 'nature'. This could easily have paved the way for an intersectional analysis of the mutual co-production of violence, gender oppression, religion, culture and socioeconomic inequality: that is, an analysis that does not simply assert the connections between phenomena, but carefully reconstructs them, never merely deducing one thing from another. The question of whether (and, if so, how) specific mechanisms for the reproduction of masculine domination and the stabilization of male rule might have been linked to cultural, religious and socio-regional dynamics, so as to shed light on the misogynistic attitudes that undeniably played a part in the attacks on New Year's Eve in Cologne, could then have been treated as an open and potentially illuminating empirical question, instead of as a foregone conclusion.

But Schwarzer does not take this route. Even if one takes into account that she is a journalist, not an academic, the problem is clear: Schwarzer has only decisive answers, no questions. She is not given to an anti-racist, intersectional-feminist vein on inquiry, and she is not interested in treating *all* cultural and symbolic norms, customs and institutions as contingent and unsettled, without exception. She evinces basically no curiosity about the means by which gender and class relations, or stratification based on ethnicity and race, became embedded in the social structure and institutional bedrock of a given society, or how this domination made itself at home in the bodies and practices of its subjects.

Even basic sensitivity, or interest in the world, or empathic understanding of the poison that is *Versämtlichung* (when things are
subsumed under the weight of negative ascriptions) remain largely
alien capacities to Schwarzer. This is a person who sits in judgment on
the world, thinking about it, not with it, in direct contravention of
Achille Mbembe's injunction to 'responsibility', visited in Chapter 1.
Nor does Schwarzer seem to care that 'words are made', to recall J. L.
Austin's famous formula.[16] Clearly, obliviousness to the performative
power of her own words, not to mention (as Judith Butler might say)
the inherently injurious powers of language, is a price Schwarzer is
willing to pay to keep her worldview intact.[17]

In any case, in 'The Consequences of False Tolerance', the subtle
but unmissable sound of othering, of violent generalization and of
Versämtlichung, follows hard upon Schwarzer's initial reservations
and concerns that 'we' might wrong the perpetrators by presuming
them criminal by nature. In the same breath as her ostensible impulse
to protect these young men from the perils of jumping to conclusions,
Schwarzer describes them as 'brutalized' and socialized – in a sense
that she declares more or less inescapable – by a 'violently traditionalist patriarchy'.[18]

That the perpetrators were Muslim is, to the author, every bit as
clear as that their being so was the principal cause of the outrages. In a
subsequently blogged essay entitled 'New Year's Eve 2015: Cologne's
Tahrir Square' – reprinted just a few months later in her edited volume
The Shock: Cologne's New Year's Eve – Schwarzer affirmed: 'They were
North Africans, Arabs, Muslims. This will certainly have been the basis
for their understanding among themselves.'[19] The aggressions that took
place in Cologne, which she describes either as 'a night of horror' or an
'inferno', were unequivocally, for her, a precursor to – if not training
towards – violent terrorist acts. 'That night,' she writes, 'the terror did
not involve Kalashnikovs or suicide bombers' vests; rather, it was deliv-
ered via firework launchers and whizzcrackers and, above all, the men's
groping hands. The boys are still only practicing.'[20]

Yet another essay, published a few weeks later (also on her
personal website), bears the title 'What Really Happened on New

Year's Eve?' Here, Schwarzer again pushed the notion of a latent terrorist threat emanating from the young men who perpetrated the harassment, and she asserted a direct link between their actions and 'political Islamism'.[21] A kind of 'jihadism from below', she called it: men had 'used social media networks to organize themselves like flashmobs for the purposes of feeling up women'. Whether these men hailed 'from Morocco or Syria', whether they had just arrived, 'lived with us for years, or were even born here', she continued, 'they are all bound together by the green stripe of Islam, which sets Sharia law above domestic law, and women beneath men.'

A year later, in the first days of 2017, that is, a few days after the subsequent New Year's Eve of 2016, Schwarzer stated in an interview with the *Frankfurter Allgemeine Zeitung* (*FAZ*) that 'the same kind of man [*sic*] as last year' had 'come to Cologne to participate in the celebrations in their particular style'.[22] Here, again, one could find traces of the same transitory ambivalence that characterized her texts of the previous year, where, under the guise of not performing character assassinations on the young men, Schwarzer points to social conditions that might lead to brutalization. It is 'traumatized, displaced, uprooted, Islamized young men' we are dealing with here.

Schwarzer can thus include the fact that something terrible has happened to these men – trauma, displacement, indoctrination – at the same time as managing to make this notion of their 'brutalization' invoke, more than anything, the extremity of *their* brutality. In addition to stressing the available geopolitical information at every opportunity – 'mainly from Algeria and Morocco'[23] – she rolls out, again and again (and despite knowing better?), the ideological topoi we've visited several times in this book before: the uncivilized, savage Muslim barbarian bent on attacking the domestic girl. 'If the police had not, this time around, acted proactively from the outset', she tells the reporter, 'sexual violence would have driven hundreds of women from the streets all over again, while the "helpless" men at their sides were humiliated anew.' Once again, in Schwarzer's hands, the imputed origins of the men from the Maghreb are made to function as floating signifiers for Islamist fundamentalism, insofar as, in her interview with *FAZ*, she reiterates her thesis that theirs was a kind of rehearsal for 'real' terrorist acts: 'These guys wanted trouble again. We are dealing, here, with a kind of terrorism: not, in this case, an attack by Kalashnikov or van, but one by means of hands and fists.'

ISLAMOPHOBIC PARANOIA

What is most striking about Schwarzer's texts is her constant use of the very same oriental topoi the West has been implementing since colonialism's heyday as a justification for subjugating Muslims and a mechanism for asserting the primacy and superiority of its own civilization. The link between self-assertion and othering is, indeed, something we have now insisted many times was constitutive of the West's imperial culture. And, as even the few selections from Schwarzer's oeuvre dissected here make clear, it is this nexus of (feminist) self-vindication and repudiation of the other that is affirmed whenever she reaches for the racially charged image of the hardened Muslim horde, troubled and sexually violent, obsessed with the imperative to subordinate women to men.

She has been at it for some time. 'Turkish', 'Muslim' and 'Islamist' have served as loose, almost interchangeable signifiers for misogyny, anti-democratic sentiment and backwardness in her publication record ever since the 1990s – the same amount of time, in fact, other feminists have been criticizing her for this. In 1993, for example, Schwarzer somehow succeeded at dragging 'Islamic fundamentalism' into an article that was ostensibly about the assassination of Gürsün İnce, Hatice Genç, Hülya Genç, Saime Genç and Gülistan Öztürk by German neo-Nazis in in Solingen. Justifying this by calling jihadism 'the oriental version of fascism', Schwarzer remarks, ominously, that 'both' kinds are 'men's business'.[24] If, back then, she was still given to parceling out guilt and innocence as universal characteristics on the basis that all women, German *and* Turkish, are victims of male violence, be they fascist or Islamist, because patriarchy is the root of all evil – today, her guns are aimed unmistakably and exclusively at 'young Muslim men' who have been 'ideologized' by a 'political version of Islam that values Sharia law above any constitution and men more than women'.

This is an image based on the idea of a fundamental incompatibility of gender regimes. It is defined by a merging of Islam, the terror threat, and the idea of fundamentalist culturalization, to the point of indistinguishability. And it plays a central role in contemporary anti-Muslim racism. The Muslim man is widely hyperdetermined as tendentially aggressive, uncivilized, misogynist and irremediably bound to inhumane traditions. 'Violence has become synonymous with "Muslim man"', contends the Berlin-based sociologist Gökçe Yurdakul.[25]

The paranoid discourse that imagines Islam as a sexually predatory force coming from 'outside' to threaten the West is a key part of a larger discourse that the English pioneer of critical race studies Liz Fekete has called 'enlightened fundamentalism'.[26] Enlightened fundamentalism is, Fekete shows, often characterized by chauvinist celebration of the supposedly exclusive legacy of secularism and reason 'as the basis of Western European culture', wherein non-Western migrants are portrayed as devoid of these particular values. It's a construction guided by the idea that its discriminatory way of addressing the 'other' is encouraging 'them' to break free of their 'backwards culture' and 'adapt to the modern, secular values of the Enlightenment'.[27] Within this imaginary, it is important to reject or at least keep these others at bay in order to ensure they do not destroy the (rightfully dominant) native culture.

Central to all this is a phenomenon we, following sociologist Stanley Cohen, feel is best described as 'moral panic'. In Cohen's influential analysis, a dynamic of moral panic takes hold when, on account of real actions and characteristics, or (more often) ones merely imputed to them, a particular social group – in this case, 'the Muslims' – is characterized by society at large as a 'threat' that needs to be neutralized in the long term.[28] The journalist Angela Nagle has described this phobic excitation as a veritable tradition among social elites ever since early modernity: 'fear of the overcrowding, over-breeding, emotionally volatile, easily cowed mass of humanity'.[29]

At the centre of the paranoia of the moral panic is the figure of the brown man.[30] He is its privileged object: a liminal figure on the threshold between barbarism and civilization. Will he succeed in making the step into civilization? Should we allow him to take such a step? How can his integration into the 'community of Western values' be assured? If it can't, then, according to the open letter to migrants penned by Dutch prime minister Mark Rutte, no doubt about it, he should just 'leave'.[31] There are women to consider – notably, brown women in the colonies – who need rescuing from his clutches and who better deserve the white man's protection. *White men saving brown women from brown men*: Gayatri Chakravorty Spivak's original formulation.[32] Only, now that the brown man has come to us, it is the white woman in the metropole who must be defended against him. She, as we know, is intended only for the white man. Thus: *white men saving white women from brown men* – and saving them from feminism, too, if necessary, should the white man feel emasculated and 'helpless' vis-à-vis the brown men, as Schwarzer suggested in her interview in *FAZ*. The motto now seems to be: *feminism saving all women from Islam*.

But this, too, reveals itself to be a topos as old as European imperialism itself. In her monograph *Women and Gender in Islam: The Historical Roots of a Modern Debate*, the gender theologian Leila Ahmed investigates the British occupation of Egypt in order to trace what she sees as the common thread and guiding tenet of colonial politics: the idea that Islam oppresses women by its very nature. The physical proof of this, for the colonizing men and women, was the practice of veiling as well as other local customs pertaining to women, such as gender-based segregation. In their eyes, these were the cause of the indisputable, universally agreed-upon backwardness of Muslim societies, and they urgently required reform. European (and, more specifically, English) gender norms were therefore hypostatized as a symbol of Western civilization's superiority, whose ultimate expression was the white Victorian image of womanhood concertedly deployed by colonialists against colonized women as a disciplinary norm.[33]

Whether these 'Western civilizers are best regarded as patriarchal colonialists, missionaries or feminists', Ahmed concludes, what is clear is that they insisted Muslims give up their customs, their faith and their modes of dress – or, at minimum, reform them according to imposed prescriptions. Thus, as Leila Ahmed commented in *Der Spiegel* in 2016, 'outside of Western societies, feminism has become the handmaiden of colonial systems, notwithstanding its history of opposition to white male supremacy within those borders.'[34]

FEMONATIONALISM

Islamophobic paranoia is not, then, the exclusive domain of right-wing reaction, conservative populisms and alt-right political currents. Rather, it has long thrived in parts of the liberal bourgeois public sphere as well as parts of feminism. The sociologist Sara Farris has proposed to call this collusion 'femonationalism', defining it further as the tacit consonance between xenophobic, nativist, racist and anti-Muslim policies, on the one hand, and feminist politics on the other.[35]

Farris focuses particularly on right-wing and rightist-populist European parties' endeavours to incorporate feminist principles and demands in their campaigns against migration and 'Islamization'. The term itself, 'femonationalism', builds upon American cultural scholar Jasbir Puar's prior theoretical innovation, 'homonationalism'. What Puar describes is 'a collusion between homosexuality and American nationalism that is generated both by national rhetoric of patriotic inclusion and by gay and queer subjects themselves.'[36] In her analysis, the principal terrain of this 'collusion' is the figuration of Islamist terrorists as enemies of US civilization in general and LGBTQI people in particular. Homonationalism, for Puar, thus describes a consciously chosen alliance between nationalist actors and gay and lesbian civil rights organizations. In slight contrast to this, what Farris argues is that femonationalism, as an alliance between feminists and nativist and/or nationalist forces, is not necessarily explicit. For one thing, Harris is rightly unwilling to designate as simple 'nationalism' the rhetoric of 'an indeterminate actor, such as Europe or "European governments" as a whole'.[37] Despite the fact that many celebrated European feminists have denounced Islam and called for a headscarf ban, for example, their rationales for doing so usually differ substantially from those of committed nationalists. Conversely, however, feminist ideas have been widely instrumentalized by nationalist parties and neoliberal governments in the legitimation of xenophobic and anti-Muslim policy-making, in the absence of any actual feminists supporting their agendas.

The phenomenon observed by Farris, of feminist arguments being pressed into the service of the 'Fortress Europe' border regime, predates 'Cologne'. The mobilization of emancipatory ideals of LGBTQI and women's equality has provided the justification of the primacy of European culture for some time. Since that watershed, however, the effect has grown markedly more aggressive and spread far beyond German borders. Now, all over Europe, xenophobic, nationalist and nativist parties and governments routinely deploy ideals of equality in a fundamentalist way, that is to say, as a means of pointing to the putative inability of male Muslim-German citizens and male non-Western migrants to respect the basic rights of women and queer people. For example, the Dutch right-wing populist Geert Wilders attempted to capitalize on the Cologne attacks in January 2017 by proposing that women should have the right to state-issued pepper spray for the purposes of self-defence against 'Islamic testosterone bombs'.[38] In the French electoral campaign of that year, Marine Le Pen passed herself off as a women's rights campaigner, specifically targeting a female constituency likely to regard the National Front as a bulwark against immigration and a borderless Europe. Le Pen has largely succeeded at presenting herself as committed to men and women's equality by marketing herself as a defender of 'laïcité', locked in battle with an aggressively expansionist Islam that, for its part, contests the separation of religion and state.[39]

In this country, in the meantime, the former AfD chairwoman Frauke Petry has likewise unexpectedly taken on the task of championing queers and other minorities.[40] As she said in a live debate between herself and the Green Party politician Katrin Göring-Eckardt:

Especially here in Berlin, gays and lesbians are now afraid again. Migration has brought with it a huge wave of anxiety for gay and lesbian people here, but also for other minorities, such as Jews. The diverse German society that you describe so positively is exactly what is endangered by the unrestrained opening of the border, the mass abuse of asylum law, and the failed internal security policy that the Greens would have liked to continue![41]

It is not only the instrumentalization of women, LGBTQI people and 'other minorities' to the ends of xenophobic politics that is so characteristic here. It is also the unique belligerence of the toxic speech that typically mediates these European right-wing populisms with their, to recall Liz Fekete's phrase, 'enlightened fundamentalism' (which by no means indicates, necessarily, that the spirit of the Enlightenment has particularly influenced the party programmes in question).

This faction's stance vis-à-vis feminism is deeply contradictory. Certainly, the fundamentalists are exploiting feminism for their own purposes, namely, racist and anti-immigrant agitation; however, they are also enrolling a very specific feminism in their battle against *other feminisms*, that is, feminisms more given to thoroughgoing critiques of sexual hegemonies and gender norms. According to this ideology, heteronormativity, the nuclear family and the gender binary are to be defended alongside other (indisputably important) putatively 'German' achievements, such as the formal legal equality of the sexes and the criminality of sexual violence. And they are to be defended not only against external threats, but against internal enemies. On the home front, as we lay out in the following section, the danger comes from Germany's queers and so-called genderistas,[42] who (so the story goes) will stop at nothing to impose their 'perverse' notions of how sex and sexuality should be lived on 'ordinary people'. Meanwhile, the danger 'abroad' is conceived in essentializing, hyperculturalist terms as a scene involving victimized, quasi-sacrificial women and an uncivilized, retrograde, unmanageable 'sex mob'.

The othering of strangers, designed to keep them at a distance, is thus directly linked to the denigration of sexual and gender minorities in society, as well as feminist dissenters. It is no coincidence that the AfD and Pegida are not only against the 'Islamization of the West': what they are equally against is the intellectual scourge they call 'genderization'.

'ALL THE THINGS ONE IS NO LONGER ALLOWED TO SAY': SPIRITUAL ALLIANCES

Femonationalism is therefore more than a name for collusion between nativist and feminist projects. More precisely speaking, it calls forth an inherently heterogeneous and dynamic version of feminism. The feminism in question is profoundly naturalistic and familial in orientation, as well as (for the most part) religious, which is to say, in almost all cases, Christian. This is how femonationalists ground their claim to have their fingers on the pulse of the common sense of 'ordinary people', their everyday practices and experience – in direct contrast with the phantasmatic and alien 'gender ideology' constantly invoked by Kelle and others, which, in their insidiously suggestive rhetoric, comes to us from far away, from strangers, from the outside. Because, you see, 'gender', so they recount, was invented in Berkeley, translated into policy in Brussels, and taught at German universities, aiming to remake all the rules.[43]

The 'us and them' opposition so central to right-wing populism – a putative opposition between 'the people' and 'the establishment' – plays a key role for this politics on the terrain of gender and sexuality, too.[44] Here, the claim is that dictates handed down from Brussels are, slowly but surely, effecting a totalitarian re-education of the 'sexed and gendered human'. An instructive example of this discourse is the copy to be found on the personal website of Catholic legal journalist Gabriele Kuby, promoting her book *The Global Sexual Revolution: Destruction of Freedom in the Name of Freedom*:

> In this book, you will find all the things one is no longer allowed to say about the UN and the EU: that they have been the instigators of the 'sexual revolution', a mass project of re-education whereby we've

become sexualized 'gender' identities, of the political rape of our language, the porn epidemic, the gay movement, the rollout of sex education in schools and kindergartens, in short: the slippery slope we're on that leads to totalitarianism in a totally new guise.[45]

Clearly, on some level, this is where Schwarzer on one side and writers like Kelle and Kuby on the other part ways. There is still much to criticize about Schwarzer's brand of feminism, not least her false universalism, her bigoted view of Islam and Muslims, and her discourse's deeply culturalist – and often outright racist – toxic 'charge'. That she has a family- and a faith-oriented appeal, however, cannot be claimed. Also, Schwarzer is unknown for crusades against Gender Studies, i.e. what Kelle and Kuby would call 'gender ideology'.

However, if we are to better capture the special poisonousness of Schwarzer's feminism, which, we argue, is what really emblematizes the current imbrication of racism, anti-feminism and feminism in our time, we have to examine how it is that it can be appropriated by right-wing populists like Kelle and Kuby. For it is this specific articulation that has contributed, perhaps more than any other, to the production of a racist everyday common sense, as discussed (following Stuart Hall) in Chapter 2. This day-to-day racist consciousness, recall, provides the guidelines for our actions; we constantly refer to it without knowing it, for it consists of a knowledge that renders the social relations, dividing lines and struggles, among which we find ourselves, plausible.

As Irene Dölling has shown, one of the cultural techniques employed by this racist common sense in order to reproduce itself has been a modern, regularly refreshed interpretation (one could also say *production*) of gender. Dölling emphasizes, as part of this, the links between a constantly updated hegemonic heteronormativity, a wider gender order and the nuclear family. These, she writes, constitute a key 'arena of negotiation about society, which appeals directly to individuals and their most immediate relationships, enrolling them in the legitimation of manifold inequalities, inclusions and exclusions crucial to their collective self-understanding'.[46] It is also the privileged site of the feminisms of Birgit Kelle, Marine Le Pen, Gabriele Kuby and Frauke Petry.

In contrast to their forebears in the history of anti-feminism, these women's ideas are rarely presented as challenges to the project of feminism and the ideal of equality generally. Kelle, Kuby, Petry and Le Pen, on the contrary, present themselves *as feminists*, not as anti-feminists; indeed, they sometimes paint themselves as the last feminists still standing willing to defend the Enlightenment's feminist achievements against the rising tide of a medieval Islamism. They do not usually make the argument that women have no claim to equal rights because they are inherently different to men. Their message, instead, tends to be that women and men are (or should be) equal in rights *despite* being fundamentally, essentially, self-evidently, *ontologically* different by nature. Feminism, in their view, must be compelled to take this ontological reality into account.

The resultant activism is a genuine historic novelty: instead of mobilizing against 'feminism', they mobilize against an academic concept: *gender*.[47] Where there was once classically anti-feminist ressentiment, there is now dread of an imagined dystopia defined by state-ordained androgyny and unisex homogeneity. Already in 2006, this vision of the future was described as 'contrary to science, religion and most people's feelings' in an editorial by Volker Zastrow, head of the *Frankfurter Allgemeine Sonntagszeitung* political supplement. Zastrow opined that it would soon become necessary for ordinary citizens to rebel against this looming 'genderism':

> And here you have it, the theoretical core of the 'gender' concept. This isn't about noticing that gendered roles and characteristics operate in society – a by now banal fact that classical feminists like Betty Friedan established long ago. No, what 'gender' alleges, in the final analysis, is that biological sex does not exist. To sort newborns according to their being boys or girls, for example, is arbitrary, since they could just as well be classified according to entirely different measures (such as big and small). Thus, even to acknowledge the existence of sex is to commit a violent imposition of identity: the

so-called heterosexual matrix. This rather heady philosophical contention, it has to be said, straightforwardly contradicts the most primary perceptions and sentiments of most people, most religions and most scientific research.⁴⁸

The battle lines Zastrow drew here influenced the rhetoric of 'political genderphobes' all across Europe, and their traces can still be discerned in myriad contexts to this day. The Catholic Church in Poland, for example, has lately resolved to develop a 'new feminism' framed in direct opposition to 'the dangerous "gender" mischief', as Bożena Chołuj has shown.⁴⁹ Meanwhile, in Germany, as an investigation by Barbara Thiessen elucidates, the Association of Evangelical Free Church Communities now makes sure to immediately educate against the dangers of questioning the naturalness of gender – and of imbibing 'gender ideology' – wherever it denounces discrimination against women (such denunciations being, themselves, 'a breeding ground for ideologies').⁵⁰

With the alliances the anti-gender turn makes possible, a quite unexpected ecumenicism has emerged. We are not dealing here with scattered, isolated voices; indeed, the extremely heterogeneous, even contradictory character of this spiritual formation proves its robustness. It encompasses: the Vatican, the German evangelical free churches, the Catholic women's movement in Poland, the Manif Pour Tous movement in France, the AfD, groups of 'concerned parents' campaigning against alleged 'early sexualization' of children, neoconservative men's rights activists, self-proclaimed 'defenders of the unborn', conservative ecologists, masculinist media figures, prominent journalists, science bloggers, various (male) professors of evolutionary biology, extreme right-wingers and the '-gida' organizing wave in Germany (the 'patriotic' anti-Islamization umbrella network Pegida comprises Bogida in Bonn, Dügida in Düsseldorf, and so on).

Gender is the new watershed. Attacks are directed against anyone who characterizes gender and sexual desire as socially constituted, historically conditioned, culturally contingent and grounded in practice. The anti-genderist position, for its part, maintains a simplistic, scientistic, epistemologically untenable and empirically debunked naturalism in the matter of gender and sexuality. Inasmuch as they recognize the historical achievements of 'feminism' at all, they regard it as a victorious and concluded movement for women's equality, beyond which the claims associated with the 'gender delusion' (as they call it) become intolerable and nonsensical.

'Gender' is, it's true, apt to unsettle and offend everyday worldly certainties. In order to understand this polarized situation, criss-crossed with defences of and attacks upon gender, it is necessary, in our opinion, to take the anti-genderist attacks seriously *as a response* to this unsettling. But 'gender' also brings into the light of politics and culture a whole host of previously invisibilized, outlawed and marginalized experiences, norms and modes of existence: lives beyond the gender binary, fluid sexualities, non-binary physical and affective embodiments of sex. All of this, of course, leads to 'gender trouble', which an open and democratic society ought to deal with reflexively and, of course, critically. But the bellicose, hateful, often ad hominem mudslinging to which gender studies in Germany has been exposed for over a decade now simply isn't that.

DETOXIFYING FEMINISM

So far, in this chapter, we have covered a series of toxic partnerships between feminisms and racism (specifically, anti-Muslim resentment). It is against this background that we now propose to return to 'Cologne' and the question of the dilemmas that arise from these appropriations of – and challenges for – feminism. What tasks does this situation create for feminism? What would the 'detox' cure for contemporary feminism look like? Once again, at the theoretical level, one way of paraphrasing this question is the problem formulated at the beginning of this chapter: How does one create a non-racist, anti-sexist discourse that is simultaneously a non-sexist, anti-racist one? How to decolonize feminism?

It ought to go without saying that society has a racism problem as well as a sexism problem. Equally, there ought to be no question (ever) of attempting to deny or minimize sexism, heterosexism, homophobia or transphobia so as to avoid falling into the trap of racist prejudice. Patriarchal, homonormative, queerphobic and misogynistic (including transmisogynistic) values and practices have to be scandalized both among 'majority' Germans and among 'migrant' communities – a distinction which is, anyway, of extremely limited empirical value. Repudiations of sexism must never be allowed to become a means of legitimating xenophobic and racist attitudes. Admittedly, this is often easier said than done.

'It sure is a balancing act, thematizing real problems that exist among Muslims, without lapsing into defamation of that population, nor garnering applause from the wrong quarters.' In her book *Emanzipation im Islam: Eine Abrechnung mit ihren Feinden* ('Emancipation in Islam: Accounting with its Enemies'), the journalist Sineb El Masrar tackles the dilemma from the perspective of a Muslim and a feminist. It almost seems, writes El Masrar, as if there were only two choices: either to generate 'anti-Muslim hate speech that curries favor with the non-migrant citizenry' or to defend Muslims against any and all criticisms, which leads to standing shoulder to shoulder not only with the 'democratic and emancipated Muslims' but with 'Salafist and other extreme Islamist groups'.[51]

Is there a path between the Scylla of a racist form of anti-sexist struggle, and the Charybdis of a sexist anti-racism? Between the false universalism in Alice Schwarzer's thought, in Kelle and Kuby's vicious salvoes, on the one hand, and the denial and relativization of sexism and sexual violence, which remains not uncommon among left-wingers, on the other? A way between demonization and relativism? Or, rather, what does that path look like – the path of an unerringly anti-essentialist praxis and thought? How do we bring differences to life without totalizing them? How might we revive widespread awareness of the character of cultures, as described by Edward Said: neither uniform nor monolithic, nor, for that matter, transcendent entities?

The necessary consciousness is one that can examine sexism and racism in all their 'monotonous likeness and endless variation'[52] (to borrow a phrase from Gayle Rubin) – neither hypostatizing them as inescapable destinies nor treating them as hermetically sealed, homogeneous formations. It should, in fact, be possible to ask 'how loosely organized groups of men of Arab origin came to commit these sexual muggings', as Mark Terkessidis recently demanded in *taz* magazine.[53] The key is not to fix these men in their identities, while also not denying that the offences took place. The question of what the Cologne crimes might have to do with the practice of masculine domination is, as such, just as legitimate as the popular question of their relationship to revanchist shifts taking place within Islam today. Indeed, the two things might be interrelated.

For us, as feminist academics trying to parse the landscape Christina Thürmer-Rohr referred to as 'this whole rotten present', there is much that resonates about the dilemma described by El Masrar (from the standpoint of a migrant, Muslim, university-educated feminist author) of feeling like the options consist of either pandering to the majority and throwing a minority under the bus, or speaking in fake relativities and aligning with the 'enemies of emancipation' that way instead. We, as cognitive labourers, are called upon to name real problems and, at the same time, to shun every possible complicity with racial or sexist discourses. It is our responsibility to contend, as we said in the first chapter, with the fact that academic accounts of the events in Cologne 'make up people', as Ian Hacking puts it, just as the accounts of Alice Schwarzer, Birgit Kelle or Harald Martenstein do.

SHOULD WE THEN BE SILENT ON WOMEN'S RIGHTS?

Feminists have found different answers to this dilemma. The English feminist political scientist Nicola Pratt, for one, has proposed a 'strategic silence on women's rights in general' so that scholars may avoid complicity with racial discourses and cooptation into the 'war on terror'. 'From the position of academia in the European and North American metropoles', writes Pratt, 'perhaps the only way to avoid becoming complicit in racializing discourses and co-opted in the pursuit of the "war on terror", is to be strategically silent about "women's rights" per se.'[54]

But is this really the only possible answer to the toxic collusion of feminism, racism and sexism? Pratt's intervention has more to say. The alternative, of course, to speaking about 'women's rights' – rights which can then be defended by military means, as some proponents of the invasion of Afghanistan enthusiastically argued in the wake of September 11 – is forging a feminism that fights militarization just as vehemently as it fights neoliberal processes of dehumanization and dispossession. This is a proposal to be supplemented by a consideration by Judith Butler in the face of cultural-essentialist racism and with regard to the exploitation of the rights of women and queers against the rights of migrants. Butler contended over a decade ago that feminists should not only care about women, but mount resistance to all kinds of projects of eugenicism or chauvinism:

> Feminism, once again, needs to care not simply about the status of women, but about opposing forms of national and racial purity and superiority. There can be no feminism within the contemporary global situation that does not actively contest the kind of nationalist violence that pervades immigration policy in Europe right now.[55]

What follows from these proposals by Pratt and Butler as regards Cologne? It seems clear enough, ethically speaking, that violence must be named as such, repudiated and sanctioned, regardless of who exercises it. This applies to sexual violence, too, no matter who is perpetrating it, no matter who is suffering it. The political and academic debate about this must be open, critical and sensitive to difference, neither prematurely anticipating links and causalities, nor excluding the possibility of interconnections as irrelevant in advance.

A proper anti-racist, feminist response to the hyperculturalization, ethnicization and orientalization of sexism and sexual violence therefore cannot be, as it was sometimes assumed to be post-Cologne, an equally relativizing 'Germanization' of the problem. Nor, as the legal scholar Ulrike Lembke has recently stated, does it do to vaguely internationalize the issue.[56] We must reject out of hand, certainly, any suggestion that the violence of Cologne be absorbed into an explanatory model called 'Islamic socialization', as Harald Martenstein would like; and we must jettison every insinuation by Alice Schwarzer that a blanket gesture towards a violent Islamic or Arab patriarchy – which coercively cranks out nothing but toxic masculinity – somehow helps, let alone suffices.

But, consequently, we must understand that neither relocating rape within 'ur-German' rituals and cultural events like the Munich Oktoberfest and the Rhenish Carnival, nor re-contextualizing matters within a transnational rape culture endemic in all societies and cultures, works as an explanation *on its own*. Regardless of how true these points are, it is wrong to stop there. Only by taking into account the concrete social and economic, political and cultural conditions of sexual violence, including, for example, the urban spatial environment and local political struggles, will we get out of the woods.[57]

Once again, what we have rammed home here is just how challenging it is to analytically apprehend sexism and racism as relations of social domination, instead of a series of thoughts or actions of isolated individuals. All too often, the two are still conceptualized as conditions with an independent existence, rather than mutually exclusive power relations that need and confirm one other as core conditions of their respective articulations. It bears repeating: sex – just like 'race' – can never exist for itself (*für sich*), but is always shaped and produced 'in relation to other social and political modes of social organization'.[58] The category of gender itself, as Judith Butler and Elizabeth Weed recalled some time ago, actively produces and reproduces 'such modes, including the family, labor, class, slavery, imperialism, immigration politics, and the state, to name a few'.[59]

We agree with the political scientist Ina Kerner that the feminist consequence of these considerations can only be a relentless search for, denunciation of and struggle against 'all constellations of power and circumstance that disadvantage women, endanger, or discriminate against them', without exception. Not because every incidence will prove to be another variation on the metanarrative of 'global sexism', and not because sexism is merely cultural or religious, but precisely because, 'on the contrary, things are much more complicated than that.'[60]

Kerner concludes by visiting a number of critiques leveled by feminist thinkers and activists from the Global South. For example, the Pakistani feminist scientist and activist Afiya Shehrbano Zia has rejected Nicola Pratt's plea that gender be de-prioritized and women's rights generally ignored as nonsensical. Zia argues that this argument is akin to the demands of ultra-religious and/or conservative Pakistani nationalists that feminists be silent about patriarchal violence in Pakistan so as not to 'wash our dirty laundry in the eyes of the West.'[61] It is itself, writes Zia, a form of racializing thinking to suggest that 'brown women cannot think for themselves, and blindly follow a white feminist agenda'. In a similar vein, the literary scholar Sadia Abbas, reworking Gayatri Spivak's dictum, has posited: 'White men may be trying to save brown women from brown men, but brown men may indeed oppress brown women, and brown women (elite and otherwise) may also collude in sustaining structures of misogyny.'[62]

RETHINKING FEMINISM

Even the relatively few dimensions of the field explored in these pages so far speak forcefully to how complex and difficult the task of 'detoxification' – that is, decolonization – presently facing feminism will be, especially when we consider that feminists are all thinking about it from different points of view: it makes a difference who is thinking about these questions. When contemplating the intertwinement of nation, gender, religion and culture, and the implications to be drawn for transnational feminism, not everybody is a white, atheist academic from the Global North, raised in the shadow of the Cold War, socialized in West Germany and sheltered from international and civil war, who – on account of having been politically educated by the second-wave feminism of the Global North – takes feminism to be a thoroughly secular project. One might also, to take just one other example, be situated, as we saw earlier, as a university-educated feminist who doesn't take feminism to be at odds with religion (or for that matter the hijab), living in a country of the Global South that is still in the midst of a violent, decades-long period of post- and/or anti-colonial struggle, where part of what matters politically is whether one was socialized as Shia or Sunni.

It is because the future of feminism is transnational, postcolonial and geographically context-specific – and because feminism will never be a Western side project – that all of us must participate in arguing over which demands feminism must take into account today. The idea that politics is feasible on behalf of all women, without producing exclusions – and without ultimately revealing somewhere down the line that the feminism alleged to include all women actually only had in mind a specific group of women after all – was ever a myth at the level of national politics. Its absurdity is even more apparent on a global scale.

The insight (this really cannot be repeated often enough) that gender relations don't exist and can't be understood (let alone changed!) independently from other social divisions – in other words, the insight of intersectionality – must be the central guideline of feminist thinking and feminist activism. As the social philosopher Gudrun-Axeli Knapp declared a decade ago, the single genus 'women', alone, tells us next to nothing about whom the myriad axes of inequality bind together and separate, how they become configurations of power and domination, and in what way they are drawn so as to connect to one another.[63]

In light of the toxic collusions discussed in this book and the fact that domination manifests, among other things, in the fact that some people just don't have to concern themselves with certain questions and problems, it seems urgent that we free feminism from the arrogance of the First World and think afresh how it can be lived under the horizon of 'anti-imperialist egalitarianism', to borrow a term from Judith Butler. It is vital we forget old certainties or, in other words, forget the privilege of ignorance. Put plainly: 'Germany' is part of the colonial constellation; it is not 'Africa' alone that has 'a colonial past'. Germans are just as ethnically constituted as 'foreigners'; it is not only 'they' who have an ethnic identity. Men have genders; it isn't just women. Likewise, it isn't just black people who have a skin colour. Straight people, too, have a sexual orientation.

A note of caution: every feminist politics, be it 'from above' or 'from below', contributes to ideas of femininity and masculinity, and to a society-wide reconstruction of gender. As a result of the gains of state-oriented 'inclusion' politics, for example, the assumption that 'woman' denotes a formally unemployed, heterosexual, 'native' German, middle-class housewife and mother changes slightly: the archetypal 'she' becomes a heterosexual wife and mother juggling her career and family. But this still requires the pretence that all women are the same, while naturalizing a hierarchical gender order and reproducing a heteronormative frame that constructs women and men as distinct groups, each with unique circumstances and interests. It is therefore a politics that conceals its own contributory role in the generation of fresh social fissures. At any rate, the focus on questions of how to 'reconcile' unpaid domestic labour and paid employment – especially in the legalistic sphere of what American legal theorist Janet Halley has called 'governance feminism'[64] – has not prevented structures of rejection and hierarchy from intensifying, and has not eradicated the yawning social divisions among women.

The voguish German 'alpha-girl' feminism of the late 2000s, with its solipsistic blueprints for the self, is not suitable for the challenges of the twenty-first century. Meredith Haaf, Susanne Klingner and Barbara Streidl, authors of the sensational *Wir Alphamädchen: Warum Feminismus das Leben schöner macht* ('We the Alpha-Girls: Why Feminism Makes Life More Beautiful'), wrote nonchalantly on the second page of their blockbuster that it is 'enough' to focus on issues that 'affect a large proportion of the young women living in Germany today'.[65] Anyone who believes this, that is to say, believes that it makes sense to exclude immigrant and migrant women, lesbians, single parents, and those who, for financial reasons, have no 'choice' to make between children and work, or for whom the word 'career' doesn't feature, has grossly misrecognized the challenges of our time.

What decolonized feminism needs first and foremost in the face of all this is the willingness to ask how feminism – at least, what goes on under its name – is implicated in the management and the production of what Foucault called 'marginal voices'.[66] It needs to be ready to take responsibility for its own thinking. That's why it's compulsory we keep a continuous account of how the world is being imagined, shaped and maintained, constantly asking, in particular: What values, voices and experiences are feminist activism and feminist theory orienting themselves towards? What battles are we centring? *Who* do we think about and act for, as feminists? Whose leadership are we facilitating, and whose are we making less likely? In short, part of decolonizing feminism is the hard task of asking these questions – of which experiences, which bodies, which desires, which needs, which modes of feeling and being, which forms of kinship are presently livable and unlivable, which sorts of alliances are possible across the borders of 'sex', and which are sabotaged – while being open to being questioned oneself.

From a feminist point of view, the most urgent problems in the world today still remain non-access to food, shelter, health care, and education; the epidemics of abuse and violence, poverty and want; the production of some people as 'surplus', abject, right-less, disposable; and structures of sexism, homophobia, transphobia, racism and xenophobia in their most diverse manifestations. That is precisely why there is no going back, for feminism, on the critiques and interventions by lesbian and black, immigrant and queer, postcolonial and trans feminists. A more complex articulation of feminism is the challenge we must rise to. For, insofar as the freedom to speak in one's true voice is a precarious and unevenly distributed political resource, the crux of our predicament is the question of who gets to speak and how, in what contexts and which conditions; who are the ones who get to define a 'state of emergency' society-wide; whose voices *count* – a question that must ceaselessly be raised anew. Now, more than ever, this means that feminism has to put up with being questioned, too, even while defending itself against nativistic appropriation.

ON YOUR MARKS!

To be sustainable and fit for purpose, feminism will have to be more than a factional 'alpha' endeavour. In order to triumph over the numerous injustices we still have to contend with, feminism will have to synthesize the experiences, accomplishments and contradictions of the second wave of women's liberation. And, under such circumstances, it has no choice but to face up publicly to its own contradictions. This is *not* about tokenistically acknowledging and signaling awareness of the limits and paradoxes at stake by issuing the disclaimer 'yes, we know that women aren't all alike', prior to simply carrying on with the usual *Versämtlichung* concerning 'women' as a universal. It's about showing up again and again to renegotiate the contradictions.

Insight into the contradictions and overlaps between 'major systems of oppression' – and the way these imbrications, like it or not, weave the very fabric of life – was exponentially advanced by the Combahee River Collective, a mid-1970s group of African-American lesbian feminists in the United States. Ever since, it has behooved every feminist to think carefully whether what is understood in the West as feminism's vindication and success is not better described as the ascent of certain privileged women into the ruling classes – the price of this being the intensification of a racially stratified international division of labour between women.

The sine qua non for us shall be our absolute willingness to repeatedly question our own 'mainstream', modifying, wherever appropriate, even things we used to deem irrefutable. Here, the open-endedness that any broad-based political project, with its constitutive ambivalences, inevitably brings with it can be seen as more of an advantage than a disadvantage. In summary, then, feminism requires three main things: openness, self-reflexiveness and a sincere readiness to unlearn what we thought was right.[67]

Openness is crucial: particularly vis-à-vis struggles and concerns, such as undocumentedness and illegality, that have previously sat fairly low on the agenda. Self-reflexivity is key because, in any broad-based political project, it is almost inevitable that internal distortions will occur, that the effects of internal power relations will unfold, and that the strategies the movement chooses for itself will lead in various unforeseen directions. For example, think of the gulf between gender mainstreaming, which clearly operates on the assumption that men and women inhabit different realities, and thus reproduces the idea of binary sexuality, and the approach of most queer critique, which seeks to destabilize that duality. Finally, we have proposed for feminism the willingness to reassess from scratch what's right and wrong. Not every tactic tried by the women's movement of the '60s and '70s is now 'outdated'. But neither are they blueprints for the present, let alone the future.

Any theory, any movement, any political project, is only as good as its ability to make sense of the questions of its time. So: off our marks, get set, go! Now is no time to linger on the starting blocks. What *won't* help is abstracting feminism from history in order to freeze and thus immunize it against criticism, or, for that matter, allowing ourselves to forget the long critical legacy of anti-essentialist feminist thought. In a world as variegated and challenging as ours, to cleave nostalgically to hallowed and heroic moments of our history, thereby forcing feminism to repeat itself in perpetuity, is no more a solution than the urge to constantly proclaim the advent of a new and improved, cooler, more radical, more (self-) righteous feminism, and to bill each newly (re-) invented version as successfully rid of all the old monsters.

The feminism of the second wave has left us an undeniably demanding and often politically, intellectually and emotionally trying inheritance. This includes the desire for freedom and happiness, a passion for participating and meddling in the world, as well as a willingness to be touched and moved by it and all that happens in it. We carry forward sensitivity to the many, many modes of physical and emotional pain, degradation and dispossession, alienation and isolation that are operative on Earth. We carry forward a belief in the right to self-determination, to equality and dignity, and the knowledge that individual and collective emancipation are indivisible. We fight not only to overcome men's domination over women, but also that of men over other men, because the fight is against all forms of oppression and violence. We commit to this ongoing struggle – notwithstanding its manifold failures – not simply to come to a better *understanding* of the intricately webbed intersectional fabric of global social, political and economic injustice, with its production of privilege on the one hand and abjection on the other. We persist in order to overcome it, never forgetting that feminisms are always bound up in the struggles of their time, which is also to say that women are co-producers of the conditions in which they live. Women are not excluded from the exercise of hegemonic rule, in fact, they are and have always been active participants in it. Neither 'women' nor 'feminism' is politically innocent.

What we do with this legacy is one of the central challenges of feminist movements and theory in the twenty-first century. Because it is of vital importance, still today, to *lead a feminist life*.[68]

5

Outsiders Within?
A Dialogue with Differences

> Advocating the mere tolerance of difference ... is the grossest reformism. It is a total denial of the creative function of difference in our lives. Difference must ... be seen as a fund of necessary polarities between which our creativity can spark like a dialectic.[1]
>
> – Audre Lorde

> My hope is that the movement we are building can further the conscious work of turning Otherness into a keen lens of empathy, that we can bring into being a politics based on concrete, heartfelt understanding of what it means to be Other.[2]
>
> – Adrienne Rich

QUESTIONING THE SAYABLE

Paula-Irene Villa (PIV): Our book was prompted by our uneasiness with both – on the one hand – the limits of the *sayable*, and the vehemence of what gets *said*, on the other. People everywhere were all putting enormous emphasis on this sexual violence 'Arab men' had perpetrated upon (German) women in public. In this sense, after the Cologne New Year's Eve, the subject of sexual violence against women was suddenly widely under mainstream discussion. And this was surprising. Of course, it's a topic that has occupied women's struggles, both feminist and queer activism, and also human rights activism, for decades. Sexual violence has also long been a central matter for gender research. But stimulating interest among a broader public has always, until now, been difficult at best. But in the spring of 2016, news about gendered violence was suddenly thick on the ground, and I found myself repeatedly getting interviewed as a 'gender expert'. Everybody wanted to go into it at great length . . . *on one condition* (at least, this was my impression). One particular issue could *not* be brought up, and that was the immense scale of sexualized violence against women worldwide; particularly the pervasiveness of sexism and 'rape culture' in Germany itself and the West more generally. I got the impression that the condition for participation in any conversation about 'that night in Cologne' was that one be unequivocal about the assessment that 'refugees/Arabs/North African men are the perpetrators, and German women are the victims', and abstain from nuancing or qualifying it. It seemed as though one could only 'see' the problem, in that sense, once it had already been outsourced. The price for talking openly about sexual violence was, paradoxically, keeping it under wraps.

Sabine Hark (SH): Yes, a veritable explosion of discourse! But the flip side of all this was that, just a few days after this New Year's Eve, many of my feminist friends were already fully aware of the need to situate themselves in relation to it. We cannot, we *must* not allow this xenophobic monopolization of feminist concerns to stand. But equally, we can't – we don't want to – keep silent about what happened in Cologne. It's intolerable that non-feminist men *and Alice Schwarzer* should determine the terms of the debate. How to get out of this gridlock was one of the challenges of the first few weeks and months after the incident. And this question remains just as alive even today.

PIV: The sheer vehemence of the sweeping, simplistic categories that were being used in discussion around Cologne honestly surprised me and, at first, left me speechless. It hardly seemed possible that now, all of a sudden, all kinds of people were indignant about patriarchy, talking about 'patriarchal cultures' – people who had never before involved themselves in the struggle against sexualized violence. It did not seem possible that people seriously thought 'the' Arab and 'the' African simply *were that way*. It did not seem possible that educated people in highbrow magazine articles were complaining about the absence of real manhood among German men.

SH: This narrative had actually already been initiated in the months before. Which is to say: by the autumn of 2015, we were already hearing constant reiterations of the warning not to let too many young men into the country, as this would pose a threat to common decency, order and morality, and put 'our' women in danger. Feminism had (allegedly) gained many new friends. I was frequently interviewed on precisely this question, namely, of what feminists were making of these new offers of solidarity coming from, for example, CDU politicians, who had not hitherto exactly excelled as supporters of women's issues. Linking a trend towards xenophobia with a feminist politics had, in fact, long been in the pipeline. That is what we have tried to reconstruct.

PIV: One of the challenges for me was that I did not want to pretend – and I don't think anyone who grapples seriously with sexual violence would ever want to pretend – that there are *no* differences in how sexual violence manifests itself in specific contexts. There *are* differences. But mentioning these differences in the months after Cologne, and perhaps even today, amounted to a kind of 'whataboutism', a rhetorical manoeuvre designed to distract from the actual circumstances.

But, at the same time, this rhetorical manoeuvre seemed somehow justified and justifiable because, in fact, nothing ever is – nor can be – adequately articulated all at once. The accusation that one failed to mention this thing or the other is always, so to speak, correct. We have both several times thrown these seesawing accusations back and forth at each other – in retrospect, these were clearly well intended: 'But what about the sexual predators at the Oktoberfest, at the carnival, at the women's shelters; what about the abuses in the boarding schools and the Catholic schools?' – 'But what about the cathedral square in Cologne, though? What about the Arab men, who apparently cannot cope with life here?' – 'But what about the concrete fears of women *here*?' – But, but . . . and so on.

In any case, it was very destabilizing for me to find myself in a position within the debate in which I was saying, 'Yes, but . . .' about sexual violence! And I was doing this not only to avoid 'sounding' racist, but also in order to contest the deeper, repressed racial attitudes and fault lines that seemed so self-evident for me: first and foremost, our ability to see sexualized violence only in 'them' and not in 'us'. The question resulting from this became central to our book: how to talk about specifics and contexts such that differences are given a name, and taken seriously, but not made absolute.

SPEAKING ABOUT DIFFERENCES

SH: I wonder whether we have, in fact, really managed to talk about differences without reification or hypostasis. Nevertheless, I would also like to mention another aspect. In our first chapter, we made the case that fact and interpretation cannot be separated, and that many things have to coincide in order for a local occurrence to become an event, i.e., what Bruno Latour calls a 'matter of concern'. In other words, besides the concrete occurrences, there have to be experiences, praxes, images, media representations, political reactions, legal measures, cultural interpretations and even academic research, for something to become a 'thing' (*Ding*). But this means that, through our very critical reflections, we are contributing to the plausibility of the social demarcations induced by Cologne. A paradox of legitimation, as it were.

PIV: Our reflections have certainly contributed, that's beyond any question for me. But I don't think it's that much of a problem. The more important question for me is whether we can *also* contribute another way, in the sense of critical reflection.

An occurrence is certainly not always of the same relevance, a 'matter of concern', for everybody. In the academic and political contexts in which we are (among others) active, there is a fairly widespread tendency to keep silent and, I would like to insist, to ignore certain sensitive areas like religion on the one hand and the indignant condemnation of racism on the other. These are contexts which understand themselves as agents of critical reflection and pluralism. When the two of us wrote our book on so-called anti-genderism in 2015, quite a few people thought it would be more intelligent *not* to write this particular book. This kind of attention and this kind of terminology (i.e., talking about anti-genderism instead of anti-feminism) would, they thought, only make the problem bigger, would only fuel the defamatory smear campaign ongoing against gender and gender studies.

I certainly struggle with this mix of well-intentioned keeping schtum about certain things while taking a clear stand about others. To simply refrain from looking at an issue does not strike me as a particularly good solution – on the contrary – even if (as it inevitably must) public discussion contributes to the very existence of the issue. There is never an innocent position to be taken, anyway.

As ever, the question remains: How might we think about a problem in such a manner that it becomes comprehensible in the broadest possible terms while, *at the same time,* critically exploring it in all its complexity?

SH: Another facet of what I have just called critical theory's 'legitimation paradox' is that we ourselves often contribute unintentionally to shoring up generalizations. Perhaps we are insufficiently aware of the internal differentiations, personal identities, histories and so on, among those whose totalizing generalizations we are trying to challenge and prevent. Perhaps we fail to see our opponents as individuals with their own desires, flaws and defects, prejudices and biases, and so on. As imperative as it is not to portray the Cologne perpetrators either as a generalized mass who helplessly obeyed an essentializing credo (as though driven by their primitive urges), *or,* on the other hand, as the domestic phalanx of an international Islamist terror network, it is equally important to acknowledge that the people in question *were* violent – that sexual violence *was* part of their repertoire. How do we discuss, how do we condemn this, in the current climate, without putting all Muslims under suspicion?

PIV: It is certainly rather difficult, in a context where an 'enlightened' community of 'Western values', and specifically 'German' culture qua 'lead' culture (*Leitkultur*), is everywhere being invoked in distinction to a reactionary, 'dark', Arab or Islamist alternative. In numerous populist (but only sometimes clearly racist) statements, we find a vague but still more or less explicit cultural-fundamendalist claim: 'they' have a 'patriarchal culture', 'they' are sexist and misogynistic – unlike us. A positive image forms, of a kind of indissoluble fraternity, linked by tradition and destiny. I call this manoeuvre 'positional fundamentalism'. Social position is ontologized as *being*, in order to be equated with a political, ethical or normative consciousness. At the same time, 'our' own cultural identity ('German-ness') is asserted as though it were an ideology. A false posit is confidently advanced, not least *because* it does not fit empirical criteria and is therefore doomed to failure anyway. I'm talking about the existence of a homogenous culture of 'being German'.

SH: For me, a good example was the heated discussion about the handshake. Leaving aside the link to putative considerations of hygiene, the question is: In whom is the reluctance to shake a woman's hand judged as misogynist, and therefore a sign of reluctance to integrate, and in whom is it regarded as a legitimate part of culture or religion that has to be respected? By the way, in the past two years, I have met many Muslims from Syria, Iraq and Afghanistan, and none of them has refused to shake my hand.

But this is just a side aspect. Besides what you call 'positional fundamentalism', there was an opportunity, after Cologne, to bring certain feminist nuances of terminology into the public debate: for example, Sara Farris's concept of 'femonationalism', which is obviously a central component in our argument. The trope has, of course, been theorized by feminists for some time prior to the coinage conceived for it by Farris.

A reminder: 'femonationalism' denotes feminism's collusion in nationalist or nativist politics. This became relevant in European colonialism insofar as feminism, in the colonies, was part of the European 'civilizing mission' right from the get-go. Katharina Walgenbach has explored this via the example of the Frauenbundes der Deutschen Kolonialgesellschaft (Women's Union of the German Colonial Society), especially in Namibia.[3] As Birgit Rommelspacher writes: 'complicity with the conquerors was instrumental to German women's emancipation.' Rommelspacher also demonstrates how the oppression of women was constantly projected onto 'the' colonized others.[4] In the same way, the invasion of Afghanistan following the terrorist attacks by Al Qaeda on 11 September 2001 – and the ongoing war against the Taliban – were justified using feminist arguments. Afghan women were to be saved from the Taliban and liberated from the burka.[5] After Cologne, it became easier to talk about these links critically, even outside of academic feminist discussions.

HOW TO TALK ABOUT SEXUAL VIOLENCE?

PIV: Indeed. The sheer visibility of the topic – sexual violence by refugees or, generally, 'others', against 'us' – could itself be taken advantage of to frame the subject differently. There was, and is, heightened attention now to feminist issues and to everything related to migration, refugees and 'culture'. We agree, I think, that the opening for this book was the chance to (finally!) come to grips with the interweaving of what might appear to be 'loose ends' in the culture, strands one too often finds, in reality, to be in knots.

Maybe, along the way, we neglected to think sufficiently about the 'actuality' of sexual violence, however. I am thinking of the material, visible dimensions of vulnerability to this violence – its concreteness as an affective experience. We have, perhaps, talked too little about the attacks themselves: about the fear and unease in public spaces that numerous empirical studies tell us are all too familiar to women in this country, in one form or another.[6] We didn't really allocate any space to these widespread phenomena: of feeling afraid in the dark, experiencing harassment on public transport, instinctively keeping an eye on your drink in the club in case it gets tampered with, dress codes and body language, the scourge of harassment on social media and much, much more. LGBTQI* people, non-white people, gender-nonconforming or otherwise 'atypical' men, and people who are

perceived as disabled all know about this structure of disenfranchise-
ment, which can often reach the level of a debilitating fear of being in
public. Now that we are finishing this book, we are receiving news
from Chechnya of deaths in 'raids on gays', as one TV news bulletin
called the attacks. Meanwhile, in the Netherlands – liberal Holland!
– two young men have just been beaten up for holding hands in the
street. And racist violence is a part of daily life in this country, which
seems to be routinely underestimated.

SH: That which you are calling the actuality of sexual violence – how
it is experienced and survived – has definitely not been the focus for
us, in this book, and we identified this limitation in our introduction.
Nor is the question of how to talk about the aftermath and the survival
of sexual violence – that is, how survivors talk about these things –
really our focus here.[7] In fact, to focus on these issues in the context of
Cologne has been exceedingly rare, as far as I can see. In the beginning, there were a small number of reports that gave some of the
affected women a chance to speak. But, in my view, these contributions tended to serve, above all, the popular fantasy that that night
had given rise to something like flash mobs, i.e., dizzying swarms of
large numbers of men coming together to pounce on German women
before melting away again into air.

PIV: Yet we have to take seriously what the interviewees articulated;
we have to treat their accounts as authentic, undeniable feelings and
experiences. If we are only willing to take into account concrete
'effects', we are committing the same mistake that underlies sexism
and rape culture, i.e., the mistake of interpreting individual experience and evaluating it according to a predetermined (ideological)
frame. It is all too easy to believe that 'that which must not be, cannot
be'. So, in that sense, you're right: those who were targeted have had
no real voice, and there has been no real dialogue with them. They
must be taken seriously, no matter how badly the subject is being
monopolized. And, equally, we have to take those people seriously
who now experience the fear that similar assaults will happen to

them. Then, and only then, might we get into questions of where these fears come from, explaining, analysing and interpreting them.

TRANSNATIONAL DYNAMICS IN SEXUAL POLITICS

SH: The voices of those directly affected by sexual violence are missing. Discussions with survivors of this violence are missing. This is perhaps the best indication we've got that, after all, Cologne was *not* about sexual violence after all; *not* about how we should deal with it socially, politically and legally. To this day, I cannot understand why, for example, there has been no so-called revolt of the decent[8] against sexual violence *among men*. Why is there no manifesto, written by men, that states: 'sexual violence affects us, it's *our* topic, we are responsible for it'? There have been numerous occasions for something like that in recent years. To name just two examples: the abuse of over 500 boys in the Regensburger Domspatzen choir, and of some 130 girls and boys at the Odenwaldschule.

After Cologne, however, the debate over how we as a society should deal with sexual violence was reduced almost exclusively to the criminal dimension and to 'security' issues. Forget improving the rape crisis infrastructure: the fact that the counseling and support services built up by the women's movement over the last century remain chronically underfunded, or that there are all too few forms of treatment available for those who have suffered sexual violence – be it as victims of rape, or survivors of childhood sexual abuse – is hardly ever even discussed.

PIV: That said, the reform of the law on sex crimes last year was an important and long overdue step – albeit somewhat poisoned by the simultaneous tightening of asylum law.

SH: True enough. But even the reform of §177 is now, as we've recently seen, being questioned by German defence lawyers. To reform the law on sexual violence might not be constitutional, the German criminal defence attorney recently stated.[9] Sometimes, the rationale is genuinely amazing. For example, it's been argued here that there has been no increase in this type of violence and that, on the contrary, the incidence of sexual violence has actually *decreased*. To take into account contradictory findings, such as the case analyses carried out by the Federal Association of Women's Counseling Centres and Shelters (Bundesverband der Frauenberatungsstellen und Frauennotrufe in Deutschland), Frauen gegen Gewalt or *bff e.V.* would, according to these people, serve only to inflame feelings, not to provide facts.

So, instead, the defence lawyers are arguing abstractly against the 'juridification' of sexuality. 'A lived sexuality that is exciting and fulfilling is everybody's right, and we must protect against attempts on the part of the state to access, control or interfere in it', the statement declared. In principle, there's little here to disagree with. But who determines what an 'exciting and fulfilling lived sexuality' is?! That's what it's all about, at the end of the day: when is a 'no' a 'no'? Who gets to define whether or not a sexual act took place by mutual agreement?

PIV: This is definitely one of the central questions (politically and empirically) of our times, and the source of endless and mushrooming controversy. Frankly, it is the very substance of the political that is being negotiated in this debate about 'consent'. What I mean by 'the political', here, is the negotiation of the question of who is (and who is not) bound by what norms. So, in the battle over 'consent', we are dealing not only with the establishment of the presence of willingness or even mutual agreement – a conversation which tends to revolve around the unsatisfactory terms 'no means no' and 'yes means yes' – but with definitions of coercion and violence. I suspect that, in the future, this altercation will only unfold even more dramatically, even more controversially, and in an even more uninhibitedly 'fundamentalist' manner.

SH: This form of governance, the exercise of power *over* difference *via* differentiation, is the essence of today's politics of 'othering and ruling'. We have long since grown accustomed to living under legal systems that implement different legal norms for different groups. And we reflected on this, to some extent, in the second chapter of this book. But it's a question that evidently requires a far more extensive treatment in the transnational context.

PIV: Exactly. When it comes to sexual violence, it seems to me that there are three overlapping dynamics that are currently operative. First, I'd point to the significantly increased prominence of thematizations of sexual violence in popular culture. Celebrities, actors, pop stars and politicians are now talking openly about their experiences of harassment, rape, assault and abuse; and about the tangible everyday sexism that structures daily life within their respective industries. Throughout Latin America, massive protests against sexual and gendered violence – especially the remarkably normalized phenomenon of 'femicide' – have been mobilizing for some years now. In Argentina, nearly 500,000 people protested violence against women in the spring of 2015.[10] Then, in 2016 and 2017, the mass demonstrations continued. In India, also, we witnessed massive protests in the wake of gang rapes that took place on trains and buses. Incidentally, male survivors have been increasingly outspoken, too: in particular as pertains to the sexual violence that takes place in the bosom of the church, as well as in state institutions such as boarding schools.

SH: At least in India, however, part of the response was a spike in nationalist, which is to say, *femo*nationalist energies, featuring actors for whom bloody vigilante justice is the tool of choice when it comes to making reparation for rape. But what I find very interesting, in this context, is the fact that women and queer people – for example, in the Arab Spring or during the Gezi Park protests in Istanbul – have come together to organize the struggle against misogyny, sexual assault, and trans- and homophobic violence.[11] As far as I can tell, some of these groups have actually succeeded in forming bonds of solidarity and critical reflexivity with and within larger social movements – thus harnessing the latter's enormous momentum – and giving rise to new, non-identity-based alignments. In the United States, too, 'rape culture' continues to be widely and strenuously discussed, especially in relation to college campuses. That is, it is not only talked about – it is beginning to sensitize and transform institutions.

PIV: Yes. Although, on the other hand, we are seeing a backlash – and this would be the second dynamic of the three I mentioned just now. Without a doubt, there's a backlash underway against this 'sensitization' you identify. In some countries, it is already eroding what little juridical and civil bulwarks against sexual violence have been accomplished to date. This is quite clear in Russia, for instance, where, at the beginning of 2017, the criminal status of domestic violence was considerably downgraded under pressure from (hyper-) culturalist arguments. Meanwhile, in the United States, the notion of 'rape culture' is being subjected to a concerted wave of ridicule, in retaliation against the fact that so much visibility and awareness around the issues have been achieved. Things are once again being said in public that I would scarcely have thought sayable anymore – for example, that women can't get pregnant as a result of a 'true' rape because their bodies somehow know how to avoid this. It was the former Republican congressman Todd Akin who initiated the resurgence of this view in 2012, when he stated, in the context of the debate on abortion law: 'If it's a legitimate rape, the female body has ways to try to shut that whole thing down.' Egregious as this might seem, actually, the positions now being mooted by the Association of German Defence Attorneys actually tend in this exact same direction.

I could list any number of further examples of these 'smear-and-ridicule' tactics aimed at eroding the social proscription against rape and softening its criminal status. However, to move on to the third (and overlapping) dynamic: we have lately seen a surge of public sexist defamation, ressentiment, intimidation and rage – especially on social media – whose sheer quantity and qualitative intensity both take the breath away. 'Gamergate', in 2014, was just one surge within this relentless tide of organized discursive violence (prominently featuring threats of actual violence) against vocal women in the public sphere. It's no trivial matter, given that veritable online guerrilla cells are coming together on social media, whose radical mode of aggression against women and unconventional masculinities is completely divorced from any law or morality. Many of these networks are, besides being viscerally misogynist, openly racist and openly antisemitic.[12] It's a reality that tends to be underestimated outside of the feminist 'tech' bubble. But the (digital) commons has successfully been turned into a violent, hostile environment – to the point that it is impossible to inhabit – for women and for men who do not conform to the hegemonic model of manhood.

So, my thesis is that these three dynamics together form a tension in which – under the rubric of sexual violence – the question of the relationship of the individual to the state, of the individual to society and the law, is being fundamentally renegotiated in all sorts of (implicit, sometimes explicit) ways.

SH: Absolutely. Sexual politics and gender politics are *central* to these processes of negotiation of the political. It is these contestations between multiple actors, each pushing for rights and social participation, that define and determine that arena; and it is by means of these constant performative acts that the dividing lines in society are (re)produced, maintained, challenged, displaced, reinterpreted and/or redrawn.

Consequently, questions like 'what is a family?' and 'what *ought* a family to be?' – questions ranging from the appropriateness of gender stereotypes, their role in linguistic and cultural representation, to the legitimacy of academic gender studies and the rights commanded by lesbian, gay and trans lifestyles – are among the most controversial issues presently up for political, ethical, legal and social debate. And there is a direct connection between this dynamic and the relative increase in freedoms among populations who explicitly did not mean their revolution to be a bourgeois, white, cis-heterosexual men's revolution.

OUTSIDER WITHIN?

PIV: A point I want to ensure gets raised is the fact that the distribution of knowledge about the political imbrications discussed in this book is incredibly uneven. Both of us are engaged in a particular kind of scholarship – research of an often quasi-activist nature – which addresses the ambiguities of strategies of 'thematization' and 'de-thematization' of various structures of social difference. The history of all social movements in the modern age, perhaps especially of the feminist movements, is a history of simultaneous emancipation and subjugation, simultaneous progress and retrenchment, and bursts of revolutionary desire simultaneous to the realization of reform. It's also the story of (good) feminism getting tangled up in (bad) antisemitism and (bad) racism. What I'm driving at here is this: you and I come from milieus and modes of learning in which the definiteness of right and wrong, good and bad, them and us, then and now, and so on, is being constantly challenged. Seemingly clear distinctions are always revealing themselves to be highly contested gestures of differentiation in which we are all, personally and collectively, implicated, to a greater or lesser extent (depending on the context), and which affect us in ways we cannot ignore. As we have repeatedly stated in the book, by virtue of the historical processes by which human beings shape them as such, these differentiations end up becoming social facts. And, while such facts are always provisional, they carry real institutional and social weight.

SH: I'm reminded of an intervention I read by Paul Mecheril, who is a scholar of migration and culture in Oldenburg. He proposes that it is important 'to be capable of taking up distance in relation to one's self', in a very fundamental sense.[13] This is closely related to what we have argued in connection with Adorno: that the goal is to *not* set up one's self, the group to which one belongs, either as positive or as the measure of everything else (which consequently gets negated). And part of that task consists simply in listening to and hearing the other, in being quiet for a while. The political power of listening appears, notably, in the writings of Christina Thürmer-Rohr. For her, listening expresses the fact that 'others concern me': that one wishes to learn something from them.[14] 'To forget how to listen', on the other hand, amounts to 'following the rules of a society based on domination'.[15]

In asking for a taking up of distance vis-à-vis the self, Mecheril is primarily addressing those he calls the 'geopolitically privileged'. We certainly belong among that number. But who are the posited 'others', here? Which voices are not heard, or cannot be heard, or do not want to be heard?

PIV: We have both, on the basis of our personal biographies, concretely experienced the fact that national and/or 'cultural' differences aren't just contingent things: they are straightforwardly ideological. Many people, including people from contexts quite different from ours, have had similar experiences, I think – and this knowledge should not be underestimated.

In both our lives, various seemingly definite social locations and ostensible affiliations have, in many cases, proved to be fluid, or broken, or not so definite in the long run after all. I, for one, cannot really answer the question of whether I'm German, or say where I'm from. It depends on what is meant. Can *you* say, unequivocally, whether you belong to the intellectual elite? Your answer would probably have to be 'hmm, yes and no'. For my part, I am white and Jewish. But what does that even mean? What follows from that? The position of the 'outsider within'[16] – as sociologist Patricia Hill Collins sketched it – is probably the best description of experiences like ours. And to designate oneself as such need not be either coy or pretentious. Rather, 'outsider within' positionality simply articulates the complexity of biographical locations, the forms of situatedness that really result from all too often being – you, me, all of us – *multiply* located, even as we transcend these positions, actively shaping them and transforming them through political analyses. And, perhaps most obviously, we have the power to shape the 'consciousness', the attitude, that informs our dealings with these positions. Our thought, our praxis, our affect, and our speech is never in any way identical to a particular subject-position or reducible to a specific experience. We *make* something of our situations, and we know about the processes of differentiation that arise from that making. One might designate those who possess knowledge of this, and who appreciate its value, as 'difference-competent'. And, given the political dynamics in play today, especially since the election of Donald Trump as president of the United States, I think one could say that there's a cultural war being waged against it. But that's just a little 'aside'.

SH: I'd perhaps rather describe what you're talking about here as 'contingency competence'. Because it's a question of acting, always, in the knowledge that things – *I*, we, everyone and everything – could be different. And maybe that, in turn, is really a question of rendering that 'yes *and* no' you mentioned much more full-throated and determined. As Stuart Hall teaches us, if we believe that we require a unified identity from birth until death, it's only because we find such narratives about ourselves deeply comforting. But, in the actual societies people have been living in for more than two centuries, at this point, a stable birth-to-death identity is not given to anyone. We are all from somewhere else, nobody is 'from here'. We should seek comfort – for there is comfort to be found – in that fact.

On these occasions, I like to say that I am 'a person with a migration background', in the phrase of the ominous governmental category. You might think I am joking. But actually, according to the definition of the Federal Office of Statistics, a 'person with a migration background' includes 'all persons who have emigrated into the present territory of the Federal Republic of Germany since 1949, and all foreigners born in Germany, as well as all Germans born in Germany whose mother and/or father is either an immigrant or a foreigner born in Germany'.[17] The fact is, I was born in Saarland. And Saarland only joined the Federal Republic of Germany in 1957, so my parents are, strictly speaking, immigrants. My eldest sister was technically born abroad, because Saarland was not part of the Federal Republic at the time of her birth. And there are other dimensions to my 'migrant background': I'm the first person in my family to graduate from high school, and I'm the only one among all my relatives ever to have forged an academic career. I live a lesbian life. All these things are manifold experiences of displacement, movement and foreignness. How can I just say, 'I'm from here'? Where exactly would that 'here' even be?

WHOM DO WE HEAR?

PIV: I would like to return to that prescription you quoted, by Paul Mecheril. On the one hand, it strikes me as quite right. But on the other hand, wouldn't that mean – and please forgive my limitless scepticism, here – writing a book in which we principally listened to, and wrote down, what the AfD has to say, or the enraged *Bürger* of German respectability, the CSU, anti-gender blogs, Frauke Petry, journalists like Harald Martenstein and Gabriele Kuby, politicians like Björn Höcke and Thilo Sarrazin, philosophers like Peter Sloterdijk, or, say, the supposedly 'woke' hyper-identitarians on Tumblr? Wouldn't 'taking up distance from oneself' equally mean, here, reproducing what they say without really knowing what it *is* that they are saying, or, for that matter, what *we* say to that? Back when we were working on our last book, on the anti-gender movement, *Anti-Genderismus*,[18] I considered conducting and publishing an interview with an actress who belongs, broadly speaking, to the faction we were critically analysing – with a view to guiding our analysis. Incidentally, I *still* talk occasionally with many of the people involved, and I try to listen to them as best I can. But that kind of listening has not been the subject of this book and, consequently, is not visible here.

SH: When it comes to 'politicizing listening', as Thürmer-Rohr demands we do, clearly, we must first learn to listen to those *other* others, that is to say, to the 'marginal voices' who are, in reality, speaking all the time, but whose speech is distorted and, as a result, not heard. After all, speech by the AfD et al. is actually listened to very, very intensely, even though it is violent in the sense that it claims to be the *only* legitimate speech, tolerating no other speech besides itself. In this sense, it is as far removed as one can get from 'thought from else-where' – the idea of an 'expanded practice of thought' – as Hannah Arendt termed it, drawing on Kant. In contrast, as I see it, what we wanted to do was write a book in which the long-standing counter-canons of 'other' knowledges – feminist, postcolonial, anti-racist, intersectional – were rendered more visible on all of these questions. They simply are not present in the public debate, since they do not sit well with (German talk show hosts sympathetic to the AfD) Frank Plasberg, Anne Will, Sandra Maischberger and all the rest of them. Whether we succeeded, however, is something for others to decide.

PIV: I want to agree with you. But I worry that things aren't that clear-cut. Empirically and sociologically speaking, we have to understand that some of these milieus, groups and individuals manifest in the same way – alienated, marginalized, excluded, detached, villainized, stigmatized, repressed, unrepresented – as do the 'others' of the system, the 'others' of hegemonic elites. And many of the loudest among these (though not all) are individuals that we have good reason to view as *part* of that hegemony in terms of their incomes, their wealth and their access to the media and formal recognition: white, heterosexual people. There are 'wages' to this whiteness and straight-ness: they – we – have something to lose in the process of expanding the sphere of subjecthood. It's not something we deal with, in the book.

Arendt's injunction applies to everyone, always. It applies to us. And this means that even our classificatory comfort zones, the ones we use for ourselves, to think with, where we distinguish (for instance) between 'them' and 'us', hegemonic and marginal, legitimate and ille-gitimate: these, too, have to be abandoned in the name of letting go of our 'securities'. We can't just expect it of everybody else. It applies to us as well.

SH: Sure. But if our role, as intellectuals, is to remake the actually existing conditions of audibility, then it doesn't take long to realize that the resources in question are unevenly distributed. I agree with

María do Mar Castro Varela in this sense, who recently argued in *taz* that the really pressing question is: *Who* gets the opportunity to advance their truth?[19] To which I would add: Who has access to what resources for making their own situation known, and to make their own voice heard? This is something that requires careful unpacking. For example: Who among us benefits from racism as a (differentiating, discriminating) resource? White people do; non-white people, for the most part, do not.

It's true, and should not be denied, that many of those who are still (in my opinion) part of societal hegemony – or, at least, 'complicit' in the sense theorized by Raewyn Connell[20] – feel that they have been hung out to dry. But why do we have to acquiesce to this, analytically? Shouldn't we be insisting that we live in an age of social inequality on a historically unprecedented scale, instead of copying the formulas of the new era of populisms? Shouldn't we be making a progressive, emancipatory offer to those who have, in fact, been economically marginalized – including those among them who feel they have been culturally silenced – rather than dismissing them as reactionaries and diehards?

I totally agree: it's right to be always asking who has the opportunity to have their concerns heard – and, I would add, who are the people exploiting those feelings and twisting them to xenophobic ends? The spokespeople for the AfD are not, for example, themselves part of the alienated and precarized middle classes they speak for; rather, at least in Berlin, they are state prosecutors, professors and judges – members of the hegemonic apparatus. What we urgently need is an alternative to the politics of blame, not to mention the even more destructive politics of confrontation and animosity that is currently so in vogue.

PIV: I've already indicated that I feel we are, all of us, deeply embroiled in a kind of 'culture war'. It's a tangible struggle over difference. Now, there are, in my view, two basic orientations: the reflexive approach that treats difference as a process of relational differentiation, and the ontological approach, where differences are treated as pre-given entities and, paradoxically, subject to attempted rescue wherever they appear to be about to disappear. The latter sums up the various identitarian movements, as well as the *völkisch* currents in some of the main political parties, not to mention the popular idea of *Leitkultur* – autochthonous culture – whereby various cultural artifacts, from ham hocks and handshakes to sleeping with the window open (to name just a few of the elements that have circulated) are understood as essential.

This kind of ontologization of difference is sometimes espoused by those who claim to speak in the name of the marginalized. Such actors are, one might say, engaged in 'self-justification'– in the sense theorized by Adorno or Mecheril – in that they render difference absolute, thereby absolutizing themselves. Unsurprisingly, their arguments end up in a fundamentalist place. I'm thinking of, for example, a certain kind of indignation and outrage one sees articulated in popular culture nowadays over 'cultural appropriation', with people arguing, for instance, that white people with dreadlocks are to be interpreted as the worst kind of racism.[21]

The underlying logic here is the same: in order to legitimate making a distinction between us and others, differences must be asserted. *They are them because they are not us, and we are us because we are not them.* And: *the reason why they are not us is because they are different.* And so on. That not even approximate forms of evidence or comprehensible reasoning seems to be required to ground these claims is part of the sickness of the present 'post-factual' age. It's a problem that goes deeper than simply people getting away with lying through their teeth.

SH: But if we are to see how far things have come, we have to treat questions of appropriation in their proper historic context, namely the centuries-long destruction of cultures and the exploitation of racialized populations that took place in the name of the Enlightenment. True, we must break through this hopeless, devastating logic of 'identity', and criticize it even where it is being deployed with the 'best' of intentions. At the same time, as I say, we must never let go of the question of who gets the chance to produce differences, from where, and how.

PIV: That's right. The production and exploitation of differences on an open market – for example, in the music or food industries – takes place within structures and parameters that are themselves already unequal, racialized and gendered. The desire to be recognized as 'different' – which is, above all, a claim to inclusion – is wholly understandable, viewed in this light. I take it very seriously and by no means wish to be understood as belittling it. But, as you point out, the ends (of inclusion and recognition) do not justify the (essentialist) means.

We would already have gained a lot, were we able – finally – to truly perceive the radical diversity of the world. There are Muslim feminists, queer activists in Arab communities, trans and gender-queer Muslims; equally, there are migrants and lesbians in the AfD, folk-nationalist gay men, and cultural purists to be found in queer urban scenes. Furthermore, the corpus of theory and commentary on the hijab and other forms of clothing at the intersection of politics, religion, gender, fashion and lifestyle is already very well developed. Thanks to this scholarship and analysis, the culturalist and essentialist construction of 'us vs. them' can readily be unmasked as the fundamentalizing error that it is.

The world is full of many things, including prominent hijabi feminist journalists deep in arguments with other Muslim women who, for their part, take a stance against the hijab (and other forms of feminine veiling) because they, too, are feminists and/or critical of organized religion. There is no one Islamic feminism, and people from predominantly Muslim regions of the world are by no means all misogynists; likewise, people who have lived in or been socialized in Germany are by no means all feminists living in total harmony with fully realized ideals of equality, recognition, anti-discrimination and sexual diversity.

SH: Yes, amazingly enough, Germany has not in fact become a feminist nation overnight. We have had to learn this all over again over the course of the last few months, in the most painful possible way – even though we haven't had a 'Pussygate' per se. Besides xenophobia, there is a lot of deeply heterosexist messaging to be found in the ressentiment-filled repertoires of today's reactionaries. If you don't believe me, take a look at the latest manifesto of the CSU (Christian Social Union)![22] Alas, the West is still a long way from fulfilling Dipesh Chakrabarty's demand that it 'provincialize' itself, by which he meant moving away from the mode of making the world in one's own image and towards the mode of sharing it with others.[23] We still have a long way to go to get to a society where we can say each person's voice is free and heard, and where people collectively 'look after one another' for the simple reason that we are all 'weak and ignorant and . . . doomed to live out a few fleeting moments on Earth', as Voltaire wrote in his polemic for tolerance.[24]

'Differences Inside Me Lie Down Together': Thinking in Difference

> Plurality does not simply bring colour into the world. It is also the source of necessary contestations, and it is reliant upon a form of coexistence that goes beyond affirmation of one's own life-world.[1]
>
> – Christina Thürmer-Rohr

What we wanted to do, in this book, was contribute to a question that seems to us to be at the centre of the constitution of modern societies once more: the political question of the production (and state reproduction) of cultural difference. Our aim was to issue a reminder that racism and sexism cannot be conceptualized through the identities or characteristics of any group or an individual, but only through the circumstances in which they are produced and rendered relevant. Racism does not exist because there are races, any more than sexism does because there is sex. It's the other way around. Instead of approaching difference in an identitarian way – that is, rather than always establishing a specific identity in advance, thereby removing it from criticism – we have tried to think *in* difference about difference, and to differentiate between differences. Our written reflection, in two voices, was guided by curiosity about the conditions, within the present power-saturated mode of production of differences, under which these differences are activated.

We will now conclude this book with a few further thoughts on the movement of thought *in* difference. We take thinking in difference to be an 'attitude' in a Foucauldian sense. Attitudes can be adopted; they can be reconsidered and tested. Sometimes they take on a life of their own, but they are never unassailable. I may opt into an attitude in order to then act, one way or another. So, an attitude comes with the obligation to vouch for one's actions and give an account of them. And this means learning to be attentive precisely to

what one has decided to disregard. It means letting go of the known
– or, at least, questioning it, while allowing others to question it – and
learning to see things from different perspectives.

These remarks about thinking in difference are inspired by – to
name only our most important sources – the poet Audre Lorde, the
theorist Judith Butler, and the political philosopher Hannah Arendt.

Audre Lorde has shown us the many – often deeply intimate –
ways that racism, sexism, homophobia and class do damage to people's
lives and kill off solidarity. Her poetry, prose and essays also tell of an
overwhelming desire to survive sexist and racist violence, and to
prevent the destruction of tenderness and eros. With extraordinary
tenacity, Lorde insists that difference is our greatest strength in the
struggle for another, better world. She demands that we neither negate
difference nor conceptualize it as something that pits people against
one another. Instead, the contradictions arising from the commin-
gling of differences within us should be viewed as a source of (richly
conflictual) learning. Lorde puts it pithily and beautifully in *A Burst of
Light*: 'I have always known I learn my most lasting lessons about
difference by closely attending the ways in which the differences
inside me lie down together.'[2]

Judith Butler, for her part, evokes for us the necessity of 'thinking
the possible'[3] – for the simple reason that we are 'social beings from
the start, dependent on what is outside ourselves, on others, on institutions, and on sustained and sustainable environments'.[4] This is at
the heart of Butler's ethics: an ethics that does not proceed from an
autonomous a priori subject but rather devotes itself to the precariousness of identity, seen as a relation to the self. Precarity, in this
context, is not a problem, but an everyday question of praxis, and an
opportunity. We are vulnerable, yes, insofar as we are dependent on
others, including structures that enable our lives: vulnerability is, as
such, perhaps the original form that social relationships take. We
depend on social, individual, legal, political and institutional recognition. But, of course, we are not all equally vulnerable. On the contrary:
precariousness is highly differentiated, unevenly distributed. The
politics of danger, mediated via institutional and legal arrangements,

social norms and economic realities, endanger and injure some of us while protecting others.

While deeply cognizant of this, Butler still turns to the experience of difference to ground an ethic based on the fact that we are all exposed to one another, informed by the knowledge that it is only 'together [that we can] create the conditions for a viable life'. For this very reason, she does not think of differences as ontological, preferring to regard them as dynamic, endlessly deferred, inherently precarious effects of processes of domination and differentiation.[5] There can never, in that sense, be a 'last word' on the question of what is female, for example, or Western, or feminist.

Finally, we owe to Hannah Arendt our commitment never to speak of 'the' human in the singular; likewise, the insight that 'the' world can only be apprehended, as she says, via 'the almost infinite diversity of its appearances'.[6] For Arendt, plurality is a cherishable fact and, at the same time, a moral one and a political demand: we should accept these plural worlds and protect them. The following, for her, are indispensable: humans' interest in building a common world, the multidimensionality of their perspectives, the non-fungibility of people, the unconditional character of individuality and, finally, the continuity of the conversation. For, as Arendt held forth in her Lessing Award speech in 1959, if we imagine that there was only one view, only one, rather than the many perspectives that first created the world between human beings, then that view would still have revolved around conversation, friendship and humanity – in short, this, our world.[7]

Thinking in difference, as we mean it, goes together with the development of an epistemic attitude as much as a political one. It relies on the rejection of totalizing and otherizing perspectives in favour of an embrace of thinking *with* the world instead of *about* it. This means thinking horizontally, on an equal footing with the 'others' we are talking about, who have the right not only to be listened to – when they spell out this otherness, reject it or relativize it – but to expect that we be affected and transformed by this otherness. Basically, we're talking about universally advocating for 'everyone's right to inherit the whole world', as Achille Mbembe says.[8] This entails, too, readiness to provincialize one's own position, especially on the part of those who, for too long, have enjoyed the privilege of belonging to an unmarked universal identity category, enabling them to shape the world in their own image.

This said, anyone who denies others the right to exist has forfeited the right to be listened to. Which is not to say it is impossible to take the rationales and frames of such – terrorist, inhumane – attitudes seriously, or even to understand them. Thinking together, however, starts from a basis of mutual recognition. Put simply: only those who take everyone involved (even potentially involved) in a conversation as seriously as they take themselves have the right to be taken seriously. For to refrain from this minimal standard, to refuse others the right to speak and be heard, is an authoritarian foreclosure and the antithesis of thinking in difference. Those who make such anti-democratic and antipluralist gestures seldom, if ever, show any willingness to transform their view of their own truth into 'an opinion among opinions'[9] – as Arendt says – that is, to allow their opinion to become an object of debate. We do not argue here for a simple relativism. There are standards by which arguments can be deemed more and less plausible than others; facts exist, as do good and bad forms of reasoning.

What we are talking about, to put it another way, is once again the putting of doubt into doubt, and the development of an ethos – in radical contrast to the constant din of media vehicles and their surrogates – that pursues the virtues of nuance and de-escalation. Such an ethos provides a concrete and practical way to make critical reference to arguments, to other people and – last but not least – to oneself. It makes possible an attitude favouring openness and questioning, while knowing very well what the difference is between empirical certainties and normative judgments. By adopting it, we make room for questions like who it is we talk about, with whom and how, while problematizing ourselves as 'autonomous subjects', as Michel Foucault laid out in (among others) his text 'What Is Enlightenment?' It is here that Foucault argues for 'the permanent reactivation of an attitude – that is, of a philosophical ethos that could be described as a permanent critique of our historical era'.[10]

Rightly understood, 'critique', then, does not refer to any substantially fixed opinion, position or viewpoint, but to an attitude of questioning, an attitude that questions. Critique, as such, means not taking things as they are, but asking, rather, how they came to be that way, and how else they might be. Again and again, we must call into question the status quo (*So-sein*) of opinions, categories and views by trying to determine what that epistemic closure bases itself on, which is to say, what it takes as non-negotiable and for granted. Thinking is a form of resistance, according to Theodor Adorno, to that which is imposed upon us.[11]

Adorno's aims are ones we share. For example, we are not interested in asserting that Muslim people's religious identities determine their individual attitudes to the issue of gender equality or inequality. Nor would we want to assert that religiosity has no bearing on an individual's relation to the gender issue. Feminism does not 'belong' to anyone, and we aren't at all sure that feminist treatments of the 'gender trouble' arising in such disparate contexts as queer nightclubs and shelters for refugees (most of which are miserable) always succeed.[12] It is precisely this rhetoric we see all around us, this fundamentalizing rhetoric that can only speak in generalizations, 'always' and 'never', either/or, for or against, everything and nothing – given to painting things as either fully deterministic or individually autonomous – that elicits our suspicions. Shorthands like these may seem fine for everyday use. But they rarely hold any water empirically and are equally rarely conducive to dialogical, multi-perspectival openings where one can look at things from a different angle. On the contrary: they close down discussion and exclude.

Resisting them, and committing to working through differentiations in dialogue, is perhaps the greatest challenge implicated in the preservation, defence and deepening of pluralist democracies today. Amid the seemingly ineluctable and often menacing spectacles of acceleration, dissolution, and hyper-mediatization, amid the multiplication of modes of existence, it is necessary to find time to undertake these necessary differentiations, these necessary disputes. Clearing time and space for such conversation is tantamount to humanizing 'that which is in the world, and that which is going on inside of us, alike' as Christina Thürmer-Rohr suggests.[13] We spell out, through this conversation, all relevant complexities, and we learn how to unlearn assumptions and certainties through the practice of (self-) questioning. The ultimate goal is a practice in which differences are not overlooked and ignored but brought relentlessly into conversation.

As naive as this may seem at first blush, it's worth noting that similar attempts to conduct such a conversation, to deal with differences, to acknowledge them and question them at the same time while preserving – developing, even – a capacity for critical action has long since been a familiar part of life and reality. In urban residential communities and rural parishes, in front of blackboards in classrooms, in churches and in mosques, in neighbourhood associations, supermarkets, volunteer-run German courses for refugees, football clubs, research projects and choirs, on subways and buses, around falafel stands, exercise machines at the gym, benches at the carpentry workshop, tables in Bavarian taverns on the corner or in family dining rooms, cooperation and conversation is taking place – sometimes well, sometimes less well – between people endowed with almost infinite difference.[14] And in these situations, as Frantz Fanon would say, people are – by recognizing and talking to one another – 'reexamining the question of man': raising their own awareness of the fact that we are 'go[ing] forward all the time, night and day, in the company of Man, in the company of all men',[15] which is to say, of all human beings.

What we can learn by doing this is the essence of the 'attitude' we wish to promulgate: an ethos given neither to idealized abstraction nor to principle for principle's sake; an ethos representing neither opinion nor assertion, and certainly not a luxury of out-of-touch academic elites. No – the attitude in question is a practice of decisive and thoroughly partisan passion towards the world, a fearless commitment both to meddling in it and to everyone else participating in that meddling in equal measure. To quote Thürmer-Rohr one last time, a passion for differentiation of this nature depends upon our being genuinely interested in a mode of 'coexistence that cannot be reduced to the affirmation of one's own life-world'.[16]

The texture of this essay is full of the kind of diffuse, discomfiting and destabilizing implications that, to many of us, signify 'Cologne'. That texture has been built, not least, by remarks and insights garnered from discussions we undertook with members of fraternities, CSU politicians, students in Neukölln, other students in the leafiest locations in Munich, students in Switzerland, and Polish taxi drivers in London. We have incorporated conversations with DJs from queer dance parties, Facebook friends, friends who are hosting unaccompanied refugee 'minors' in their homes, waiters in Rostock, neighbours in the Ruhr area, our siblings, our (worried) parents and, finally, people who have hurled personal abuse at us via email, sometimes insulting us in obscene, racist or homophobic style.

One thing that none of us needs, when it comes to living together in a pluralistic democracy, however, is a politics that elevates 'action' as though it had inherent value. There exists a tendency to valourize 'acts', even if the act is neither reflexively weighed in advance nor grounded in thoughtful differentiation. Here, the benchmark of the political becomes not the search for the most innovative vision or the best solution, but the simple fact of winning – an attitude that despises anything that looks like weakness. And the last thing we need is a blind 'decisionism' of this nature, which feeds on denigration, revenge and antagonism, and which wants nothing to do with empathy.[17]

What *is* needed, on the other hand, is openness to the world, and willingness to be touched and moved by what is happening in it. What we are crying out for is togetherness, a grammar of coexistence of the different, a readiness to expose oneself to worlds that might be different from the realities of one's own life. What will it take to get there? The art of encountering others without erasing their otherness.

Bibliography

Abbas, Sadia, *At Freedom's Limit: Islam and the Postcolonial Predicament*, New York: Fordham University Press, 2014.

Adelson, Leslie, 'The Price of Feminism: Of Women and Turks', 305–19 in Patricia Herminghouse and Magda Mueller, eds, *Gender and Germanness: Cultural Productions of Nation*, Providence/Oxford: Berghahn, 1997.

Adichie, Chimamanda Ngozi, 'Now Is the Time to Talk About What We Are Actually Talking About', *New Yorker*, 2 December 2016, newyorker.com.

Adorno, Theodor, *Negative Dialectics*, New York: Continuum, 2007.

Adorno, Theodor, *Problems of Moral Philosophy*, trans. Rodney Livingstone, ed. Thomas Schroder, Stanford: Stanford University Press, 2000.

Ahmed, Leila, *Women and Gender in Islam: Historical Roots of a Modern Debate*, New Haven: Yale University Press, 1992.

Ahmed, Sara, 'Collective Feelings: Or, the Impressions Left by Others', *Theory, Culture & Society* 21(2): 25–42, 2004.

Ahmed, Sara, *Living a Feminist Life*, London/Durham, NC: Duke University Press, 2017.

Alexander, Robin, *The Driven Ones: Merkel and Refugee Policy: Report from Inside the Centre of Power*, Berlin: Siedler Verlag, 2017.

Anthias, Floya and Nira Yuval-Davis, *Racialized Boundaries: Race, Nation, Gender, Colour and Class in the Anti-Racist Struggle*, New York/London: Routledge, 1993.

Arendt, Hannah, 'Freedom and Politics' in Hannah Arendt, *Between Past and Future*, New York: Viking Press, 1961.

Arendt, Hannah, 'On Humanity in Dark Times: Thoughts about Lessing', trans. Clara and Richard Winston, 3–31 in *Men in Dark Times*, New York: Harcourt Brace, 1993.

Arendt, Hannah, *The Life of the Mind, Volume 1: Thinking*, London: Secker and Warburg, 1978.

Arendt, Hannah, *Thinking Without a Banister: Essays in Understanding, 1953–1975*, London: Schocken, 2018.

Ateş, Seyran, *Der Multikulti-Irrtum*, Berlin: Perlentaucher, 2008.

Attia, Iman, *Die »westliche Kultur« und ihr Anderes: Zur Dekonstruktion von Orientalismus und antimuslimischem Rassismus*, Bielefeld: transcript, 2009.

Austin, J. L., *How to Do Things with Words*, Cambridge, MA: Harvard University Press, 1962.

Bargetz, Brigitte, 'Jenseits emotionaler Eindeutigkeiten: Überlegungen zu einer politischen Grammatik der Gefühle', 117–36 in Angelika Baier, Christa Binswanger, Jana Häberlein, Yv Nay and Andrea Zimmermann, eds, *Affekt und Geschlecht: Eine einführende Anthologie*, Vienna: Böhlau, 2014.

Bauman, Zygmunt, 'Der neue Hass aufs Establishment und die Sehnsucht nach dem Feind', *Blätter für deutsche und internationale Politik* 2, 2017.

Bauman, Zygmunt, *Modernity and Ambivalence*, Ithaca, NY: Cornell University Press, 1991.

Becker-Schmidt, Regina, '"Class", "gender", "ethnicity", "race": Logiken der Differenzsetzung, Verschränkung von Ungleichheitslagen und gesellschaftliche Strukturierun', 56–83 in Cornelia Klinger, Gudrun-Axeli Knapp and Birgit Sauer, eds, *Achsen der Ungleichheit: Zum Verhältnis von Klasse, Geschlecht und Ethnizität*, Frankfurt/New York: Berghahn, 2007.

Berger, John, *Ways of Seeing*, London: Penguin, 1977.

Bourdieu, Pierre, *Distinction: A Social Critique of the Judgement of Taste*, London: Routledge, 1986.

Bourdieu, Pierre, 'Language and Symbolic Power, an English Translation of "Ce que parler veut dire"', trans. Gino Raymond and Matthew Adamson, 32–159 in John Thompson, ed., *Language and Symbolic Power and Other Essays by Pierre Bourdieu*, Cambridge: Polity, 1993.

Brah, Avtar, *Cartographies of Diaspora: Contesting Identities*, London/New York: Routledge, 1996.

Brown, Wendy, *Undoing the Demos: Neoliberalism's Stealth Revolution*, New York: Zone, 2015.

Brubaker, Rogers, *Trans: Gender and Race in an Age of Unsettled Identities*, Princeton: Princeton University Press, 2016.

Bude, Heinz, *Die Ausgeschlossenen: Das Ende vom Traum einer gerechten Gesellschaft*, Hamburg: Perlentaucher, 2008.

Bührmann, Andrea, *Das authentische Geschlecht: Die Sexualitätsdebatte der Neuen Frauenbewegung und die Foucaultsche Machtanalyse*, Münster: Unrast, 1995.

Butler, Judith, *Bodies That Matter: On the Discursive Limits of Sex*, London: Routledge, 1993.

Butler, Judith, 'Can One Lead a Good Life in a Bad Life?', Adorno Prize Lecture, *Radical Philosophy* 176 (Nov/Dec): 9–18, 2012.

Butler, Judith, *Excitable Speech: A Politics of the Performative.* New York: Routledge, 1997.

Butler, Judith, *Frames of War: When is Life Grievable?*, London: Verso, 2009.

Butler, Judith, *Giving an Account of Oneself*, New York: Fordham University Press, 2005.

Butler, Judith, 'Merely Cultural', *Social Text* 52/53: 265–77, 1997.

Butler, Judith, 'Performativity's Social Magic', 113–28 in Richard Shusterman, ed., *Bourdieu: A Critical Reader*, Oxford: Blackwell, 1999.

Butler, Judith, *Precarious Life: The Powers of Mourning and Violence*, London: Verso, 2004.

Butler, Judith, *Undoing Gender*, London: Routledge, 2004.

Butler, Judith and Elizabeth Weed, 'Introduction', 1–8 in Judith Butler and Elizabeth Weed, eds, *The Question of Gender: Joan W. Scott's Critical Feminism*, Bloomington: Indiana University Press, 2011.

Butler, Judith, Zeynep Gambetti and Leticia Sabsay, eds, *Vulnerability in Resistance*, Durham, NC: Duke University Press, 2016.

Castro Varela, María do Mar and Paul Mecheril, eds, *Die Dämonisierung der Anderen: Rassismuskritik der Gegenwart*, Bielefeld: transcript, 2016.

Chakrabarty, Dipesh, *Provincializing Europe: Postcolonial Thought and Historical Difference*, Princeton: Princeton University Press, 2000.

Chołuj, Bożena, "'Gender-Ideologie": ein Schlüsselbegriff des polnischen Anti-Genderismus', 219–37 in Hark and Villa, eds, *Anti-Genderismus*, 2015.

Cohen, Stanley, *Folk Devils and Moral Panics: The Creation of the Mods and Rockers*, London: Routledge, 2002 [1972].

Combahee River Collective, 'The Combahee River Collective Statement', 272–82 in Barbara Smith, ed., *Home Girls: A Black Feminist Anthology*, New York: Rutgers University Press, 1983.

Connell, Raewyn, *Masculinities* (2nd edition), Berkeley: University of California Press, 2005.

Demirović, Alex, *Der nonkonformistische Intellektuelle: die Entwicklung der Kritischen Theorie zur Frankfurter Schule* ['The Nonconformist Critical Intellectual'], Frankfurt am Main: Suhrkamp, 1999.

Dierbach, Stefan, *Jung – rechts – unpolitisch? Die Ausblendung des Politischen im Diskurs über Rechte Gewalt*, Bielefeld: transcript, 2010.

Dietze, Gabriele, 'Das Ereignis Köln', 93–102 in *femina politica* 1, 2016.

Dietze, Gabriele, 'Ethnosexismus: Sex-Mob-Narrative um die Kölner Silvesternacht' in *movements: Journal für kritische Migrations – und Grenzregimeforschung* 2(1): 177–86, 2016.

Dohm, Hedwig, *Der Frauen Natur und Recht*, Zürich, 1976 [1876].

Dohm, Hedwig, *Die Mütter: Beitrag zur Erziehungsfrage*, Berlin, 1903.

Dölling, Irene, 'Eva-Prinzip? Neuer Feminismus? Aktuelle Verschiebungen in Geschlechterleitbildern im Kontext gesellschaftlicher Umbruchsprozesse', 24–41 in Marburger Gender-Kolleg, ed., *Geschlecht Macht Arbeit: Interdisziplinäre Perspektiven und politische Intervention*, Münster: Unrast, 2008.

Duggan, Lisa and Nan D. Hunter, *Sex Wars: Sexual Dissent and Political Culture,* London/New York: Routledge, 1995.

Durkheim, Emile, *The Rules of Sociological Method*, trans. W. D. Halls, ed. Steven Lukes, New York: Free Press, 1982.

Eggers, Maureen Maisha, Grada Kilomba, Peggy Piesche and Susan

Arndt, eds, *Mythen, Masken und Subjekte: Kritische Weißseinsforschung in Deutschland*, Münster: Unrast, 2005.

El Masrar, Sineb, *Emanzipation im Islam: Eine Abrechnung mit ihren Feinden*, Freiburg: Herder, 2016.

El-Tayeb, Fatima, *Undeutsch: Die Konstruktion des Anderen in der Postmigrantischen Gesellschaft*, Bielefeld: transcript, 2016.

Elias, Norbert, *The Civilizing Process: Sociogenetic and Psychogenetic Investigations*, Oxford: Blackwell, 1994 [1939].

Engel, Antke, *Bilder von Sexualität und Ökonomie: Queere Kulturelle Politiken im Neoliberalismus*, Bielefeld: transcript, 2009.

Erdem, Esra, 'In der Falle einer Politik des Ressentiments: Feminismus und die Integrationsdebatte', 187–206 in Sabine Hess, Jana Binder and Johannes Moser, eds, *No Integration? Kulturwissenschaftliche Beiträge zur Integrationsdebatte in Europa*, Bielefeld: transcript, 2009.

Eshahangizi, Kijan, Sabine Jess, Juliane Karakayali, Bernd Kasparek, Simona Pagan, Mayjias Rodatz and Vassilis Tsianos, 'Rassismus in der postmigrantischen Gesellschaft: Zur Einleitung', *movements: Journal für kritische Migrations- und Grenzregimeforschung* 2(1): 9–24, 2016.

Fanon, Frantz, *Black Skin, White Masks*, trans. Richard Philcox, New York: Grove Press, 1952.

Fanon, Frantz, *The Wretched of the Earth*, Grove Press, New York, 1961.

Farris, Sara, 'Die politische Ökonomie des Femonationalismus', *feministische studien* 2: 321–34, 2011.

Farris, Sara, *In the Name of Women's Rights: The Rise of Femonationalism*, London/Durham: Duke University Press, 2017.

Fekete, Liz, 'Enlightened Fundamentalism? Immigration, Feminism and the Right', *Race & Class* 48(2): 1–22, 2006.

Foucault, Michel, '*Discourse and Truth*' and '*Parresia*', Chicago: University of Chicago Press, 2019.

Foucault, Michel, *Power/Knowledge: Selected Interviews and Other Writings, 1972–1977*, ed./trans. Colin Gordon, New York: Pantheon, 1980.

Foucault, Michel, 'What is Critique?', 41–82 in Michel Foucault, *The Politics of Truth*, Los Angeles: Semiotext(e), 1997.

Foucault, Michel, 'What is Enlightenment?', 32–50 in Paul Rabinow, ed., *The Foucault Reader*, New York: Pantheon Books, 1984.

Franck, Georg, 'The scientific economy of attention: A novel approach to the collective rationality of science', *Scientometrics* 55(1): 3–26, 2002.

Fromm, Erich, *Beyond the Chains of Illusion: My Encounter with Marx and Freud*, London: Bloomsbury, 1962.

Goodman, Nelson, *Ways of Worldmaking*, London: Hackett, 1978.

Gramsci, Antonio, *Prison Notebooks, Volume 2*, trans. Joseph Buttigieg, New York: Columbia University Press, 2011.

Gunda-Werner-Institut and Sabine Hark, eds, *Die Freundschaft zur Welt nicht verlernen: Texte für Christina Thürmer-Rohr*, Berlin: Institut der Heinrich Böll-Stiftung, 2016.

Haaf, Meredith, Susanne Klingner and Barbara Streidl, *Wir Alpha-Mädchen: Warum Feminismus das Leben schöner macht*, Hamburg: Hoffman & Campe, 2008.

Habermas, Jürgen, 'The New Obscurity: The Crisis of the Welfare State and the Exhaustion of Utopian Energies', trans. Phillip Jacobs, *Philosophy and Social Criticism* 11: 1–18, 1986.

Habermas, Rebekka, *Skandal in Togo: Ein Kapitel deutscher Kolonialherrschaft*, Frankfurt am Main: S Fischer, 2016.

Hacking, Ian, 'Making Up People', in T. L. Heller, M. Sosna and D. E. Wellbery, eds, *Reconstructing Individualism*, Stanford, CA: Stanford University Press, 1985.

Hage, Ghassan, 'Der unregierbare Muslim: Jenseits der Bipolarität von Multikulturalismus und Assimilation', 73–94 in Sabine Hess, Jana Binder and Johannes Moser, eds, *No Integration? Kulturwissenschaftliche Beiträge zur Integrationsdebatte in Europa*, Bielefeld: transcript, 2009.

Hagemann-White, Carol, 'European Research on the Prevalence of Violence Against Women', *Violence Against Women*, 7(7): 732–59, 2001.

Hagemann-White, Carol, 'Gewalt im Geschlechterverhältnis als

Gegenstand sozialwissenschafttlicher Forschung und Theoriebildung: Rückblick, gegenwärtiger Stand, Ausblick', 29–52 in Regina-Maria Dackweiler, ed., *Gewalt-Verhältnisse*, Frankfurt: campus, 2000.

Hall, Stuart, 'Popular-democratic vs authoritarian populism: two ways of taking democracy seriously', 157–85 in Alan Hunt, ed., *Marxism and Democracy*, London: Lawrence and Wishart, 1980.

Hall, Stuart, 'The Spectacle of the "Other"', 225–39 in Hall, Stuart, ed., *Representation: Cultural Representations and Signifying Practices*, London: Thousand Oaks, 1997.

Hall, Stuart, 'The West and the Rest: Discourse and Power', 184–227 in Stuart Hall et al., eds, *Modernity: An Introduction to Modern Societies*, Cambridge, MA: Blackwell, 1996.

Hall, Stuart, and Lawrence Grossberg, 'On Postmodernism and Articulation: An Interview with Stuart Hall', *Journal of Communication Inquiry* 10(2): 45–60.

Hammar, Tomas, *Democracy and the Nation State: Aliens, Denizens, and Citizens in a World of International Migration*, Aldershot: Avebury, 1990.

Haraway, Donna, *Simians, Cyborgs, and Women: The Reinvention of Nature*, London: Free Association Books, 1991.

Haraway, Donna, 'Situated Knowledges: The Science Question in Feminism and the Privilege of Partial Perspective', *Feminist Studies* 14(3): 575–99, 1988.

Harding, Sandra, *Sciences from Below: Feminisms, Postcolonialities, and Modernities*, Durham, NC: Duke University Press, 2008.

Hark, Sabine, 'Das ethische Regime der Bilder oder: Wie leben Bilder?', 53–8 in Angelika Bartl, Josch Hoenes, Patricia Mühr and Kea Wienand, eds, *Sehen – Macht – Wissen: ReSaVoir. Bilder im Spannungsfeld von Kultur, Politik und Erinnerung*, Bielefeld: transcript, 2011.

Hark, Sabine, 'Deviante Subjekte – Normalisierung und Subjektformierung', 219–42 in Michael Corsten and Michael Kauppert, eds, *Der Mensch – nach Rücksprache mit der Soziologie*, Frankfurt/New York: Campus, 2013.

Hark, Sabine, 'Die Vermessung des Schweigens – oder: Was heißt sprechen?', 285–96 in Iman Attia, Swantje Köbsell and Nivedita Prasad, eds, *Dominanzkultur Reloaded: Neue Texte zu gesellschaftlichen Machtverhältnissen und ihren Wechselwirkungen*, Bielefeld: transcript, 2015.

Hark, Sabine, ed., *Dis/Kontinuitäten: Feministische Theorie*, Wiesbaden: Springer, 2007.

Hark, Sabine, *Dissidente Partizipation: Eine Diskursgeschichte des Feminismus*, Frankfurt am Main: Suhrkamp, 2005.

Hark, Sabine, '"Überflüssig": Negative Klassifikationen – Elemente symbolischer Delegitimierung im soziologischen Diskurs', 151–62 in Cornelia Klinger, Gudrun-Axeli Knapp and Birgit Sauer, eds, *Achsen der Ungleichheit: Zum Verhältnis von Klasse, Geschlecht und Ethnizität*, Frankfurt am Main/New York: Campus, 2007.

Hark, Sabine, 'Vom Erfolg verwöhnt: Feministische Ambivalenzen der Gegenwart', 76–91 in Deniz Hänzi, Hildegard Matthies and Dagmar Simon, eds, *Erfolg: Konstellationen und Paradoxien einer gesellschaftlichen Leitorientierung*, Leviathan Sonderband 29, 2014.

Hark, Sabine and the Gunda-Werner-Institut, eds, *Die Freundschaft zur Welt nicht verlernen: Texte für Christina Thürmer-Rohr*, Berlin: Gunda Werner Institut, 2016.

Hark, Sabine and Paula-Irene Villa, eds, *Anti-Genderismus: Sexualität und Geschlecht als Schauplätze aktueller politischer Auseinandersetzungen*, Bielefeld: transcript, 2015.

Hausen, Karin, 'Die Polarisierung der »Geschlechtscharaktere«. Eine Spiegelung der Dissoziation von Erwerbs- und Familienleben', 173–96 in Sabine Hark, ed., *Dis/Kontinuitäten: Feministische Theorie*, Wiesbaden: Springer, 2007 [1976].

Henning, Anja, 'Political genderphobia in Europe: Accounting for right-wing political-religious alliances against gender-sensitive education reforms since 2012', *Z Religion Ges Polit.*, 2(2): 193–219, 2018.

Hensel, Jana, and Elisabeth Raether, *Neue deutsche Mädchen*, Reinbek: Rowohlt, 2008.

Hentschel, Linda, ed., *Bilderpolitik in Zeiten von Krieg und Terror:*

Medien, Macht und Geschlechterverhältnisse, Berlin: b-books, 2008.

Hirschman, Albert, 'Morality and the Social Sciences', in *The Essential Hirschman*, ed. Jeremy Adelman, Princeton: Princeton University Press, 2013.

Honegger, Claudia, *Die Ordnung der Geschlechter: Die Wissenschaften vom Menschen und das Weib*, Frankfurt: Suhrkamp, 1991.

Honegger, Claudia, 'Weiblichkeit als Kulturform: Zur Codierung der Geschlechter in der Moderne', 197–210 in Sabine Hark, ed., *Dis/ Kontinuitäten: Feministische Theorie*, Wiesbaden: Springer, 2007.

Huntington, Samuel, *The Clash of Civilizations and the Remaking of World Order* (21st century edition), New York: Simon and Schuster, 2011.

Jäger, Margarete, 'Feministische Argumente zur Untermauerung von Rassismus: Warum liegt Deutschen die Stellung der Einwanderinnen so am Herzen?', 248–61 in Christoph Butterwege and Siegfried Jäger, eds, *Rassismus in Europa*, Köln: Bund-Verlag, 1993.

Jameson, Fredric, 'On Cultural Studies', *Social Text* 34: 17–52, 1993.

Kaddor, Lamya, 'Verschleierung von Haut und Haar – ein Interview', *sozialmagazin* 42(1–2): 28–35, 2017.

Kant, Immanuel, *Critique of Pure Reason* (Revised Edition), London: Penguin, 2008.

Karakayali, Serhat, 'Reflexiver Eurozentrismus: Zwischen diskursiver Kombinatorik und Latenz', 96–113 in Sebastian Friedrich, ed., *Rassismus in der Leistungsgesellschaft: Analysen und kritische Perspektiven zu den rassistischen Normalisierungsprozessen in der »Sarrazindebatte«*, Münster: Unrast, 2011.

Kerner, Ina, *Differenzen und Macht: Zur Anatomie von Rassismus und Sexismus*, Frankfurt: Suhrkamp, 2009.

Kerner, Ina, 'Religion, Culture, and the Complexities of Feminist Solidarity', Paper presented at the International Symposium 'Hermeneutic Conflict, Cultural Entanglement and Social Inequality: Power of Interpretation in Intersectional Perspective', Rostock, 22–24 September 2016.

Knapp, Gudrun-Axeli, 'Die vergessene Differenz', 263–84 in Sabine

Hark, ed., *Dis/ Kontinuitäten: Feministische Theorie*, Wiesbaden: Springer, 2007 [1988].

Knapp, Gudrun-Axeli, 'Macht und Geschlecht: Neuere Entwicklungen in der feministischen Macht und Herrschaftsdiskussion', 287–325 in Gudrun-Axeli Knapp and Angelika Wetterer, eds, *Traditionen, Brüche: Entwicklungen feministischer Theorie*, Freiburg: Kore, 1992.

Knapp, Gudrun-Axeli, 'Verhältnisbestimmungen: Geschlecht, Klasse, Ethnizität in gesellschaftstheoretischer Perspektive', 138–70 in Gudrun-Axeli Knapp and Cornelia Klinger, eds, *ÜberKreuzungen: Fremdheit, Ungleichheit, Differenz, Forum Frauen- und Geschlechterforschung* 23, Münster: Unrast, 2008.

Köttig, Michaela, Renate Bitzan and Andrea Petö, *Gender and Far-Right Politics in Europe*, Cham: Springer, 2017.

Krais, Beate and Gunter Gebauer, *Habitus*, Bielefeld: transcript Verlag, 2002.

Kramer, Caroline and Anina Mischau, 'Städtische Angst-Räume von Frauen am Beispiel der Stadt Heidelberg', 45–63 in *ZUMA Nachrichten* 17, 1993.

Latour, Bruno 'Why Has Critique Run out of Steam? From Matters of Fact to Matters of Concern', *Critical Inquiry* 30(2): 225–48, 2004.

de Lauretis, Teresa, 'The Technology of Gender', in Teresa de Lauretis, *Technologies of Gender Essays on Theory, Film, and Fiction*, Bloomington: Indiana University Press, 1987.

Lembke, Ulrike, 'Weibliche Verletzbarkeit, orientalisierter Sexismus und die Egalität des Konsums: gender-race-class als verschränkte Herrschafts strukturen im öffentlichen Raum', 30–57 in *Bulletin – Texte* (43), Zentrum für transdisziplinäre Geschlechterstudien, HU Berlin, 2017.

Lenz, Ilse, ed., *Die Neue Frauenbewegung in Deutschland: Abschied vom kleinen Unterschied: Eine Quellensammlung*, Wiesbaden: Springer, 2008.

Linton, Ralph, 'Nativistic Movements', *American Anthropologist* 45(2): 230–40, 1943.

Lorde, Audre, *A Burst of Light*, Ithaca/New York: Firebrand Books, 1988.

Lorde, Audre, 'The Master's Tools Will Never Dismantle the Master's House' [1979], 110–12 in *Sister Outsider*, California: Berkeley University Press, 2007.

Luhmann, Niklas, 'Paradigm Lost: On the Ethical Reflection of Morality: Speech on the Occasion of the Award of the Hegel Prize 1988', *Thesis Eleven*, 29(1): 82–94, 1991.

Luhmann, Niklas, 'The Sociology of the Moral and Ethics', *International Sociology* 11(1): 27–36, 1996.

Lutz, Helma, 'Rassismus und Sexismus, Unterschiede und Gemeinsamkeiten', in Andreas Foitzik et al., eds, »*Ein Herrenvolk von Untertanen*«. *Rassismus– Nationalismus – Sexismus*, Duisburg: DISS, 1992.

Maihofer, Andrea, 'Sara Ahmed: Kollektive Gefühle – Elemente des westlichen hegemonialen Gefühlsregimes', 253–72 in Angelika Baier, Christa Binswanger, Jana Häberlein, Yv Nay and Andrea Zimmermann, eds, *Affekt und Geschlecht: Eine einführende Anthologie*, Vienna: Böhlau, 2014.

Mayer, Stefanie, Itzok Šori and Birgit Sauer, 'Gendering "the People": Heteronormativity and "Ethnomasochism" in Populist Imaginary', 84–104 in Mara Ranieri, ed., *Populism, Media, and Education: Challenging Discrimination in Contemporary Digital Societies*, New York, 2016.

Mayreder, Rosa, *A Survey of the Woman Problem*, trans. Herman Scheffauer, London: Heinemann, 1913.

Mbembe, Achille, *Critique of Black Reason*, Durham, NC: Duke University Press, 2017.

Mbembe, Achille, *Out of the Dark Night: Essays on Decolonization*, New York: Columbia University Press, 2019.

McClintock, Anne, *Imperial Leather: Race, Gender, and Sexuality in the Colonial Context*, New York/London: Routledge, 1995.

McRobbie, Angela, 'Top Girls?: Young women and the post-feminist sexual contract', *Cultural Studies* 21(4–5): 718–37, 2007.

Mecheril, Paul, 'Flucht, Sex und Diskurse: Gastrede im Rahmen des Neujahrsempfang der Stadt Bremen', *Zeitschrift des*

Informations- und Dokumentationszentrums für Antirassismusarbeit in Nordrhein-Westfalen 22(1): 3–7, 2016.

Mercer, Kobena, *Welcome to the Jungle: New Positions in Black Cultural Studies*, New York/London: Routledge, 1994.

Merton, Robert, 'The Normative Structure of Science', 223–67 in Robert Merton, ed., *The Sociology of Science: Theoretical and Empirical Investigations*, Chicago: University of Chicago Press, 1973.

Messerschmidt, Astrid, 'Nach Köln – Zusammenhänge von Sexismus und Rassismus thematisieren', 159–72 in María do Mar Castro Varela and Paul Mecheril, eds, *Die Dämonisierung der Anderen: Rassismuskritik der Gegenwart*, Bielefeld: transcript, 2016.

Morrison, Toni, 'Home', 3–12 in Wahneema Lubiano, ed., *The House that Race Built: Original Essays by Toni Morrison, Angela Y. Davis, Cornel West, and Others on Black Americans and Politics in America Today*, New York: Vintage, 1997.

Mouffe, Chantal, *On the Political*, London/New York: Routledge, 2005.

Münkler, Herfried and Marina Münkler, *Die neuen Deutschen: Ein Land vor seiner Zukunft*, Berlin: Rowohlt, 2016.

Nachtwey, Oliver, *Germany's Hidden Crisis: Social Decline in the Heart of Europe*, trans. Loren Balhorn and David Fernbach, London: Verso, 2018.

Neckel, Sighard and Ferdinand Sutterlüty, 'Negative Klassifikationen: Konflikte um die symbolische Ordnung sozialer Ungleichheit', 409–28 in Wilhelm Heitmeyer and Peter Imbusch, eds, *Integrationspotenziale einer modernen Gesellschaft: Analysen zu gesellschaftlicher Integration und Desintegration*, Wiesbaden: Suhrkamp 2005.

Nietzsche, Friedrich, *The Gay Science*, trans. Walter Kauffman, London: Penguin, 1974.

Pratt, Nicola, 'Weaponising feminism for the "war on terror" versus employing strategic silence', *Critical Studies on Terrorism* 6: 327–33, 2013.

Puar, Jasbir, *Terrorist Assemblages: Homonationalism in Queer Times*, Durham, NC: Duke University Press, 2007.

Rancière, Jacques, *The Politics of Aesthetics: The Distribution of the Sensible*, New York: Continuum, 2005.

Ranieri, Mara, ed., *Populism, Media, and Education: Challenging Discrimination in Contemporary Digital Societies*, New York: Routledge, 2016.

Reuter, Julia, *Ordnungen des Anderen: Zum Problem des Eigenen in der Soziologie des Fremden*, Bielefeld: transcript, 2002.

Rich, Adrienne, *Blood, Bread and Poetry: Selected Prose 1979–1985*, London: Norton, 1986.

Riley, Denise, *Am I That Name? Feminism and the Category of 'Women' in History*, London: Palgrave, 1988.

Rommelspacher, Birgit, *Anerkennung und Ausgrenzung: Deutschland als multikulturelle Gesellschaft*, Frankfurt: campus, 2002.

Rommelspacher, Birgit, *Dominanzkultur: Texte zu Fremdheit und Macht*, Berlin: Orlanda Frauenverlag, 1995.

Rommelspacher, Birgit, 'Sexismus und Rassismus im Bild der "Anderen"', 49–64 in Annemarie Hürlimann, Martin Roth and Klaus Vogel, eds, *Fremdkörper – Fremde Körper: Von unvermeidlichen Kontakten und widerstreitenden Gefühlen*, Ostfildern: restlos, 1999.

Rubin, Gayle, 'The Traffic in Women: Notes on the "Political Economy" of Sex', 157–210 in Rayna Reiter, ed., *Toward an Anthropology of Women*, New York: Monthly Review Press, 1975.

Said, Edward, *Culture and Imperialism*, New York: Knopf, 1993.

Sarrazin, Thilo, *Deutschland schafft sich ab: Wie wir unser Land aufs Spielsetzen*, München: Deutsche Verlags-Anstalt, 2010.

Sauer, Birgit, 'Transformationen von öffentlich und privat: Eine gesellschaftsund affekttheoretische Perspektive auf Geschlechterdemokratie', 12–29 in *Bulletin – Texte 43*, Berlin: Zentrum für transdisziplinäre Geschlechterstudien HU Berlin, 2017.

Scharff, Christina, 'The New German Feminisms: Of Wetlands and Alpha-Girls', 265–78 in Rosalind Gill and Christina Scharff, eds,

New Femininities: Postmodernism, Neoliberalism and Subjectivity, London: Palgrave Macmillan, 2011.

Scheer, Monique, ed., *Bindestrich-Deutsche? Mehrfachzugehörigkeit und Beheimatungspraktiken im Alltag*, Tübingen: Tübinger Vereinig, 2014.

Schiffauer, Werner, Anne Eiler and Marlene Rudloff, eds, *So schaffen wir das – eine Zivilgesellschaft im Aufbruch: 90 wegweisende Projekte mit Geflüchteten*, Bielefeld: transcript, 2017.

Schröter, Susanne, 'Gewaltlegitimierende Gendernormen brechen', *UniReport*, Johann Wolfgang Goethe-Universität, 2(2).

Schwarzer, Alice, ed., *Der Schock: Die Silvesternacht von Köln*, Köln: Rowohlt, 2016.

Schwarzer, Alice, ed., *Sexualität – Ein EMMA-Buch*, Köln: Rowohlt, 1982.

Scott, Joan, 'After History?' in Joan Scott and Debra Keates, eds, *Schools of Thought: Twenty-Five Years of Interpretive Social Science*, Princeton: Princeton University Press, 2001.

Searle, John, *The Construction of Social Reality*, New York: The Free Press, 1995.

Shooman, Yasemin, 'Einblick gewähren in die Welt der Muslime: "Authentische Stimmen" und "Kronzeugenschaft" in antimuslimischen Diskursen', 47–58 in Iman Attia, Swantje Köbsell and Nivedita Prasad, eds, *Dominanzkultur Reloaded: Neue Texte zu gesellschaftlichen Machtverhältnissen und ihren Wechselwirkungen*, Bielefeld: transcript, 2015.

Sontag, Susan, *Regarding the Pain of Others*, New York: Farrar, Straus and Giroux, 2003.

Spivak, Gayatri Chakravorty, *Can the Subaltern Speak?*, Basingstoke: Macmillan, 1988.

Spivak, Gayatri Chakravorty, 'Displacement and the Discourse of Woman', 169–96 in Mark Krupnick, ed., *Displacement: Derrida and After*, Bloomington: Indiana University Press, 1983.

Spivak, Gayatri Chakravorty, *The Post-Colonial Critic: Interviews, Strategies, Dialogues*, New York/London: Routledge, 1990.

Stokowski, Margarete, *Untenrum frei*, Reinbek: Rowohlt, 2016.

Stoler, Ann, *Race and the Education of Desire*, Durham, NC: Duke University Press, 1995.

Streeck, Wolfgang, *Buying Time: The Delayed Crisis of Democratic Capitalism*, trans. Patrick Camiller and David Fernbach, London: Verso, 2014.

Thiessen, Barbara, 'Gender Trouble evangelisch: Analyse und Standortbestimmung', 149–68 in Hark and Villa, eds, *Antigenderismus*, 2015.

Thürmer-Rohr, Christina, 'Abscheu vor dem Paradies', 21–37 in *Vagabundinnen*, Berlin, 1987.

Thürmer-Rohr, Christina, 'Achtlose Ohren: Zur Politisierung des Zuhörens', 111–29 in *Narrenfreiheit: Essays*, Berlin, 1994.

Thürmer-Rohr, Christina, 'Eine »Welt in Scherben«? Gender, Nation und Pluralität', unpublished manuscript of a speech, Berlin, 2017.

Thürmer-Rohr, Christina, 'Feminisierung der Gesellschaft – Weiblichkeit als Putz – und Entseuchungsmittel', 106–22 in *Vagabundinnen*, Berlin, 1987.

Toprak, Ahmet, *'Unsere Ehre ist uns heilig': Muslimische Familien in Deutschland*, Freiburg: Herder, 2012.

Treibel, Annette, *Integriert Euch! Neue Perspektiven für die Deutschen*, Frankfurt/New York: campus, 2015.

Tunç, Michael, 'Männlichkeiten und (Flucht-)Migrationserfahrungen: Kritik und Emanzipation', *IDA-NRW* 1: 15–19, 2016.

Villa, Paula-Irene, 'Anerkennung und Verwundbarkeit: Das Social Flesh der Gegenwart', in Ilse Lenz et al., eds, *Geschlecht im Flexibilisierten Kapitalismus*, Wiesbaden: Springer, 2017.

Villa, Paula-Irene, 'Habe den Mut, Dich Deines Körpers zu bedienen! Thesen zur Körperarbeit in der Gegenwart zwischen Selbstermächtigung und Selbstunterwerfung', 245–72 in Paula-Irene Villa, ed., *Schön Normal: Manipulationen am Körper als Technologien des Selbst*, Bielefeld: transcript, 2008.

Villa, Paula-Irene, 'Pornofeminismus? Soziologische Überlegungen zur Fleischbeschau im Pop', 229–48 in Villa et al., eds, *Banale Kämpfe? Perspektiven auf Populärkultur und Geschlecht*, Wiesbaden: Springer, 2012.

Voltaire, *Treatise on Tolerance and other Writings*, trans. Brian Masters, ed. Simon Harvey, Cambridge: Cambridge University Press, 2000.

Wagner, Peter, *A Sociology of Modernity: Liberty and Discipline*, London: Routledge, 1993.

Waldenfels, Bernhard, *Order in the Twilight*, trans. David Parent, Athens, OH: Swallow Press, 1996.

Walgenbach, Katharina, *Die weiße Frau als Trägerin deutscher Kultur: Koloniale Diskurse über Geschlecht, 'Rasse' und Klasse im Kaiserreich*, Frankfurt: campus, 2005.

Weber, Max, *The Protestant Ethic and the Spirit of Capitalism*, trans. Talcott Parsons, London: Routedge, 2005 [1930].

Wekker, Gloria, *White Innocence: Paradoxes of Colonialism and Race*, Durham, NC: Duke University Press, 2016.

Wenk, Silke, *Versteinerte Weiblichkeit – Allegorien in der Skulptur der Moderne* [Petrified Femininity – Allegories in Modern Sculpture], Köln: Böhlau Verlag, 1996.

Wertschulte, Christian, 'Nach Köln ist wie vor Köln', *Aus Politik und Zeitgeschichte*, 67(1–3): 10–17, 2016.

Wieviorka, Michel, 'The Making of Differences', *International Sociology* 19(3): 281–97, 2004.

Williams, John Thomas Mitchell, *What Do Pictures Want? The Lives and Loves of Images*, Chicago: University of Chicago Press, 2005.

Wodak, Ruth, *The Politics of Fear: What Right-Wing Populist Discourses Mean*, London: Sage, 2016.

Wodak, Ruth, Majid KhosraviNik and Brigitte Mral, eds, *Right-Wing Populism in Europe: Politics and Discourse*, London: Bloomsbury, 2013.

Wodak, Ruth, Teun A. Van Dijk, Ineke Van der Valk, Martin Reisigl, and Jessica Ter Wal, eds, *Racism at the Top: Parliamentary Discourses on Ethnic Issues in Six European States*, Klagenfurt/Celovec: Drava, 2000.

Woolf, Virginia, *A Room of One's Own*, San Diego: Harcourt Brace Jovanovich, 1989 [1957].

Yurdakul, Gökce, 'Governance Feminism und Rassismus: Wie führende Vertreterinnen von Immigranten die antimuslimische Diskussion in Westeuropa und Nordamerika befördern', 111–27 in Gökce Yurdakul and Michal Bodemann, eds, *Staatsbürgerschaft, Migration und Minderheiten*, Münster: Springer, 2010.

Yuval-Davis, Nira, 'Nationalist Projects and Gender Relations', *Nar: umjet* 40(1): 9–36, 2003.

Yuval-Davis, Nira, 'Gender and Nation', *Ethnic and Racial Studies* 16(4): 621–32, 1993.

Zia, Afiya Shehrbano, 'A response to Nicola Pratt's call for "strategic silence"', *Critical Studies on Terrorism* 6(2): 332–33, 2013.

Notes

NOTES TO PREFACE TO THE ENGLISH EDITION

1 'Germany Shocked by Cologne New Year Gang Assaults on Women', BBC News, 5 January 2016, bbc.com.

2 'Germany on the Brink', *New York Times*, 9 January 2016, nytimes. com.

3 Stefan Aust et al., 'Die Nacht, die alles verändert' ['The night that changes everything'], *Welt am Sonntag*, 10 January 2016.

4 Kobena Mercer, 'Introduction', in Stuart Hall, *The Fateful Triangle: Race, Ethnicity, Nation*, Cambridge, MA: Harvard University Press, 2017, 10.

5 Michel Foucault, *The History of Sexuality, Volume 1*, trans. Robert Hurley, London: Penguin, 1990 [1976], 103.

6 Ibid.

7 Circular 16/14450, 16th legislative session, final report of the Parliamentary Committee of Inquiry IV, landtag.nrw.de/portal/ WWW/dokumentenarchiv/Dokument/MMD16-14450.pdf.

8 See 'UN-women: Ending Violence Against Women – What We Do', unwomen.org, OECD, 2019, Violence Against Women Indicator. See also Alexa Yakubovich et al., 'Prospective risk and protective factors for intimate partner violence victimisation among women: a systematic review and meta-analysis', *The Lancet* 390, 13: 2017; Getachew Kassa and Amanuel Abajobir, 'Prevalence of Violence Against Women in Ethiopia: A Meta-Analysis', *Trauma, Violence and Abuse*, 2018; Michele Decker et al., 'Gender-Based Violence Against Adolescent and Young Adult Women in Low- and Middle-Income Countries', *Journal of Adolescent Health* 56, 2015, 188–96; and Sylvia Walby et al., *The Concept and Measurement of Violence Against Women and Men*, Bristol: Policy Press, 2019.

9 Alice Schwarzer, in her lecture on 'Sexual violence and power among societies living in parallel' on 28 April 2019, in the Düsseldorf Schauspielhaus (Grand Theatre), vimeo.com/ 333390553. The North Rhine-Westphalia parliamentary

committee's final report refers to 'at least one thousand people': namely, 'predominantly male adolescents, adolescents and young adults' who could be identified, 'in outward appearance at least, as being of North African and Arab extraction'. (Circular 16/14450).

10 On this question, see: Anne Wiezorek, *Weil ein #Aufschrei nicht reicht: Für einen Feminismus von heute*, Frankfurt am Main, 2014.

11 See Paula-Irene Villa, 'Women, the Powerless Sex? #MeToo and Us', *Public History Weekly* 6:3, 2018.

12 According to the UNHCR, the total number of people fleeing violence, persecution, disaster and war (civil or otherwise) was 51.2 million in 2013; over 60 million in 2014; 65.3 million in 2015; 65.6 million in 2016; and 68.5 million in 2017. Those among them seeking refuge in Europe have represented just over 10 percent of these numbers – about 2.643 million people every year. In 2015, the number of people who entered the EU illegally was around 1.05 million people, compared to 230,000 in 2014. See the UNHCR report 'Forced Displacements' for the most up-to-date information, year by year: unhcr.org/figures-at-a-glance.html.

13 Navid Kermani, *Upheaval: The Refugee Trek through Europe*, London: Polity, 2017, 40.

14 'Foto eines toten Jungen wird zum Symbol der Flüchtlingskrise' ['Photo of a dead boy becomes a symbol of the refugee crisis'], *Die Zeit*, 3 September 2015, zeit.de.

15 'Mit Wucht durch den Wahrnehmungspanzer' ['Shattering our anti-shockability armour'], *Die Zeit*, 3 September 2015, zeit.de.

16 See, for example, Doris Akrap in *The Guardian*, 6 September 2015; or Katrin Bennhold in the *New York Times*, 23 September 2015.

17 'Gutmensch ist Unwort des Jahres' ['"Gutmensch" is the word of the year'] *Der Spiegel*, 2015, spiegel.de.

18 'Umgang mit Migration ist für Seehofer Mutter aller politischen Probleme' ['Dealing with migration is the mother of all political problems for Seehofer'], *Handelsblatt*, 6 September 2018, handelsblatt.com.

19 'Seehofer provoziert mit Äußerungen zu Flüchtlingen' ['Seehofer's remarks about refugees provoke indignation'], *rp-online*, 25 June 2015, rp-online.de.

20 'Bundestag stimmt Reform von Staatsangehörigkeitsrecht zu' ['Bundestag agrees to reform of citizenship law'], *Die Zeit*, 27 June 2019, zeit.de.

21 See, for example, Aladin El-Mafaalani, *Das Integrationsparadox: Warum mehr Integration zu mehr Konflikten führt*, Kiepenheuer & Witsch, 2018; Fatma Aydemir und Hengameh Yaghoobifarah, eds, *Eure Heimat ist unser Alptraum*, Berlin: Ullstein, 2019; Max Czollek, *Desintegriert Euch*, Carl Hanser Verlag, 2018; and Ferda Ataman, *Hört auf zu fragen: Ich bin von hier*, Frankfurt-am-Main: Fischer, 2019.

22 'National Socialist Underground', en.wikipedia.org.

23 'Hoyerswerda Riots', en.wikipedia.org.

24 'Rostock – Lichtenhagen Riots', en.wikipedia.org.

25 'Mordanschlag von Mölln', de.wikipedia.org.

26 '1993 Solingen Arson Attack', en.wikipedia.org.

27 'Marwa El Sherbini', de.wikipedia.org.

28 Maurice Blanchot, *The Writing of the Disaster*, trans. Ann Smock, Lincoln: University of Nebraska Press, 1986, 1.

NOTES TO PREFACE: OTHER AND RULE (AN ESSAY)

1 Joan Scott, 'After History?', in Joan Scott and Debra Keates, eds, *Schools of Thought: Twenty-Five Years of Interpretive Social Science*, Princeton: Princeton University Press, 2001, 91.

2 As it is used (unofficially) by the police in Germany, the word 'Nafri' represents a shortening of 'Nordafrikanische Intensivtäter', that is to say, 'multiple offender of North African descent'. The civic controversy over its use kicked off on 4 January 2016, when many, having learned of it for the first time (for instance, the blogger Nadia Shehadeh – see: shehadistan.com), rightly denounced it as discriminatory and racist.

3 Ernest Laclau and Chantal Mouffe, *Hegemony and Socialist Strategy: Towards a Radical Democratic Politics*, London: Verso, 1985, 128.

4 'Was geschah wirklich?' ['What REALLY happened?'], *ZEIT* 27, 28 June 2016, zeit.de.

5 That a signifier – a referent – be 'empty' at the same time as it overflows with meaning is, strangely enough, nothing special. For Jacques Derrida, for instance, that contradiction is actually the normal condition of meaning-making, for meaning arises in his view through a movement of deferral or postponement that is tightly linked to the referential *context* of every conceptual referent. It must be said (departing from Derrida), however, that all

references are not equally effective. See Jacques Derrida, *Writing and Difference*, trans. Alan Bass, Chicago: University of Chicago Press, 1978.

6 Laclau and Mouffe, 1985, 139.

7 Scott, 1997, 14.

8 Hannah Arendt, *Thinking Without a Banister: Essays in Understanding, 1953–1975*, London: Schocken, 2018.

9 Naturally, we have not entirely renounced, here, the usual protocols of scientific reference and academic citation; far from it. However, in our use of these, we strive to be deliberately economical and selective. We do not pretend to represent a comprehensive debate or sum up the state of current research. We have striven to quote whatever we are referring to directly, as well as quoting, wherever possible, those voices that have hitherto been most marginalised in the debates.

10 On the overlaps and differences between racism and sexism, see Ina Kerner, *Differenzen und Macht: Zur Anatomie von Rassismus und Sexismus*, Frankfurt: Campus, 2009.

11 Rogers Brubaker. *Trans: Gender and Race in an Age of Unsettled Identities*, Princeton: Princeton University Press, 2016.

12 We are loosely referencing, here, sociologist Norbert Elias's understanding of figuration as a dynamic social network of interdependent individuals. Norbert Elias, *The Civilizing Process: Sociogenetic and Psychogenetic Investigations*, Oxford: Blackwell, 1994 [1939].

13 Edward Said, *Culture and Imperialism*, New York: Knopf, 1993, 11.

14 Max Weber, *The Protestant Ethic and the Spirit of Capitalism*, trans. Talcott Parsons, London: Routledge, 2005 [1930], 123.

NOTES TO CHAPTER ONE

1 Christina Thürmer-Rohr, 'Abscheu vor dem Paradies' ['Revulsion for Paradise'], 21–37 in *Vagabundinnen: Feministische Essays* [*Vagabond: Feminist Essays*], Berlin: Orlanda Frauenverlag, 1987, 29. Christina Thürmer-Rohr, *Vagabonding: Feminist Thinking Cut Loose*, trans. Lise Weil, Boston: Beacon Press, 1991.

2 Nelson Goodman, *Ways of Worldmaking*, London: Hackett, 1978, 71.

3 Ibid., 111–12.

4 Ibid., 91.

5 Ibid., 94.

6 Friedrich Nietzsche, *The Gay Science*, trans. Walter Kauffman, London: Penguin, 1974, 122.

7 Pierre Bourdieu, 'Language and Symbolic power, an English translation of "Ce que parler veut dire"', trans. Gino Raymond and Matthew Adamson, 32–159 in John Thompson, ed., *Language and Symbolic Power and Other Essays by Pierre Bourdieu*, Cambridge: Polity, 1993; Judith Butler, *Excitable Speech: A Politics of the Performative*, London: Routledge, 1997; Judith Butler, 'Performativity's Social Magic', 113–28 in Richard Shusterman, ed., *Bourdieu: A Critical Reader*, Oxford: Blackwell, 1999.

8 John Searle, *The Construction of Social Reality*, New York: The Free Press, 1995.

9 Bernhard Waldenfels, *Order in the Twilight*, trans. David Parent, Athens, OH: Swallow Press, 1996. On modernity and contingency, see also Sabine Hark, 'Deviant Subjects: Normalization and Subject Formation' [Deviante Subjekte – Normalisierung und Subjektformierung], 219–42 in Michael Corsten and Michael Kauppert, eds, *Der Mensch – nach Rücksprache mit der Soziologie*, Frankfurt/New York: Campus, 2013.

10 Robert Merton, 'The Normative Structure of Science', 223–67 in Robert Merton, ed., *The Sociology of Science: Theoretical and Empirical Investigations*, Chicago: University of Chicago Press, 1973.

11 Jürgen Habermas, 'The New Obscurity: The Crisis of the Welfare State and the Exhaustion of Utopian Energies', trans. Phillip Jacobs, *Philosophy and Social Criticism* 11, 1986, 1–18.

12 Stuart Hall, 'The Spectacle of the "Other"', 225–39 in Stuart Hall, ed., *Representation: Cultural Representations and Signifying Practices*, London: Thousand Oaks, 1997, 232.

13 Stuart Hall, 'The West and the Rest: Discourse and Power', 184–227 in Stuart Hall et al., eds, *Modernity: An Introduction to Modern Societies*, Cambridge, MA: Blackwell, 1996.

14 Alex Demirović, *Der nonkonformistische Intellektuelle: die Entwicklung der Kritischen Theorie zur Frankfurter Schule* ['The Nonconformist Critical Intellectual'], Frankfurt am Main: Suhrkamp, 1999, 39.

15 For a historical example of how sexual politics became an apparatus of racist truth production, as a kind of mirror image of Cologne, see Rebekka Habermas's monograph on a case of sexual violence

perpetrated by a German colonial official on a Togolese woman: *Skandal in Togo: Ein Kapitel deutscher Kolonialherrschaft*, Frankfurt am Main: S Fischer, 2016.

16 One example of this is the proposal put forward by the Berlin CDU member Kai Wegner for a 'gender' or women's quota pertaining to Germany's reception of refugees: 'Warum eine Geschlechterquote bei der Einreise von Flüchtlingen sinnvoll ist', kai-wegner.de.

17 'Wir sind nicht Burka', *Frankfurter Allgemeine Zeitung*, 30 April 2017.

18 Samuel Huntington, *The Clash of Civilizations and the Remaking of World Order*, 21st c. ed., New York: Simon and Schuster, 2011.

19 Michel Foucault, *'Discourse and Truth' and 'Parresia'*, Chicago: University of Chicago Press, 2019.

20 Gayatri Chakravorty Spivak, 'Scattered Speculations on the Question of Culture Studies', in *Outside in the Teaching Machine*, London: Routledge, 1993, 281.

21 Teresa de Lauretis, 'The Technology of Gender' in Teresa de Lauretis, *Technologies of Gender Essays on Theory, Film, and Fiction*, Bloomington: Indiana University Press, 1987, 25.

22 Gayatri Chakravorty Spivak, 'Displacement and the Discourse of Woman,' 169–96 in Mark Krupnick, ed., *Displacement: Derrida and After*, Bloomington: Indiana University Press, 1983, 184.

23 Denise Riley, *Am I That Name? Feminism and the Category of 'Women' in History*, London: Palgrave, 1988.

24 bell hooks, *Ain't I a Woman?: Black Women and Feminism*, New York: South End Press, 1981. See also: Paula-Irene Villa, 'Anerkennung und Verwundbarkeit: Das Social Flesh der Gegenwart', in Ilse Lenz et al., eds, *Geschlecht im flexibilisierten Kapitalismus*, Wiesbaden: Springer, 2017.

25 Judith Butler, *Bodies That Matter: On the Discursive Limits of Sex*, London: Routledge, 1993, 117.

26 Ibid.

27 Ibid.

28 Bruno Latour, 'Why Has Critique Run out of Steam? From Matters of Fact to Matters of Concern', *Critical Inquiry* 30(2): 2004, 225–48.

29 Chimamanda Ngozi Adichie, 'Now Is the Time to Talk About What We Are Actually Talking About', *New Yorker*, 2 December 2016, newyorker.com.

30 Ian Hacking, 'Making Up People', in T. L. Heller, M. Sosna and D. E.

Wellbery, eds, *Reconstructing Individualism*, Stanford, CA: Stanford University Press, 1985.

31 Sighard Neckel and Ferdinand Sutterlüty, 'Negative Klassifikationen: Konflikte um die symbolische Ordnung sozialer Ungleichheit', 409–28 in Wilhelm Heitmeyer and Peter Imbusch, eds, *Integrationspotenziale einer modernen Gesellschaft: Analysen zu gesellschaftlicher Integration und Desintegration*, Wiesbaden: Suhrkamp, 2005, 413.

32 The fact that many Germans are wont to speak quite casually of so-called Hartz IV populations, for example, illustrates how a legal manoeuvre can directly result in widespread social adoption and essentialisation of a category. The reform known as Hartz IV was a 2005 reform to the German welfare system, subsuming the provision of social security as a whole into the unemployment benefit system.

33 Regina Becker-Schmidt, '"Class", "gender", "ethnicity", "race": Logiken der Differenzsetzung, Verschränkung von Ungleichheitslagen und gesellschaftliche Strukturierun', 56–83 in Cornelia Klinger, Gudrun-Axeli Knapp and Birgit Sauer, eds, *Achsen der Ungleichheit: Zum Verhältnis von Klasse, Geschlecht und Ethnizität*, Frankfurt am Main/ New York, 2007, 60. On the reification of social inequalities via scientific classification and social categorisation, see also Sabine Hark, '"Überflüssig": Negative Klassifikationen – Elemente symbolischer Delegitimierung im soziologischen Diskurs', 151–62 in the same volume.

34 Donna Haraway, *Simians, Cyborgs, and Women: The Reinvention of Nature*, London: Free Association Books, 1991.

35 Donna Haraway, 'Situated Knowledges: The Science Question in Feminism and the Privilege of Partial Perspective', *Feminist Studies* 14(3): 1988, 575–99.

36 Paula-Irene Villa, 'Eure Gefühle sind mir schnuppe' ['I don't give a damn about your feelings'], *Zeit* (online), 10 February 2017, zeit.de.

37 Donna Haraway, 'Situated Knowledges', 584.

38 Ibid., 579.

39 Achille Mbembe, *Out of the Dark Night: Essays on Decolonization*, New York: Columbia University Press, 2019.

40 Theodor Adorno, *Negative Dialectics*, New York: Continuum, 2007. On dissident practices of knowledge production, see also: Sabine Hark, *Dissidente Partizipation: Eine Diskursgeschichte des*

Feminismus [*Dissident Participation: A Discursive History of Feminism*], Frankfurt: Suhrkamp, 2005.

41 Judith Butler, 'Can one lead a good life in a bad life?', Adorno Prize Lecture, *Radical Philosophy* 176 (Nov/Dec): 2012, 9.

42 Sandra Harding, *Sciences from Below: Feminisms, Postcolonialities, and Modernities*, Durham: Duke University Press, 2008.

43 On 'Household Air Pollution', see the World Health Organization's dedicated page: who.int/indoorair/en/. See also: Sabine Hark, 'Tödliches Kochen', *faz.net*, 1 April 2015, blogs.faz.net.

44 Sabine Hark und Ines Kappert, 'Die Freundschaft zur Welt nicht verlernen – Ein Gespräch mit Christina Thürmer-Rohr' ['"Don't Unlearn How to be Friends with the World": A Conversation with Christina Thürmer-Rohr'], 27–38 in Gunda Werner and Sabine Hark, eds, *Die Freundschaft zur Welt nicht verlernen: Texte für Christina Thürmer-Rohr*, Berlin, 2016.

45 Hannah Arendt, 'On Humanity in Dark Times: Thoughts about Lessing', trans. Clara and Richard Winston, in *Men in Dark Times*, New York: Harcourt Brace, 1993, 3–31.

46 Georg Franck, 'The scientific economy of attention: a novel approach to the collective rationality of science', *Scientometrics* 55(1), 2002, 3–26.

47 Pierre Bourdieu, *Distinction: A Social Critique of the Judgement of Taste*, London: Routledge, 1986.

48 Michel Foucault, *Power/Knowledge: Selected Interviews and Other Writings, 1972–1977*, ed./trans. Colin Gordon, New York: Pantheon.

49 For examples of this, see the arguments of Mark Lilla, 'The End of Identity Liberalism', *New York Times*, 10 November 2016; or Adam Soboczynski, 'Vielfalt von oben?', *Die Zeit*, 26 November 2016, zeit. de.

50 Parvin Sadigh, 'Wahlkampf mit Burka' ['Campaigning with the burka'], *Zeit Online*, 22 February 2017, zeit.de. See also Joseph Micallef, 'Bikinis Not Burkas: The German Election Earthquake', *Huffington Post*, 26 September 2017, huffingtonpost.com.

51 The German political magazine *Monitor* has published a report on how migration, asylum-seeking, Islam, terrorism and violence were, throughout 2016, extensively linked together in talk shows disseminated on channels operated by the public broadcasters ARD and ZDF: wdr.de/tv/applications/daserste/monitor/pdf/2017/manuskript -talkshows.pdf.

52 On the media's inability to call the recent Nazi murders either 'murders' or 'Nazi', see Fabian Virchow, Tanja Thomas, and Elke Grittmann, 'Das "Unwort" erklärt die "Untat": Die Berichterstattung über die NSU-Morde – eine Medienkritik' ['A non-word to explain a non-deed: a critique of media coverage of the NSU murders'], Otto Brenner-Stiftung, 2015, otto-brenner-shop.de.

53 On the erasure of the political in discourses about German right-wing violence, see Stefan Dierbach, *Jung – rechts – unpolitisch? Die Ausblendung des Politischen im Diskurs über Rechte Gewalt* ['Young, right-wing, apolitical?: On the erasure of the political in discourses about right-wing violence'], Bielefeld: transcript, 2010.

54 On this phenomenon of Germans feeling shut out, disenfranchised and excluded from politics, see Heinz Bude, *Die Ausgeschlossenen: Das Ende vom Traum einer gerechten Gesellschaft* ['Shut out: the end of the dream of a just society'], Hamburg: Perlentaucher, 2008; and Herfried Münkler and Marina Münkler, *Die neuen Deutschen: Ein Land vor seiner Zukunft* ['The new Germans: a country before its own future'], Berlin: Rowohlt, 2016.

55 Oliver Nachtwey, *Germany's Hidden Crisis: Social Decline in the Heart of Europe*, trans. Loren Balhorn and David Fernbach, London: Verso, 2018, 1.

56 Albert Hirschman, 'Morality and the Social Sciences', in *The Essential Hirschman*, ed. Jeremy Adelman, Princeton: Princeton University Press, 2013, 342.

57 Christina Thürmer-Rohr, 'Feminisierung der Gesellschaft – Weiblichkeit als Putz- und Entseuchungsmittel' ['The feminisation of society: femininity as means of cleansing and decontamination'], 106–22 in Christina Thürmer-Rohr, *Vagabundinnen*.

58 Ibid., 118.

59 Hannah Arendt, *The Life of the Mind, Volume 1: Thinking*, London: Secker and Warburg, 1978, 19. See also: 'Freedom and Politics' in Hannah Arendt, *Between Past and Future*, New York: Viking Press, 1961.

60 Christina Thürmer-Rohr, 'Eine "Welt in Scherben"? Gender, Nation und Pluralität' ['A "world in smithereens"? Gender, nation and plurality'], unpublished manuscript, 2017. (Sophie Lewis's translation.)

61 Birgit Rommelspacher, *Dominanzkultur: Texte zu Fremdheit und Macht*, Berlin: Orlanda, 1995.

62 Ibid., 22.

63 Michel Wieviorka, 'The Making of Differences', *International Sociology* 19:3, 2004, 281–97. See also (in the original French): Michel Wieviorka, *La différence*, Paris: Balland, 2001.

64 Rommelspacher, 1995.

65 Ibid., 22.

66 Ibid.

67 Beate Krais and Gunter Gebauer, *Habitus*, Bielefeld: transcript Verlag, 2002, 10. (Sophie Lewis's translation.)

68 Judith Butler, 'Merely Cultural', *Social Text* 52/53, 1997, 265–77.

69 Wieviorka, 'The Making of Differences'.

70 Avtar Brah, *Cartographies of Diaspora: Contesting Identities*, London /New York: Routledge, 1996, 110.

71 Stuart Hall and Lawrence Grossberg, 'On Postmodernism and Articulation: An Interview with Stuart Hall', *Journal of Communication Inquiry*, 10(2): 45–60.

72 Fredric Jameson, 'On Cultural Studies', *Social Text* 34, 1993, 17–52.

NOTES TO CHAPTER TWO

1 Toni Morrison, 'Home', 3–12 in Wahneema Lubiano, ed., *The House that Race Built: Original Essays by Toni Morrison, Angela Y. Davis, Cornel West, and Others on Black Americans and Politics in America Today*, New York: Vintage, 1997.

2 Stefan Aust et al., 'Die Nacht, die alles verändert' [The night that changes everything], *Welt am Sonntag*, 10 January 2016, welt.de.

3 On the significance of 'law and order' discourse within 'authoritarian populisms', see Stuart Hall, 'Popular-democratic vs authoritarian populism: two ways of taking democracy seriously', 157–85 in Alan Hunt, ed., *Marxism and Democracy*, London: Lawrence and Wishart, 1980.

4 Stefan Aust et al., 'Die Nacht, die alles verändert'.

5 Birgit Kelle, 'Eskalation mit Ansage' ['An escalation, and a threat'], wirtschaftswunder.at. The same text appeared shortly afterwards in the German magazine *Focus* under the title '"Ihr könnt mir nichts": Übergriffe von Köln sind dreiste Ansage gegen den Rechtsstaat' ['"You can't help me": The Cologne attacks are bold assaults on the rule of law'], *Focus*, 9 January 2016, focus.de.

6 Ibid.

7 Harald Martenstein, 'Es geht um den Islam, nicht um Flüchtlinge'
   ['This is about Islam, not refugees'], *Der Tagesspiegel*, 10 January
   2016, tagesspiegel.de.

8 Ibid.

9 Ibid.

10 Further examples can be found in Christian Werthschulte's essay
   '"Nach" Köln ist wie "vor" Köln' ['"After Cologne" is just like "before
   Cologne"'], *Aus Politik und Zeitgeschichte*, 67(1–3): 2017, 10–17.

11 We concern ourselves with this intervention and the dilemmas for
   feminism arising from it in Chapter 4.

12 Stuart Hall, 'Introduction', in Stuart Hall, ed., *Representation: Cultural
   Representations and Signifying Practices*, London: Sage, 1997.

13 Among the large number of publications attentive to this question
   of the other and othering, those we would particularly like to high-
   light are: María do Mar Castro Varela and Paul Mecheril, eds, *Die
   Dämonisierung der Anderen: Rassismuskritik der Gegenwart*,
   Bielefeld: transcript, 2016; Iman Attia, *Die 'westliche Kultur' und ihr
   Anderes: Zur Dekonstruktion von Orientalismus und antimuslimis-
   chem Rassismus*, Bielefeld: transcript, 2009; Maureen Maisha Eggers,
   Grada Kilomba, Peggy Piesche and Susan Arndt, eds, *Mythen,
   Masken und Subjekte: Kritische Weißseinsforschung in Deutschland*,
   Münster: Unrast, 2005; Julia Reuter, *Ordnungen des Anderen: Zum
   Problem des Eigenen in der Soziologie des Fremden*, Bielefeld: tran-
   script, 2002. For more recent contributions to research on racism,
   migration and borders, please see the journal *movements*, inaugurated in 2015.

14 Zygmunt Bauman, *Modernity and Ambivalence*, Ithaca, NY: Cornell
   University Press, 1991.

15 Claudia Honegger, *Die Ordnung der Geschlechter: Die Wissenschaften
   vom Menschen und das Weib*, Frankfurt: Suhrkamp, 1991.

16 Achille Mbembe, *Critique of Black Reason*, Durham, NC: Duke
   University Press, 2017, 55.

17 Ann Stoler, *Race and the Education of Desire*, Durham, NC: Duke
   University Press, 1995.

18 Political movements can be described as 'nativist' if they fight for the
   rights of a 'national' majority born in the same country, as defined in
   opposition to the claims of an alien minority and against immigration. The American sociologist Ralph Linton went further, defining
   nativism as any conscious, organized attempt by members of a

society to reproduce or continue select aspects of their culture. See: Ralph Linton, 'Nativistic Movements', *American Anthropologist* 45(2): 230–40, 1943.

19 On this, see Mara Ranieri, ed., *Populism, Media, and Education: Challenging Discrimination in Contemporary Digital Societies*, New York: Routledge, 2016; Ruth Wodak, Majid KhosraviNik and Brigitte Mral, eds, *Right-Wing Populism in Europe: Politics and Discourse*, London: Bloomsbury, 2013; Ruth Wodak, *The Politics of Fear: What Right-Wing Populist Discourses Mean*, London: Sage, 2016. For a critique of the Manichaeanism operating even within anti-racist discourse, see the dialogue between George Yancy and Paul Gilroy: 'What "Black Lives" Means in Britain', *New York Times*, 1 October 2015, opinionator.blogs.nytimes.com.

20 In his analysis of the emergence of authoritarian populism in England, Stuart Hall illustrates Manichaean constructions with reference to the British National Front slogan 'Against the Bosses, Against the Blacks'. Already in the 1970s, Hall identified the invocation of the 'nation', 'national culture' and 'our people' as the 'respectable' versions of a virulent racism. Stuart Hall, 'Popular-democratic vs authoritarian populism: two ways of taking democracy seriously', 157–85 in Alan Hunt, ed., *Marxism and Democracy*, London: Lawrence and Wishart, 1980.

21 Chantal Mouffe, *On the Political*, London/New York: Routledge, 2005, 77.

22 Zygmunt Bauman, 'Der neue Hass aufs Establishment und die Sehnsucht nach dem Feind', *Blätter für deutsche und internationale Politik* 2: 77–82, 2017, 81.

23 Zygmunt Bauman and Aleksandra Kania, 'That West meant to be declining', *Thesis Eleven*, 149(1): 91–99, 2018, 98.

24 Ibid.

25 Ruth Wodak, Teun A. Van Dijk, Ineke Van der Valk, Martin Reisigl, and Jessica Ter Wal, eds, *Racism at the Top: Parliamentary Discourses on Ethnic Issues in Six European States*, Klagenfurt/Celovec: Drava, 2000. See also: Nora Fritzsche, 'Antimuslimischer Rassismus im offiziellen Einwanderungsdiskurs', Working Paper 13, June 2016, Center for North African and Middle Eastern Politics, Freie Universität Berlin, polsoz.fu-berlin.de. For two examples from the early 2000s of a distinction drawn in favour of 'economically useful' immigrants and migrants that 'benefit us', see Kerstin Müller's op

-ed, 'We need more immigration', *Frankfurter Rundschau,* 14 March 2001, which argues for 'flexible quotas for regulating immigration according to pre-determined needs for certain skills and qualifications, or on the basis of concrete job openings'; and Günther Beckstein's contention that 'We must make sure that fewer foreigners come to Germany overall, but we must welcome *more* of the type that benefits us' (quoted in *Süddeutsche Zeitung,* 4 July 2000). An echo of this argument based on usefulness, efficiency and willingness to work is also to be found in the liberal-humanitarian plea for a 'non-ethnic' conceptualization of the nation advanced by Herfried Münkler and Marina Münkler: 'Germany is an open and meritocratic society that will have to become even more open and even more meritocratic in the coming years and decades if it wants to maintain its position within the world economy and its prosperity at home. German society relies on immigration and competes with other societies for the most skilled and capable individuals. The desire to attract and prioritize these hard-working, highly skilled people does not rule out welcoming those who are unlikely to belong in that category – people, that is, who can only be integrated into the German labour market with considerable effort – in emergency situations, on humanitarian grounds. Of course, our capacity to economically afford such humanitarian acts depends in turn on our prior success in competing for the most skilled and hard-working immigrants – to which end, the less an "ethnic" concept of the nation has served as an exclusionary filter, the better.' Herfried Münkler and Marina Münkler, *Die neuen Deutschen: Ein Land vor seiner Zukunft* ['The new Germans: a country before its own future'], Berlin: Rowohlt, 2016, 289.

26 Tomas Hammar uses the term 'denizen' to describe 'non-citizens with permanent residence', i.e., those who either cannot be naturalized – for example, because they are being denied dual nationality – or because the nation-states in which they reside simply will not recognize them as citizens. Tomas Hammar, *Democracy and the Nation State: Aliens, Denizens, and Citizens in a World of International Migration,* Avebury: Gower, 1990.

27 Wendy Brown, *Undoing the Demos: Neoliberalism's Stealth Revolution,* New York: Zone Books. See also: Wolfgang Streeck's *Buying Time: The Delayed Crisis of Democratic Capitalism,* trans. Camiller and Fernbach, London: Verso, 2017.

28 Peter Wagner, *A Sociology of Modernity: Liberty and Discipline*, Lonon: Routledge, 1993, 58.

29 The editorial collective of the journal *movements* has argued, for example, that while the expansion of naturalization in Germany has indeed 'turned many former "foreigners" into citizens with full political rights', this move has gone hand in hand with a 'restrictive paradigm of integration' that has not created the 'political, institutional and social preconditions' for that integration to actually take place (such as anti-discrimination measures in labour and housing markets, for example). See: Kijan Eshahangizi, Sabine Jess, Juliane Karakayali, Bernd Kasparek, Simona Pagan, Mayjias Rodatz and Vassilis Tsianos, 'Rassismus in der postmigrantischen Gesellschaft: Zur Einleitung', *movements: Journal für kritische Migrations- und Grenzregimeforschung* 2(1): 9–24, 2016.

30 Margarete Jäger, 'Ethnisierung von Sexismus im Einwanderungsdiskurs: Analyse einer Diskursverschränkung' ['Racializing Sexism in the Immigration Conversation: Analyzing a Discursive Entanglement'], 16 September 1999, diss-duisburg.de. A 'racist mode of argumentation, whereby the supposed lack of equality endured by women among immigrant populations serves somehow as a reason to exclude them, is everyday fare in the Federal Republic', wrote Jäger in 1993. Here, already, we see 'feminist arguments' underpinning racism. For more on this question and the related one of 'why Germans are so attached to the plight of immigrant women', see: Margarete Jäger, 'Feministische Argumente zur Untermauerung von Rassismus: Warum liegt Deutschen die Stellung der Einwanderinnen so am Herzen?', 248–61 in Christoph Butterwege and Siegfried Jäger, eds, *Rassismus in Europa*, Köln: Bund-Verlag, 1993.

31 Ibid.

32 Serhat Karakayali, 'Reflexiver Eurozentrismus' Zwischen diskursiver Kombinatorik und Latenz', 96–113 in Sebastian Friedrich, ed., *Rassismus in der Leistungsgesellschaft: Analysen und kritische Perspektiven zu den rassistischen Normalisierungsprozessen in der »Sarrazindebatte«*, Münster: Unrast, 2011.

33 Monique Scheer, ed., *Bindestrich-Deutsche? Mehrfachzugehörigkeit und Beheimatungspraktiken im Alltag* ['Hyphenated Germans? Plural citizenship and assimilation practices in everyday life'], Tübingen: Tübinger Vereinig, 2014.

34 Even soi-disant feminists like Alice Schwarzer participated in this
   racist turn. We go into detail on this in Chapter 4.

35 For an example, see: Claudius Seidl, 'Wo sind die echten Männer?'
   ['Where are all the *real* men?'], *Frankfurter Allgemeine Zeitung*, 1
   March 2016, faz.net.

36 On the sexualization of subjugated male populations in the colonial
   context, see Anne McClintock, *Imperial Leather: Race, Gender, and
   Sexuality in the Colonial Context*, New York/London: Routledge,
   1995. On the sexualization of race generally, see María do Mar
   Castro Varela and Paul Mecheril, eds, *Die Dämonisierung der
   Anderen: Rassismuskritik der Gegenwart*, Bielefeld: transcript, 2016.

37 See Ghassan Hage, 'Der unregierbare Muslim: Jenseits der
   Bipolarität von Multikulturalismus und Assimilation', 73–94 in
   Sabine Hess, Jana Binder and Johannes Moser, eds, *No integration?
   Kulturwissenschaftliche Beiträge zur Integrationsdebatte in Europa*,
   Bielefeld: transcript, 2009.

38 We explore the simultaneous infantilization and sexualization of the
   other further in Chapter 3.

39 Gabriele Dietze, 'Das Ereignis Köln' ['The Cologne Incident'],
   93–102 in *femina politica* 1, 2016. (Sophie Lewis's translation.)

40 Gabriele Dietze, 'Ethnosexismus: Sex-Mob-Narrative um die Kölner
   Silvesternacht' ['Ethnosexism: Sex-Mob Narratives around the New
   Year's Eve Events in Cologne'], *movements: Journal für kritische
   Migrations- und Grenzregimeforschung*, 2(1): 177–86, 2016. Dietze
   cites a particularly insidious example of this trope of a 'detoxified
   German masculinity' from the journalist Bernd Ulrich, writing in
   Zeit: 'Following on from two wars lost both militarily and morally,
   following years of anti-authoritarian and anti-patriarchal struggle,
   Germany has developed an immense capacity for detoxifying
   masculinity.' No one, for Ulrich, escapes this legacy of Germanness
   'in the long run'. Bernd Ulrich, 'Wer ist der arabische Mann?' ['Who
   is the Arab man?'], *Zeit Online*, 17 January 2016, zeit.de.

41 As Claudia Honegger demonstrates, the link between femaleness
   and the 'level of civilisation' of a culture or nation goes back at least
   as far as the writings of Johann Gottfried von Herder, the thinker
   who is commonly considered to be the inventor of the modern
   concept of culture. Honegger: 'For Herder, the theorist of culture's
   historicity, the intimate linkage between levels of cultural "development" and the status of women is key. All "uncultured nations" are,

according to Herder, characterized by a "contempt for women". In this view, it was the forward march of culture – progress – that freed women from "slavery" and rendered them equal to men via a process of "rational education".' Claudia Honegger, 'Weiblichkeit als Kulturform: Zur Codierung der Geschlechter in der Moderne', 197–210 in Sabine Hark, ed., *Dis/Kontinuitäten: Feministische Theorie*, Wiesbaden: Springer, 2007.

42 Stefanie Mayer, Itzok Šori and Birgit Sauer, 'Gendering "the People": Heteronormativity and "Ethnomasochism" in the Populist Imaginary', 84–104 in Mara Ranieri, ed., *Populism, Media, and Education*.

43 'Jahresrueckblick-vom-29-dezember-2016', 29 December 2016, beatrixvostorch.de. (Sophie Lewis's translation.)

44 Birgit Kelle, #Aufschrei 0.0 – 'Wenn die feministische Empörung ausbleibt' ['When feminist indignation fails'], djb.de.

45 ausnahmslos.org ('Ausnahmslos' means 'unexceptional', in the sense of 'unsurprising').

46 Pierre Bourdieu, *Masculine Domination*, Stanford: Stanford University Press, 2001.

47 On this point, see Astrid Messerschmidt, 'Nach Köln – Zusammenhänge von Sexismus und Rassismus thematisieren', 159–72 in María do Mar Castro Varela and Paul Mecheril, eds, *Die Dämonisierung der Anderen: Rassismuskritik der Gegenwart*, Bielefeld: transcript, 2016.

48 Susanne Schröter, 'Gewaltlegitimierende Gendernormen brechen', *UniReport*, Johann Wolfgang Goethe-Universität, 2(2). (Sophie Lewis's translation.)

49 On this, see Ricarda Drüeke's commentary for the Gunda Werner-Institut, part of Heinrich Böll-Stiftung, Richard Drüeke, 'Die TV-Berichterstattung in ARD und ZDF über die Silvesternacht 2015/16 in Köln', boell.de.

50 'Justizminister Maas hält Ausweisung der Täter für denkbar' ['The Justice Minister Considers Deporting the Perpetrators'], *Spiegel Online*, 7 January 2016, spiegel.de.

51 Nico Fried, 'Ein Wort zu viel' ['A Claim Too Far'], *Süddeutsche Zeitung*, 7 January 2016, sueddeutsche.de.

52 See Andrea Dernbach, 'Willkommen und Abschiebung für Flüchtlinge', *Der Tagesspiegel*, 25 February 2016, tagesspiegel.de. It is important to grasp that the interior minister Thomas de

Maizière's claim, in the autumn of 2016, that Cologne was a political 'turning point', has no basis whatsoever in fact. (See 'De Maizière calls Cologne's New Year's Eve "turning point"', *Spiegel Online*, 25 October 2016, spiegel.de). The so-called Asylum Packages I and II, like the so-called Integration Act of July 2016, very much represent a continuity in German immigration legislation from the 1990s on. With the one exception of the temporary suspension of the Dublin II Agreement in the summer of 2015, all changes in asylum legislation – since the reformulation of Germany's Basic Law Article 16a in 1993 – have made it more difficult to apply for asylum, rather than easier. In March 2017, the Federal Council rejected the proposed federal law whereby Morocco, Tunisia and Algeria would have been declared safe countries of origin.

53 See, for example, the following case study of gaps in the application of German sexual criminal law in its provision for adult victims: 'Was Ihnen widerfahren ist, ist in Deutschland nicht strafbar' ['What has happened to you is not punishable in Germany'], by Katja Grieger, Christina Clemm, Anita Eckhardt and Anna Hartmann on behalf of Women Against Violence, the Federal Association of Women's Counseling Centres and Shelters (Bundesverbandes der Frauenberatungsstellen und Frauennotrufe in Deutschland (bff e.V.) – Frauen gegen Gewalt), frauen-gegengewalt.de.

54 The defence attorney's report '"Immer wieder Köln?": Von Frauenrechten, Sexualität und Strafbarkeitslücken' ['"Again and again Cologne?" On women's rights, sexuality and criminal liability'], explains that the reform of §177 goes againt several established laws in several respects, notably: 'The reforms of §§177 nF, §184 i and §184 j StGB are highly questionable from a constitutional point of view, if not outright unconstitutional. The new regulations do not conform with the principle of certainty, the principle of equality, the principle of the rule of law and – because of the overregulation it mandates – the fundamental right to freedom.' strafverteidigertag.de.

55 Council of Europe Convention on the Protection of Children against Sexual Exploitation and Sexual Abuse, coe.int.

56 The Convention Against Violence Against Women came into force on 1 August 2014. See '(Gesetzlicher) Änderungsbedarf in Deutschland' ['A need for (legal) change in Germany'], the German Institute for Human Rights, 31 July 2014, institut-fuer-menschenrechte.de.

57 'Bundeskabinett – beschliesst – ratifi zierung – der – istanbul – konvention', bmfsfj.de.

58 'Schriftliche Stellungnahme', 28 January 2015, bundestag.de.

59 Tatjana Hörnle, 'Menschenrechtliche Verpflichtungen aus der Istanbul-Konvention: Ein Gutachten zur Reform des § 177 StGB', Deutsches Institut für Menschenrechte, institut-fuer-menschenrechte.de.

60 An overview of the actions taken by women's organisations on this issue can be found on the website of the bff: frauen-gegen-gewalt.de /Sexualstrafrecht-bundesweite-Aktionen.html.

61 Written statement by Christina Clemm and Barbara Wessel before the public hearing of the Committee on Legal Affairs and Consumer Protection of the German Bundestag, 28 January 2015, bundestag. de/blob/357220/275289b6b4ea7ccc32f2123164a22fdd/clemm- data.pdf.

62 Federal Ministry of Justice and Consumer Protection, bmjv.de/SharedDocs /Artikel/DE/2015/02202015_Stn_Reform_Sexualstrafrecht.html.

63 Draft Act Amending the Criminal Code: Implementation of European Provisions on Sexual Criminal Law (Ministerial Draft of the Federal Ministry of Justice and Consumer Protection), bmjv.de/SharedDocs/Gesetzgebungsverfahren/documents/ law-change-StGB-conversion-European-defaults-to-sexual- criminal.pdf.

64 As recently as 1997, over 130 members of the CDU/CSU party had voted against the punishability of marital rape, including Horst Seehofer, Erika Steinbach, Volker Kauder and Peter Ramsauer: dipbt.bundestag.de/doc/btp/13/13175.pdf#P.15798.   The legal scholar Ulrike Lembke has contextualized this in terms of the 'racist appropriation of feminist legal policies'; see Ulrike Lembke, 'Weibliche Verletzbarkeit, orientalisierter Sexismus und die Egalität des Konsums: gender-race-class als verschränkte Herrschafts struk- turen im öffentlichen Raum', *Bulletin – Texte* 43, 30–57, Zentrum für transdisziplinäre Geschlechterstudien, HU Berlin, 2017.

65 On this putative 'hospitality culture', see Werner Schiffauer, Anne Eiler and Marlene Rudloff, eds, *So schaffen wir das – eine Zivilgesellschaft im Aufbruch: 90 wegweisende Projekte mit Geflüchteten*, Bielefeld: transcript, 2017.

66 Achille Mbembe, *Critique of Black Reason*, Durham, NC: Duke University Press, 2017, 183.

67 Paul Mecheril, 'Flucht, Sex und Diskurse: Gastrede im Rahmen des Neujahrsempfang der Stadt Bremen', *Zeitschrift des Informations - und Dokumentationszentrums für Antirassismusarbeit in Nordrhein-Westfalen*, 22(1): 2016, 3–7. Gabriele Dietze was already speaking critically of 'Willkommenskultur' in the summer of 2015. See her blog post 'Deutsche Exzeptionalismen: Willkommenskultur und Austerität' ['German exceptionalisms: Willkommenskultur and austerity'], blog.feministische-studien.de. (Sophie Lewis's translation.)

68 In early March 2017, citing the book *The Driven Ones* (*Die Getriebenen*) by journalist Robin Alexander, *Die Welt* reported that, in autumn 2015, a government order to close the borders was issued, but neither the federal chancellor nor the Cabinet were willing to take responsibility for it, citing legal concerns – so it was never implemented. See 'Fast hätte Merkel die Grenze geschlossen' ['Merkel almost closed the border'], *Die Welt*, 5 March 2017, welt. de.

69 'Das tödlichste Jahr' ['The deadliest year'], *Zeit Online*, 31 May 2016, zeit.de.

70 Kijan Eshahangizi, Sabine Jess, Juliane Karakayali, Bernd Kasparek, Simona Pagan, Mayjias Rodatz and Vassilis Tsianos, 'Rassismus in der postmigrantischen Gesellschaft: Zur Einleitung', *movements: Journal für kritische Migrations- und Grenzregimeforschung* 2(1): 9–24, 2016, 17. (Sophie Lewis's translation.)

71 Antonio Gramsci, *Prison Notebooks*, volume 2, trans. Joseph Buttigieg, New York: Columbia University Press, 2011, 179.

72 Fromm uses the term 'social unconscious' to denote how 'each society determines which thoughts and feelings shall be permitted to arrive at the level of awareness and which have to remain unconscious'. Erich Fromm, *Beyond the Chains of Illusion: My Encounter with Marx and Freud*, London: Bloomsbury, 1962, 70.

73 By 'topos' we mean a linguistic commonplace, a stereotypical locution or preconceived image. For an overview of key topoi circulating within anti-Muslim racism, see: Iman Attia, *Die 'westliche Kultur' und ihr Anderes: Zur Dekonstruktion von Orientalismus und antimuslimischem Rassismus*, Bielefeld: transcript, 2009; and Yasemin Shooman, 'Einblick gewähren in die Welt der Muslime: "Authentische Stimmen" und "Kronzeugenschaft" in antimuslimischen Diskursen', 47–58, in Iman Attia, Swantje Köbsell and Nivedita Prasad, eds,

Dominanzkultur Reloaded: Neue Texte zu gesellschaftlichen Machtverhältnissen und ihren Wechselwirkungen, Bielefeld: transcript, 2015.

74 There were, of course, exceptions. See, for instance, the contribution of Armin Nassehi, who helpfully identified a dubious 'masculinization' of the debate following Cologne, especially among 'older men, for whom the events seem to have unleashed an irrepressible desire to indulge in ressentiments they would never, as good liberals, have entertained before (at least not in public).' Armin Nassehi, 'Die Ressentiments Der Alten Männer' ['The Old Men's Resentments'], *Die Welt*, 8 February 2016, welt.de.

75 Gabriele Dietze, 'Ethnosexismus: Sex-Mob-Narrative um die Kölner Silvesternacht' ['Ethnosexism: Sex-Mob Narratives around the New Year's Eve Events in Cologne'], *movements: Journal für kritische Migrations- und Grenzregimeforschung*, 2(1): 177–86, 2016, 177.

76 Jakob Augstein, 'Männer, Monster, Muslime' ['Men, Monsters, Muslims'], *Spiegel Online*, 2 November 2015, spiegel.de.

77 On this, see Ulrike Lembke, 'Weibliche Verletzbarkeit, orientalisierter Sexismus und die Egalität des Konsums: gender-race-class als verschränkte Herrschafts strukturen im öffentlichen Raum', 30–57 in *Bulletin – Texte* (43), Zentrum für transdisziplinäre Geschlechterstudien, HU Berlin, 2017; as well as the report of the European Union on Fundamental Rights, 'Violence against Women: An EU Survey', fra.europa.eu.

78 Fatima El-Tayeb, *Undeutsch: Die Konstruktion des Anderen in der postmigrantischen Gesellschaft*, Bielefeld: transcript, 2016, 34.

79 Stefanie Mayer, Itzok Šori and Birgit Sauer, 'Gendering "the People": Heteronormativity and "Ethnomasochism" in the Populist Imaginary', 84–104 in Mara Ranieri, ed., *Populism, Media, and Education*.

80 Brigitte Geiger advances a similar argument in her blog post 'Nach Köln: Ein Blick auf Entwicklungen und Kontexte feministischer Gewaltdebatten' ['After Cologne: A look at recent developments and contexts in feminist debates on violence'], blog.feministische-studien.de.

81 Carol Hagemann-White, 'Gewalt im Geschlechterverhältnis als Gegenstand sozialwissenschaftlicher Forschung und Theoriebildung: Rückblick, gegenwärtiger Stand, Ausblick', 29–52 in Regina-Maria Dackweiler, ed., *Gewalt-Verhältnisse*, Frankfurt: campus, 2000.

82 On this, see Anabel Wahba's smart and nuanced discussion '"Mein arabischer Vater": mit "dem" arabischen Mann und "seinen" Werten auseinander' ['"My Arab Father": on "the" Arab man and "his values"'], *Zeit Online*, 29 April 2016, zeit.de. See also: Ahmet Toprak, *'Unsere Ehre ist uns heilig': Muslimische Familien in Deutschland*, Freiburg: Herder, 2012.

83 Jost Müller-Neuhof, 'Frauen mit Kopftüchern sind auch nur Menschen' ['Women who wear Headscarfs are still only People'], *Der Tagesspiegel*, 9 February 2017, tagesspiegel.de.

84 Achille Mbembe, *Critique of Black Reason*, 27.

85 Gloria Wekker, *White Innocence: Paradoxes of Colonialism and Race*, Durham, NC: Duke University Press, 2016, 2.

86 Achille Mbembe, *Critique of Black Reason*, 73.

87 Ibid., 20–21.

88 Ibid., 24.

89 Hedwig Dohm, *Die Mütter: Beitrag zur Erziehungsfrage*, Berlin, 1903. [Sophie Lewis's translation.]

90 Rosa Mayreder, *A Survey of the Woman Problem*, trans. Herman Scheffauer, London: Hyperion, 1913, 2.

91 Virginia Woolf, *A Room of One's Own*. San Diego: Harcourt Brace Jovanovich, 1989 [1957], 27.

92 Gudrun-Axeli Knapp, 'Macht und Geschlecht: Neuere Entwicklungen in der feministischen Macht- und Herrschaftsdiskussion', 287–325 in Gudrun-Axeli Knapp and Angelika Wetterer, eds, *Traditionen, Brüche: Entwicklungen feministischer Theorie*, Freiburg: Kore, 1992.

93 Gudrun-Axeli Knapp, 'Die vergessene Differenz', 263–84 in Sabine Hark, ed., *Dis/ Kontinuitäten: Feministische Theorie*, Wiesbaden: Springer, 2007 [1988]. (Sophie Lewis's translation.)

94 Karin Hausen, 'Die Polarisierung der »Geschlechtscharaktere«: Eine Spiegelung der Dissoziation von Erwerbs- und Familienleben', 173–96 in Sabine Hark, ed., *Dis/Kontinuitäten: Feministische Theorie*, Wiesbaden: Springer, 2007 [1976].

95 Gudrun-Axeli Knapp, 'Die vergessene Differenz', 276.

96 Bruno Latour, 'Why Has Critique Run Out of Steam? From Matters of Fact to Matters of Concern', *Critical Inquiry* 30(2): 225–48, 2004, 246.

97 The 'great waves of enthusiasm, indignation and pity', according to Durkheim, 'have their seat in no one individual consciousness',

rather, they 'come to us from outside'. Emile Durkheim, *The Rules of Sociological Method*, trans. W. D. Halls, ed. Steven Lukes, New York: Free Press, 1982, 22.

98 Birgit Sauer, 'Transformationen von öffentlich und privat: Eine gesellschafts- und affekttheoretische Perspektive auf Geschlechterdemokratie', *Bulletin – Texte 43*, Berlin: Zentrum für transdisziplinäre Geschlechterstudien HU Berlin, 2017, 12–29.

99 Andrea Maihofer, 'Sara Ahmed: Kollektive Gefühle – Elemente des westlichen hegemonialen Gefühlsregimes', 253–72 in Angelika Baier, Christa Binswanger, Jana Häberlein, Yv Nay and Andrea Zimmermann, eds, *Affekt und Geschlecht: Eine einführende Anthologie*, Vienna: Böhlau, 2014.

100 Sara Ahmed, 'Collective Feelings: Or, the Impressions Left by Others', *Theory, Culture & Society*, 21(2): 25–42, 2004, 25.

101 Ibid., 28.

102 Brigitte Bargetz, 'Jenseits emotionaler Eindeutigkeiten: Überlegungen zu einer politischen Grammatik der Gefühle', 117–36 in Angelika Baier, et.al., eds, *Affekt und Geschlecht*.

103 Andrea Maihofer, 'Sara Ahmed'.

104 Ibid.

105 Ibid., 270. (Sophie Lewis's translation.)

106 Angela McRobbie uses the phrase 'new deal' to describe New Labour's offer of 'female individualization and the new meritocracy at the expense of feminist politics'. See Angela McRobbie, 'Post-Feminism and Popular Culture', *Feminist Media Studies* 4(3): 255–64, 2004, 258.

107 Niklas Luhmann, 'The Sociology of the Moral and Ethics', *International Sociology* 11(1): 27–36, 1996.

108 Hannah Arendt, *Denktagebuch: 1950–1973*, Munich: Piper, 2002.

109 Ibid., 54. (Sophie Lewis's translation.)

110 'Heroes' is the name of a charitable initiative in Berlin committed to 'fighting honour-based oppression'. Heroes works with young Arab-German and Turkish-German men who have had experiences of exclusion, oppression and violence perpetrated in the name of 'honour', and who have an interest in grappling with topics like culture, equality and human rights. The Heroes website declares: 'We stand for a society in which every human being has the same opportunities and rights, regardless of gender and cultural background. We are not a movement against religion,

moral values or culture. We are committed to a diverse, open and equal way of living together. We believe in talking about controversial subjects with our peers, expressing our opinions, and having the courage to question things. We are young men, and there are many like us in society – only, as isolated individuals, we never get noticed. Together, we can have a voice, a face.' strohhalm -ev.de/heroes.

111 See in particular, on this, Said's foreword in Edward Said, *Culture and Imperialism*, New York: Knopf, 1993.

112 Theodor Adorno, *Problems of Moral Philosophy*, trans. Rodney Livingstone, ed. Thomas Schroder, Stanford: Stanford University Press, 2000, 169.

113 Niklas Luhmann, 'Paradigm Lost: On the Ethical Reflection of Morality: Speech on the Occasion of the Award of the Hegel Prize 1988', *Thesis Eleven*, 29(1): 82–94, 1991, 90.

NOTES TO CHAPTER THREE

1 John Berger, *Ways of Seeing*, London: Penguin, 1977.

2 William J. T. Mitchell, *What Do Pictures Want? The Lives and Loves of Images*, Chicago: University of Chicago Press, 2005.

3 Sabine Hark, 'Das ethische Regime der Bilder oder: Wie leben Bilder?' ['The Ethical Regime of Images, or, How Do Images Live?'], 53–8 in Angelika Bartl, Josch Hoenes, Patricia Mühr and Kea Wienand, eds, *Sehen – Macht – Wissen. ReSaVoir. Bilder im Spannungsfeld von Kultur, Politik und Erinnerung*, Bielefeld: transcript, 2011. See also: Sigrid Schade and Silke Wenk, *Studien zur visuellen Kultur*, Bielefeld: transcript, 2011.

4 Judith Butler, *Precarious Life: The Powers of Mourning and Violence*, London: Verso, 2004, 141.

5 Jacques Rancière, *The Politics of Aesthetics: The Distribution of the Sensible*, New York: Continuum, 2005, 16.

6 For a detailed interrogation of the ethical complexity and narrativity of images, particularly photographs, see Susan Sontag, *Regarding the Pain of Others*, New York: Farrar, Straus and Giroux, 2003.

7 Birgit Rommelspacher, *Dominanzkultur: Texte zu Fremdheit und Macht*, Berlin: Orlanda, 1995. (Sophie Lewis's translation.)

8 Stuart Hall, ed., *Representation: Cultural Representations and Signifying Practices*, London: Sage, 1997.

9   Judith Butler, *Excitable Speech: A Politics of the Performative*, New York: Routledge, 1997.
10 Antke Engel, *Bilder von Sexualität und Ökonomie. Queere kulturelle Politiken im Neoliberalismus*, Bielefeld: transcript, 2009, 31. (Sophie Lewis's translation.)
11 Silke Wenk, *Versteinerte Weiblichkeit – Allegorien in der Skulptur der Moderne* [Petrified Femininity – Allegories in Modern Sculpture], Köln: Böhlau Verlag, 1996.
12 Nira Yuval-Davis, 'Gender and Nation', *Ethnic and Racial Studies* 16(4): 621–32, 1993, 621. See also: Floya Anthias and Nira Yuval-Davis, *Racialized Boundaries: Race, Nation, Gender, Colour and Class in the Anti-Racist Struggle*, New York/London: Routledge, 1993.
13 Pierre Bourdieu, 'Language and Symbolic Power, an English Translation of "Ce que parler veut dire"', trans. Gino Raymond and Matthew Adamson, 32–159 in John Thompson, ed., *Language and Symbolic Power and Other Essays by Pierre Bourdieu*, Cambridge: Polity, 1993.
14 For similar arguments, see Gabriele Dietze, 'Ethnosexismus: Sex-Mob-Narrative um die Kölner Silvesternacht' in *movements: Journal für kritische Migrations- und Grenzregimeforschung*, 2(1): 177–86, 2016; and Michael Tunç, 'Männlichkeiten und (Flucht-)Migrationserfahrungen: Kritik und Emanzipation', *IDA-NRW* 1: 15–19, 2016.
15 See also the careful analysis of this by Heide Oestreich in *taz*, 15 June 2016. In the 8 January 2016 print edition of *Süddeutsche Zeitung (SZ)*, the image really did appear without the caption. SZ has, in any case, deployed the combination of picture and commentary we have analyzed here many times before, especially on social media, via the special formula '(front page) image + op-ed'. For coverage of the apology, see spiegel.de/kultur/gesellschaft/focus-und-sueddeutsche-zeitung-eine-entschuldigung-einerechtferti-gung-fuer-titel-a-1071334.html.
16 The question of whether 'showing' or 'repeating' violent speech (racist, sexist or antisemitic hate speech) – where 'speech', here, includes images – is itself violent has been the subject of political and theoretical controversy for decades. The arguments on the subject of pornography are particularly instructive here. See Judith Butler, *Excitable Speech: A Politics of the Performative*, London:

Routledge, 1997. On the many important questions associated with representation in war, especially the question of whether images of wartime violence repeat that same violence, see the essays gathered in Linda Hentschel, ed., *Bilderpolitik in Zeiten von Krieg und Terror: Medien, Macht und Geschlechterverhältnisse*, Berlin: b-books, 2008.

17 Angela McRobbie, 'Top Girls: Young women and the post-feminist sexual contract', *Cultural Studies* 21(4–5): 2007, 718–37.

18 See Ricarda Drüeke's quantitative and qualitative analysis of the TV news coverage of Cologne's New Year's Eve: 'In the media coverage, "the" perpetrators become a homogenized group of offenders that in turn became "the" Other ("the Maghreb", "Refugees" etc.) thus culturalizing sexism and sexual violence.' Ricarda Drüeke, 'Die TV-Berichterstattung in ARD und ZDF über die Silvesternacht 2015/16 in Köln' ['The TV coverage by ARD and ZDF of the New Year's Eve 2015/16 in Cologne'], Gunda Werner Institute, Heinrich Böll Foundation, boell.de.

19 See, for instance, the report by the BKA (Bundeskriminalamt): 'Crime in the context of immigration, 30 January–September 2016: Key messages', bka.de. However, it is clear that offences of this nature do happen and that problems exist. Police statistics are, after all, necessarily complicated abstractions of real differences. But experts tend to point out that offences against a person's sexual autonomy are rarely 'monocausal'. An N-TV report states: 'Research on the perpetrators of violent crime demonstrates that poverty, poor education and unemployment – especially where the subjects have been victims of violence themselves – correlate with further violence. One criminologist, Pfeiffer, contends that the men most likely to become sexual murderers later in life are those whose educations were marked by 'sadism and powerlessness . . . It has nothing to do with machismo. That's why forms of prevention, like education on sex and anti-violence, constitute the best "cure". It's more a question of milieu than of culture.' N-TV, 'Sind Flüchtlinge häufiger Sexualstraftäter?', 15 December 2016, n-tv.de.

20 'Gutmensch' (i.e., 'good Samaritan' in the sense of 'do-gooder') was even voted 'worst word of the year', rp-online.de/nrw/staedte/koeln /unwort-gutmensch-koeln-wockt-ressentiments-aid-1.5687462.

21 See the book by that title edited by María do Mar Castro Varela and Paul Mecheril: *Die Dämonisierung der Anderen: Rassismuskritik der Gegenwart*, Bielefeld: transcript, 2016.

22 Sonja Alvarez, Medien-Diskussion geht weiter: 'Wir bilden ab, was leiderpassiert ist', *Berliner Tagesspiegel*, 11 January 2016, tagesspiegel. de; see also Ulrike Bergermann, 'Köln/Rape Culture', zfm gender blog, 2016, zfmedienwissenschaft.de; Gabriele Dietze, 'Ethnosexismus: Sex-Mob-Narrative um die Kölner Silvesternacht' ['Ethnosexism: Sex-Mob Narratives around the New Year's Eve Events in Cologne'] in *movements: Journal für kritische Migrations- und Grenzregimeforschung*, 2(1): 177–86, 2016.

23 A wealth of good research – of all different shades and perspectives – has long accrued on this, which it would be absurd to overlook. For decades, multiple approaches to preventative, educational and therapeutic progress in this area have been advanced in both political and clinical contexts. Lest we forget, sexual violence has been a central theme of feminist politics since the 1970s.

24 One example is the statement of the so-called Cologne Embassy, composed in January 2016 by a group of minor celebrities and public figures (from sports, art, science, the church and the media) from Cologne, Bonn and Düsseldorf. The signatories expressed their vehement opposition to all forms of sexual violence *and* to xenophobia and racism. The statement can be found in the *Kölner Stadtanzeiger* of 21 January 2016 and online at ksta.de.

25 ausnahmslos.org.

26 We owe our analysis of the 'adobe' – alabaster – whiteness of the female body within this imaginary to Anna-Katharina Messmer.

27 See the report by Kira Kosnick, 'Köln und die Folgen', archived at Johann Wolfgang Goethe-Universität, UniReport 1(2), 2016.

28 Gabriele Dietze, 'Ethnosexismus', 179. (Sophie Lewis's translation.)

29 Ibid., 178.

30 Frantz Fanon, *Black Skin, White Masks*, trans. Richard Philcox, New York: Grove Press, 1952, 139.

31 Ibid.

32 Kobena Mercer, 'Reading Racial Fetishism', in *Welcome to the Jungle: New Positions in Black Cultural Studies*, New York/London: Routledge, 1994, 185.

33 Birgit Rommelspacher, *Anerkennung und Ausgrenzung. Deutschland als multikulturelle Gesellschaft*, Frankfurt: campus, 2002, 102. (Sophie Lewis's translation.)

34 Jürgen Mannke, 'Flüchtlingsdebatte: Anpassung an unsere

Grundwerte erforderlich', lead article in the *Zeitschrift des Philologenverbandes Sachsen-Anhalt*, 12 March 2015. (Sophie Lewis's translation.) Mannke had to resign as president of the federation in the wake of these statements.

35 Christiane Hoffmans, 'Streit übers Kopftuch kam, als Studentinnen es trugen' ['The Fight Over the Hijab Started, When Students Started Wearing It'], interview with Aladin El-Mafaalani, *Die Welt*, 8 March 2016, welt.de. (Sophie Lewis's translation.)

36 Statement of the Committee of Women from Turkey [1981] (abridged version), in Ilse Lenz, ed., *Die Neue Frauenbewegung in Deutschland – Abschied vom kleinen Unterschied: Eine Quellensammlung*, Wiesbaden: Springer, 2008. (Sophie Lewis's translation.)

37 For more on this, refer to the official report of the First Joint Congress of Immigrant and German Women, entitled 'Sind Wir Uns Denn So Fremd?' ['Are we really so alien to one another?']. The congress took place on 23–25 March 1984 in Frankfurt am Main.

38 Rommelspacher, 'Anerkennung und Ausgrenzung, 113. (Sophie Lewis's translation.)

39 Lamya Kaddor, 'Verschleierung von Haut und Haar – ein Interview', *sozialmagazin* 42(1–2): 28–35, 2017. (Sophie Lewis's translation.)

40 On 'hyperculturalization', see Andreas Reckwitz, 'Zwischen Hyperkultur und Kulturessenzialismus', *soziopolis*, 24 October 2016, soziopolis.de.

41 Nira Yuval-Davis, 'Nationalist Projects and Gender Relations'. *Nar. umjet*, 40 (1): 9–36, 2003.

42 Birgit Rommelspacher, 'Sexismus und Rassismus im Bild der "Anderen"', 49–64 in Annemarie Hürlimann, Martin Roth and Klaus Vogel, eds, *Fremdkörper – Fremde Körper. Von unvermeidlichen Kontakten und widerstreitenden Gefühlen*, Ostfildern: restlos, 1999. (Sophie Lewis's translation.)

43 Biological forms of racism have, on the other hand, by no means disappeared. For a lurid example, see Thilo Sarrazin, *Deutschland schafft sich ab: Wie wir unser Land aufs Spielsetzen*, München: Deutsche Verlags-Anstalt, 2010.

44 See Kirsten Wiese in *Legal Tribune Online*, 1 July 2014.

45 'Polizei stellt frau am Strand zur Rede', spiegel.de. (Sophie Lewis's translation.)

46 On these dynamics, see Paula-Irene Villa, 'Rohstoffisierung: Zur

De-Ontologisierung des Geschlechtskörpers', 225–40 in René John, Jana Rückert-John and Elena Esposito, eds, *Ontologien der Moderne*, Wiesbaden: Suhrkamp, 2013; and Paula-Irene Villa, 'Habe den Mut, Dich Deines Körpers zu bedienen! Thesen zur Körperarbeit in der Gegenwart zwischen Selbstermächtigung und Selbstunterwerfung', 245–72 in Paula-Irene Villa, ed., *Schön Normal: Manipulationen am Körper als Technologien des Selbst*, Bielefeld: transcript, 2008.

47   Ilse Lenz, ed., *Die Neue Frauenbewegung in Deutschland – Abschied vom kleinen Unterschied: Eine Quellensammlung*, Wiesbaden: Springer, 2008. See also: Andrea Bührmann, *Das authentische Geschlecht: Die Sexualitätsdebatte der Neuen Frauenbewegung und die Foucaultsche Machtanalyse*, Münster: Unrast, 1995; Alice Schwarzer, ed., *Sexualität – Ein EMMA-Buch*, Köln: Rowohlt, 1982. For a more up-to-date analysis, see Margarete Stokowski, *Untenrum frei*, Reinbek: Rowohlt, 2016.

48   For even here 'at home', in the modern era, among 'us', women's bodies are marked as the other, the particular, the sexual and the 'outside' of the general and the rational. See: Claudia Honegger, *Die Ordnung der Geschlechter: Die Wissenschaften vom Menschen und das Weib*, Frankfurt am Main: Suhrkamp, 1991.

49   McRobbie, 'Top Girls'.

50   Paula-Irene Villa, 'Pornofeminismus? Soziologische Überlegungen zur Fleischbeschau im Pop', 229–48 in Paula-Irene Villa et al., eds, *Banale Kämpfe? Perspektiven auf Populärkultur und Geschlecht*, Wiesbaden: Springer, 2012.

51   Lisa Duggan and Hunter D. Nan, *Sex Wars: Sexual Dissent and Political Culture*, London/New York: Routledge, 1995.

NOTES TO CHAPTER FOUR

1   Audre Lorde, 'The Master's Tools Will Never Dismantle the Master's House', 110–12 in *Sister Outsider*, California: Berkeley University Press, 2007. The text develops the presentation Lorde gave at a conference on Simone de Beauvoir in New York in September 1979.

2   Combahee River Collective, 'The Combahee River Collective Statement', 272–82 in Barbara Smith, ed., *Home Girls: A Black Feminist Anthology*, New York: Kitchen Table – Women of Color Press, 1983. The statement was composed in April 1977.

3 Seyran Ateş, *Der Multikulti-Irrtum*, Berlin: Perlentaucher, 2008. On Ateş and other 'authentic' (Muslim) Islamo-critical voices of that ilk, see Yasemin Shooman, 'Einblick gewähren in die Welt der Muslime: "Authentische Stimmen" und "Kronzeugenschaft" in antimuslimischen Diskursen', 47–58 in Iman Attia, Swantje Köbsell and Nivedita Prasad, eds, *Dominanzkultur Reloaded: Neue Texte zu gesellschaftlichen Machtverhältnissen und ihren Wechselwirkungen*, Bielefeld: transcript, 2015.

4 Ina Kerner, *Differenzen und Macht: Zur Anatonie von Rassismus und Sexismus*, Frankfurt: Campus, 2009, 364. Kerner here examines, in detail, the question of Schwarzer's – indeed *EMMA* magazine's as a whole – ethnicising and, indeed, racialising brand of sexism.

5 For a related, early critique of *EMMA*, see Helma Lutz, 'Rassismus und Sexismus, Unterschiede und Gemeinsamkeiten', in Andreas Foitzik et al., eds, *'Ein Herrenvolk von Untertanen'. Rassismus–Nationalismus – Sexismus*, Duisburg: DISS, 1992.

6 'Flüchtlinge: Was jetzt passieren muss' ['Refugees: What Has To Happen Now'], *EMMA*, 7 October 2015, emma.de. (Sophie Lewis's translation.)

7 Ina Kerner, *Differenzen und Macht*, 362.

8 As we have indicated repeatedly, these entanglements are widely studied among feminist scholars. For further references, simply peruse the endnotes throughout the text.

9 Adrienne Rich, 'Notes Towards a Politics of Location', in Adrienne Rich, *Blood, Bread and Poetry: Selected Prose 1979–1985*, London: Norton, 1986.

10 For more on this, see the interview with the sociologist Armin Nassehi in Berlin's *taz* magazine: 'Die Diskussion ist vergiftet: Interview mit Armin Nassehi', *taz*, 31 December 2016, taz.de.

11 Esra Erdem, 'In der Falle einer Politik des Ressentiments: Feminismus und die Integrationsdebatte', 187–206 in Sabine Hess, Jana Binder and Johannes Moser, eds, *No Integration? Kulturwissenschaftliche Beiträge zur Integrationsdebatte in Europa*, Bielefeld: transcript, 2009.

12 Ibid., 189. (Sophie Lewis's translation.)

13 Angela McRobbie, 'Top Girls'. See also: Sabine Hark, 'Vom Erfolg verwöhnt: Feministische Ambivalenzen der Gegenwart', 76–91 in Deniz Hänzi, Hildegard Matthies and Dagmar Simon, eds, *Erfolg: Konstellationen und Paradoxien einer gesellschaftlichen Leitorientierung*, Leviathan Sonderband 29, 2014.

14 It is a core contention of so-called anti-genderism and the 'gender-critical' movement that feminist values have acceded historically to hegemonic status: that they have become a core part of the realm of the unquestionable, part of objectivity itself, inscribed in institutional guidelines and supranational policy. However, there is some truth to this contention. To illustrate the phenomenon of 'state institutionalization' of women's politics from the 1980s onward, one need only point to the plethora of laws and regulations designed to further gender equality or the ever-growing international body of both governmental and non-governmental organizations dedicated to strengthening 'women's rights'. Prominent examples of this are the both supranational (EU) and national gender mainstreaming policies aiming at 'gender mainstreaming'. Equal rights between the sexes are now widely regarded as a *fait accompli* or, at least, as a goal very much within reach of most women and men in the Western world today. To value gender equality is widely regarded today as the sine qua non of keeping good company and having good taste.

15 Alice Schwarzer, 'Die Folgen der falschen Toleranz', 5 January 2016, aliceschwarzer.de. (Sophie Lewis's translation.)

16 J. L. Austin, *How to Do Things with Words*, Harvard University Press, 1962.

17 Judith Butler, *Excitable Speech: A Politics of the Performative*, New York: Routledge, 1997.

18 It seems worth noting that Schwarzer's formulation bears an unmistakeable affinity with Harald Martenstein's phrase 'Islamic socialization', which we encountered in Chapter 2.

19 Alice Schwarzer, 'Silvester 2015, Tahrir-Platz in Köln' ['New Year's Eve 2015, Cologne's Tahrir Square'], in *Der Schock: Die Silvesternacht von Köln*, Köln: Kiwi Verlag, 2016.

20 Alice Schwarzer, 'Die Folgen der falschen Toleranz'. (Sophie Lewis's translation.)

21 Alice Schwarzer, 'Was geschah wirklich an Silvester?', 25 February 2016, aliceschwarzer.de. (Sophie Lewis's translation.)

22 Reiner Burger, 'Auf einen Tanz mit der Staatsmacht' ['Dancing with State Power'], *Frankfurter Allgemeine Zeitung*, 4 January 2017, faz. net. (Sophie Lewis's translation.)

23 The misapprehension that those who had gathered in Cologne on New Year's Eve 2016 were, in the main, young men from the

Maghreb was corrected by the Cologne police a few days later. Most of those apprehended by the police hailed from Syria, Iraq and Afghanistan. wdr.de/nachrichten/rheinland/koeln-silvester-syrien-irak-100.html.

24 Alice Schwarzer, 'Hass: Wir gedenken der Opfer von Solingen', *EMMA* 4, 1993, 34–5, emma.de. For a detailed analysis of Schwarzer's earlier arguments, see Leslie Adelson, 'The Price of Feminism: Of Women and Turks', 305–19 in Patricia Herminghouse and Magda Mueller, eds, *Gender and Germanness: Cultural Productions of Nation*, Providence/Oxford: Berghahn, 1997.

25 Gökce Yurdakul, 'Governance Feminism und Rassismus: Wie führende Vertreterinnen von Immigranten die antimuslimische Diskussion in Westeuropa und Nordamerika befördern', 111–27 in Gökce Yurdakul and Michal Bodemann, eds, *Staatsbürgerschaft, Migration und Minderheiten*, Münster: Springer, 2010.

26 Liz Fekete, 'Enlightened Fundamentalism? Immigration, Feminism and the Right', *Race & Class* 48(2): 2006, 1–22.

27 Ibid., 6.

28 Stanley Cohen, *Folk Devils and Moral Panics: The Creation of the Mods and Rockers*, London: Routledge, 2002 [1972].

29 Angela Nagle, 'Enemies of the People: How Hatred of the Masses Bridges Our Bipartisan Divide', *The Baffler* 34, 2017, thebaffler.com.

30 The 'brown man' in question might, in reality, be black, brown, Indian, Arab, Turkish, Muslim or North African.

31 'Behave like normal people or else get out', wrote Rutte on 22 January 2017, in a full-page advertisement published in seven Dutch daily newspapers. Quoted in Ute Schürings, 'Die Freiheit der Niederlande: Vom Gründungsmythos der Nation zum Kampfbegriff der Nationalisten', *Le Monde Diplomatique*, April 2017, 9.

32 The famous phrase 'white men saving brown women from brown men' comes, of course, from Gayatri Chakravorty Spivak's *Can the Subaltern Speak?* Basingstoke: Macmillan, 1988.

33 Leila Ahmed, *Women and Gender in Islam: Historical Roots of a Modern Debate*, New Haven: Yale University Press, 1992, 150.

34 'Colonialism continually abused feminism in order to justify invasions. Still today, whoever claims to speak in the name of women's rights is cementing their own discursive superiority', said Leila Ahmed in an interview in January 2016. See 'Die Männer wussten genau, wie sie den Westen treffen: Ein Interview mit Leila Ahmed',

Spiegel Online, 20 January 2016, spiegel.de. (Sophie Lewis's translation.)

35 Sara Farris, 'Die politische Ökonomie des Femonationalismus', *feministische studien* 2: 321–34, 2011. See also Sara Farris, *In the Name of Women's Rights: The Rise of Femonationalism*, London/Durham, NC: Duke University Press, 2017.

36 Jasbir Puar, *Terrorist Assemblages: Homonationalism in Queer Times*, Durham, NC: Duke University Press, 2007, 39.

37 Sara Farris, 'Die politische Ökonowie des Femanationalismus', 323.

38 'Geert Wilders pepper-sprays women', NTV, 23 January 2016, n -tv.de.

39 Barbara Kostelnik, 'Le Pen als Kämpferin für Frauenrechte' ['Le Pen as feminist warrior'], *Deutschlandfunk*, 8 March 2017, deutschlandfunk.de.

40 Between 2015 and 2017, Frauke Petry was chairwoman of the AfD. She stepped back from all political offices and left the party after intense internal power struggles between her more 'moderate' position and the ever since growing more radical right-wing strand of the party. Petry founded a new party, which has gone unnoticed since.

41 'Es gehört nicht jeder dazu' ['It's Not For Everybody'] – 'Ein Schreckensgedanke' ['Project Fear'] – 'Ein Streitgespräch zwischen Frauke Petry (AfD) und Katrin Göring-Eckardt (Grüne)', *Zeit Online*, 9 February 2017, zeit.de. (Sophie Lewis's translation.)

42 On the so-called anti-gender movement, see Sabine Hark and Paula -Irene Villa, eds, *Anti-Genderismus: Sexualität und Geschlecht als Schauplätze aktueller politischer Auseinandersetzungen*, Bielefeld: transcript, 2015.

43 'The destabilization of the sex/gender order [is] threatening to the core agenda of the cultural right, which is centered on the defense of the family.' Rogers Brubaker, *Trans: Gender and Race in an Age of Unsettled Identities*, Princeton: Princeton University Press, 2016, 32.

44 Michaela Köttig, Renate Bitzan and Andrea Petö, *Gender and Far-Right Politics in Europe*, Cham: Springer, 2017.

45 gabriele-kuby.de. (Sophie Lewis's translation.)

46 Irene Dölling, 'Eva-Prinzip? Neuer Feminismus? Aktuelle Verschiebungen in Geschlechterleitbildern im Kontext gesellschaftlicher Umbruchsprozesse', 24–41 in Marburger Gender-Kolleg, ed., *Geschlecht Macht Arbeit: Interdisziplinäre Perspektiven und*

politische Intervention, Münster: Unrast, 2008. (Sophie Lewis's translation.)

47 For an updated account of this mobilization, published a few years after our book on the subject, see: Anja Henning, 'Political gender-phobia in Europe: accounting for right-wing political-religious alliances against gender-sensitive education reforms since 2012', *Z Religion Ges Polit*, 2(2): 193–219, 2018.

48 Volker Zastrow, 'Politische Geschlechtsumwandlung', *Frankfurter Allgemeine Zeitung*, 20 June 2006, faz.net. (Sophie Lewis's translation.)

49 Bożena Chołuj, '"Gender-Ideologie" – ein Schlüsselbegriff des polnischen Anti-Genderismus', 219–37 in Sabine Hark and Paula-Irene Villa, eds, *Anti-Genderismus: Sexualität und Geschlecht als Schauplätze aktueller politischer Auseinandersetzungen*, Bielefeld: transcript, 2015.

50 Barbara Thiessen, 'Gender Trouble evangelisch: Analyse und Standortbestimmung', 149–68 in Sabine Hark and Paula-Irene Villa, eds, *Antigenderismus*, 2015.

51 Sineb El Masrar, *Emanzipation im Islam: Eine Abrechnung mit ihren Feinden*, Freiburg: Herder, 2016.

52 Gayle Rubin, 'The Traffic in Women: Notes on the "Political Economy" of Sex', 157–210 in Rayna Reiter, ed., *Toward an Anthropology of Women*, New York: Monthly Review Press, 1975, 160.

53 Mark Terkessidis, 'Da war doch was' ['Something was up'], *taz*, 20 February 2017, taz.de. (Sophie Lewis's translation.)

54 Nicola Pratt, 'Weaponising feminism for the "war on terror" versus employing strategic silence', *Critical Studies on Terrorism*, 6: 327–33, 2013.

55 Judith Butler, 'Feminism should not resign in the Face of such Instrumentalization', interview with Renate Solbach, *Iablis, Jahrbuch für europäische Prozesse*, 2006, themen.iablis.de/2006/butler06.html.

56 Ulrike Lembke, 'Weibliche Verletzbarkeit, orientalisierter Sexismus und die Egalität des Konsums: gender-race-class als verschränkte Herrschafts strukturen im öffentlichen Raum', *Bulletin – Texte* (43); 30–57, Zentrum für transdisziplinäre Geschlechterstudien, HU Berlin, 2017, 48.

57 On this, see: Angie Abdelmonem, Rahma Esther Bavelaar, Elisa Wynne-Hughes and Susana Galán, 'The "Taharrush" Connection:

Xenophobia, Islamophobia, and Sexual Violence in Germany and Beyond', jadaliyya.com. The authors critically analyze the supposed 'parallel' between the events in Cologne and the incidents of sexual violence in Tahrir Square during the Egyptian revolution, an analogy drawn repeatedly by Alice Schwarzer (among others).

58 Judith Butler and Elizabeth Weed, 'Introduction', 1–8 in Butler and Weed, eds, *The Question of Gender: Joan W. Scott's Critical Feminism*, Bloomington: Indiana University Press, 2011, 4.

59 Ibid.

60 Ina Kerner, 'Religion, Culture, and the Complexities of Feminist Solidarity', presented at the International Symposium 'Hermeneutic Conflict, Cultural Entanglement and Social Inequality: Power of Interpretation in Intersectional Perspective', Rostock, 22–24 September 2016.

61 Afiya Shehrbano Zia, 'A response to Nicola Pratt's call for "strategic silence"', *Critical Studies on Terrorism* 6: 332–33, 2013.

62 Sadia Abbas, *At Freedom's Limit: Islam and the Postcolonial Predicament*, New York: Fordham University Press, 2014, 71.

63 Gudrun-Axeli Knapp, 'Verhältnisbestimmungen: Geschlecht, Klasse, Ethnizität in gesellschaftstheoretischer Perspektive', 138–70 in Knapp and Klinger, eds, *ÜberKreuzungen: Fremdheit, Ungleichheit, Differenz, Forum Frauen- und Geschlechterforschung*, 23, Münster: Unrast, 2008.

64 Janet Halley, *Split Decisions: How and Why to Take a Break from Feminism*, Princeton: Princeton University Press, 2006.

65 Meredith Haaf, Susanne Klingner and Barbara Streidl, *Wir Alphamädchen: Warum Feminismus das Leben schöner macht*, Hamburg: Hoffman & Campe, 2008. On the new German 'girl power' feminism, see also Jana Hensel and Elisabeth Raether, *Neue deutsche Mädchen*, Reinbek: Rowohlt, 2008; and Christina Scharff, 'The New German Feminisms: Of Wetlands and Alpha-Girls', 265–78 in Rosalind Gill and Christina Scharff, eds, *New Femininities: Postmodernism, Neoliberalism and Subjectivity*, London: Palgrave Macmillan, 2011

66 Michel Foucault, 'What is Critique?', 41–82 in *The Politics of Truth*, Los Angeles: Semiotext(e), 1997. On the production of 'marginal voices' and the meaning of silence as a dimension of epistemic violence, see Sabine Hark, 'Die Vermessung des Schweigens – oder: Was heißt sprechen?', 285–96 in Iman Attia, Swantje Köbsell and Nivedita Prasad, eds, *Dominanzkultur Reloaded: Neue Texte zu*

gesellschaftlichen Machtverhältnissen und ihren Wechselwirkungen, Bielefeld: transcript, 2015.

67 Ina Kerner and Sabine Hark formulated their initial thoughts on these three principles in an article entitled 'Eine andere Frau ist möglich' ['Another Woman Is Possible'] in *Der Freitag*, 21 July 2007, freitag.de.

68 Sara Ahmed, *Living a Feminist Life*, London/Durham, NC: Duke University Press, 2017.

NOTES TO CHAPTER FIVE

1 Audre Lorde, 'The Master's Tools Will Never Dismantle the Master's House', 110–112 in *Sister Outsider*, California, Berkeley University Press, 2007, 111.

2 Adrienne Rich, 'If not with others, how?', 202–9 in Adrienne Rich, *Blood, Bread and Poetry: Selected Prose 1979–1985*, London: Norton, 1986, 203.

3 Katharina Walgenbach, *Die weiße Frau als Trägerin deutscher Kultur: Koloniale Diskurse über Geschlecht, 'Rasse' und Klasse im Kaiserreich* ['The white woman as repository of German culture: colonial discourses on gender, race and class in the German Empire'], Frankfurt: campus, 2005.

4 Birgit Rommelspacher, *Anerkennung und Ausgrenzung: Deutschland als multikulturelle Gesellschaft*, Frankfurt: campus, 2002, 117. (Sophie Lewis's translation.)

5 In a radio address, the erstwhile first lady of the United States, Laura Bush, justified the invasion with reference to women's rights: 'Because of our recent military gains, in much of Afghanistan, women are no longer imprisoned in their homes. They can listen to music and teach their daughters without fear of punishment. Yet the terrorists who helped rule that country now plot and plan in many countries, and they must be stopped. The fight against terrorism is also a fight for the rights and dignity of women.'

6 As a corrective, see, for example (to choose just two among plentiful examples), Caroline Kramer and Anina Mischau, 'Städtische Angst -Räume von Frauen am Beispiel der Stadt Heidelberg', 45–63 in *ZUMA Nachrichten* 17, 1993; and Carol Hagemann-White, 'European Research on the Prevalence of Violence Against Women', *Violence Against Women*, 7(7): 732–59, 2001.

7 See Mithu Sanyal and Marie Albrecht, 'Du Opfer!' ['You victim!'], *taz*, 13 February 2017, taz.de; as well as the critical riposte by 'Die Störenfriedas' in their 'Open letter against the trivialization of the language of rape' on 18 February 2017, diestoerenfriedas.de/offener -brief-gegen-die-sprachliche-verharmlosung-sexueller-gewalt/; and, finally, mediating between the two positions, Marion Detjen, 'Gewalt ohne Namen', *Zeit Online*, 27 February 2017, zeit.de.

8 When, in 2000, prompted by an arson attack on a synagogue in Düsseldorf, the then-federal chancellor Gerhard Schröder called for a mobilization against antisemitic violence, he called it a 'revolt of the respectable' ['Aufstand der Anständigen'].

9 See the 41st Defence Attorney's report '"Immer wieder Köln?": Von Frauenrechten, Sexualität und Strafbarkeitslücken', Strafver-teidigertag, Bremen, 24–26 March 2017, strafverteidigervereinigun-gen.org.

10 #NiUnaMenos.

11 See Judith Butler, Zeynep Gambetti and Leticia Sabsay, eds, *Vulnerability in Resistance*, London/Durham, NC: Duke University Press, 2016.

12 Some pieces of investigative journalism worth reading on the subject of the alt-right in the United States (both on- and offline) include: M Abdekar, 'The Aesthetics of the Alt-Right', *Post-Office Art Journal*, 11 February 2017, baltimore-art.com; Laurie Penny, 'On the Milo Bus with the Lost Boys of America', *Pacific Standard Magazine*, 21 February 2017, psmag.com; and Michael Seeman, 'Das Regime der demokratischen Wahrheit IV – "It's the culture, stupid"', @ *ctrl+Verlust*, 20 March 2017, ctrl-verlust.net.

13 Paul Mecheril, 'Flucht, Sex und Diskurse: Gastrede im Rahmen des Neujahrsempfang der Stadt Bremen', 3–7 in *Zeitschrift des Informations- und Dokumentationszentrums für Antirassismusarbeit in Nordrhein-Westfalen*, 22(1), 2016, 7. (Sophie Lewis's translation.)

14 Christina Thürmer-Rohr, 'Achtlose Ohren: Zur Politisierung des Zuhörens', 111–29 in *Narrenfreiheit: Essays*, Berlin, 1994.

15 Ibid., 126. (Sophie Lewis's translation.)

16 Patricia Hill Collins, 'Learning from the Outsider Within: The Sociological Significance of Black Feminist Thought', 103–26 in Sandra Harding, ed., *The Feminist Standpoint Theory Reader: Intellectual & Political Controversies*, New York/London: Routledge, 2004.

17 German Federal Office of Statistics report on 'populations with a migration background', Wiesbaden: Destatis, 2007, 6.

18 Sabine Hark and Paula-Irene Villa, eds, *Anti-Genderismus: Sexualität und Geschlect als Schauplätze aktueller politische Auseinandersetzang*, Bielefield: transcript, 2015.

19 María do Mar Castro Varela, 'Eine Geste des Grenzdenkens', *taz*, 17 February 2017, taz.de.

20 Raewyn Connell, *Masculinities*, Cambridge: Polity Press, 1993.

21 Hengameh Yaghoobifarah, 'Fusion Revisited: Karneval der Kulturlosen', *Missy Magazine*, 5 July 2016, missy-magazine.de.

22 'Order', 2016 Manifesto of the CSU, csu.de/common/download/ CSU_Grundsatzprogramm_Parteitag_MUC_2016_ES.pdf.

23 Dipesh Chakrabarty, *Provincializing Europe: Postcolonial Thought and Historical Difference*, Princeton: Princeton University Press, 2007.

24 Voltaire, *Treatise on Tolerance and other Writings*, trans. Brian Masters, ed. Simon Harvey, Cambridge: Cambridge University Press, 2000, 100.

NOTES TO EPILOGUE

1 Christina Thürmer-Rohr, 'Eine "Welt in Scherben?" Gender, Nation und Pluralität' ['A "world in smithereens"? Gender, nation and plurality'], unpublished manuscript, 2017.

2 Audre Lorde, *A Burst of Light*, Ithaca/New York: Firebrand, 1988, 116.

3 Judith Butler, *Undoing Gender*, New York: Routledge, 2004, 31.

4 Judith Butler, *Frames of War: When is Life Grievable?* London: Verso, 2009, 23.

5 Judith Butler, 'Can one lead a good life in a bad life?' Adorno Prize Lecture, *Radical Philosophy* 176 (Nov/Dec): 9–18, 2012. See also: Judith Buter, *Giving an Account of Oneself*, New York: Fordham University Press, 2005.

6 Hannah Arendt, *The Life of the Mind, Volume 1: Thinking*, London: Secker and Warburg, 1978, 20.

7 Hannah Arendt, 'On Humanity in Dark Times: Thoughts about Lessing', 1993.

8 Achille Mbembe, *Out of the Dark Night: Essays on Decolonization*, New York: Columbia University Press, 2019.

9 Hannah Arendt, 'Philosophy and Politics', *Social Research* 57(1): 73–103, 1990, 78.

10 Michel Foucault, 'What is Enlightenment?', 32–50 in Paul Rabinow, ed., *The Foucault Reader*, New York: Pantheon Books, 1984.

11 Theodor Adorno, *Negative Dialectics*, New York: Continuum, 2007.

12 In the autumn of 2016, social media erupted around a sexist, transphobic and homophobic incident that took place at a queer party in a large German city. It was not, in this case, an incident of direct physical violence, but a situation involving disrespectful, intrusive, shaming behaviours and body language that had clearly violated the implicit and explicit rules of the subcultural space in question. It was clear, in this case, that the perpetrators were young men who were refugees from majority Muslim lands. To us, it was a positive surprise to observe how critical and nuanced the online discussion around these incidents turned out to be. See the adequate, if somewhat foreshortened, account by Anna Gauto, 'Weisst du, was "schwul" heisst?' ['Do you know what "gay" means?'] *Handelsblatt*, 28 March 2017, handelsblatt.com.

13 Christina Thürmer-Rohr, 'Eine "Welt in Scherben"?'

14 For this perspective on Germany qua 'immigration society', see Annette Treibel, *Integriert Euch! Neue Perspektiven für die Deutschen*, Frankfurt/New York: campus, 2015.

15 Frantz Fanon, *The Wretched of the Earth*, New York: Grover Press, 1961, 237.

16 Christina Thürmer-Rohr, 'Eine "Welt in Scherben"?'

17 See also: Paula-Irene Villa, 'Die Rückkehr männlicher Härte' ['The return of "manly" hardness'], Deutschland Radio Kultur, 4 April 2017, deutschlandradiokultur.de.